Depression and Bipolar Disorder:

Your Guide to Recovery

William R. Marchand, MD

Bull Publishing Company
Boulder, Colorado

Published by Bull Publishing Company
P.O. Box 1377
Boulder, CO, USA 80306
www.bullpub.com

Library of Congress Cataloging-in-Publication Data

Marchand, William R.
   Depression and bipolar disorder : your guide to recovery / William R. Marchand. -- 1st ed.
   p. cm.
   Includes bibliographical references and index.
   ISBN 978-1-933503-99-8 (pbk.)
   1. Manic-depressive illness--Popular works. 2. Depression, Mental--Popular works.
   3. Self-care, Health. I. Title.
   RC516.M374 2012
   616.85'27--dc23

                                                            2012012064

First Edition

17 16 15 14 13 12   10 9 8 7 6 5 4 3 2 1

Interior design and project management: Dovetail Publishing Services
Cover design: Shannon Bodie, Lightbourne, Inc.

*This book is lovingly
dedicated to my readers.*

Contents

Chapter 3 Do You Have a Mood Disorder?   43

Chapter 5   How and Where to Find Help   117

Chapter 6   Collaborating with Your Team   133

Chapter 7 The Diagnostic Evaluation 145

Chapter 8 Medication and Other Biological Treatments 169

Chapter 9   Psychotherapy   199

Chapter 14   Maintenance Treatment and Relapse Prevention   297

Introduction

BECAUSE YOU ARE READING THIS, chances are that you have a mood disorder or think that you might have one. Or perhaps you are seeking information because you have a loved one with a mood disorder. People who have depression or bipolar disorder frequently have lots of questions. Unfortunately, answers may be hard to find. Appointments with doctors can be rushed, and it may seem like there isn't enough time to ask questions. Many doctors aren't great communicators. The medical and mental health literature is difficult to understand (frequently even for professionals) and often contradictory. The bookstore shelves are filled with self-help titles, but few provide the comprehensive information that you need. This book is the "missing manual" you may have been looking for.

Affective (or mood) disorders are primarily disorders of emotion and come in two basic categories: depressive and bipolar disorders (much more about this later). Depressive disorders cause excessive sadness along with other symptoms. In contrast, people who suffer from bipolar disorders

---

Table I.1   Ways this book can help you

Reading this book can help you:

+ Determine whether professional treatment is needed

+ Find out about evidence-based treatment options and determine which ones may be best for you

+ Seek help and work effectively with your treatment team

+ Maximize treatment benefits

+ Avoid common obstacles to recovery

+ Develop a comprehensive recovery plan

+ Understand the biological and psychological causes of mood disorders

+ Learn about the benefits of practicing mindfulness

+ Select additional books and other resources to support your recovery

---

experience both extreme highs and lows. This book provides critical information to support your recovery from either type of disorder. It will also be helpful if you have an adult loved one with a mood disorder. Table I.1 provides a summary of how this book can help. There is saying that "information is power." This book is about empowerment. It provides facts that can empower you to take charge of your recovery and get well.

Why you need this book

Mood disorders are very serious and disabling conditions. Worldwide surveys indicate that depression is the fourth leading cause of disability. In fact, depressed individuals spend more time in bed than those with many serious medical conditions, such as high blood pressure, diabetes, chronic lung disease, or arthritis.[1] Bipolar disorders are equally disabling and often much more so. The good news is that effective treatments are available and there are many things you can do on your own to support your recovery. This book will serve as your guide to implement a comprehensive recovery plan.

Unfortunately, many of you may not get better and stay well unless you take control of your recovery. Why? Studies indicate that there are a number of obstacles to getting better. This book directly addresses many of these barriers by providing the information you need to manage your recovery. It provides the information you need in order to get the best possible treatment and optimize the use of complementary approaches. The sole purpose of this book is to empower you to overcome obstacles to getting better.

The following section will help you understand why some people don't achieve full recovery from mood disorders. This information will explain why the strategies recommended in the rest of the book can help you. But, before you read on, one more thing: The next two sections contain a lot of numbers. I think that having detailed information available can be helpful. However, the numbers are not as nearly as important as the message. So I want to be sure the message is clear. These are the take-home points:

- Many people with mood disorders don't get the help they need.

- Misdiagnosis and inadequate treatment can keep those who get treatment from getting completely better.

- Having knowledge can empower you to take charge of your recovery and maximize your chances of obtaining full remission.

Not receiving treatment

Unfortunately, many people who have a mood disorder either never get help at all or delay starting treatment. Ann is an example. She experienced depression for many years before getting treatment. She was diagnosed when she sought psychotherapy for other reasons. "I was shocked," she recalls. "I knew something was wrong but it never occurred to me that it was depression." Ann is now receiving treatment, which has been helpful for her.

Ann's story is not unusual. Among people with any kind of mood disorder, a major study found that only about half ever received treatment.[2] In regard to specific disorders, the same study found that the rates of receiving treatment were about 57% for major depression, 68% for dysthymic disorder, and 56% for bipolar disorder. The study quoted above, published in 2005, is considered one of the best, but it is becoming dated. More recent evidence doesn't suggest much improvement, however. A 2009 report by the Substance Abuse and Mental Health Services Administration[3] found that only about two-thirds of adults with major depression had received any treatment. These studies tell us that 30%–40% of those with mood disorders aren't getting any help. Please don't be one of these people.

Why don't people with mood disorders seek help? Sometimes when we're sick, we wait to see if things will get better without treatment. Depression can occasionally get better without treatment, but this tends to occur within the first few months. The possibility of spontaneous (without treatment) remission is, at best, around 50%.[4] Some studies suggest that spontaneous remission rates are lower[5] and may even be around 20% or less.[6, 7] So, there is a chance your depression might go away on its own, but there is at least a 50% chance that it won't. What if depression doesn't go away in the first few months? We know less about what happens over time, but at least 12% have not recovered after five years.[4] You should also know that the chances of recurrence are high. After a person has had one episode of major depression, the risk of having another is about 50% within the following two years and may be as high as 90% within the next six years.[4] What does this information mean for you? Most, if not all, individuals with depression will need to take action in order to get better. The same is true for people with bipolar disorder. If you have symptoms of depression that don't go away within a few weeks, please don't wait to see if things will improve on their own. Start down the road to recovery today. This book will guide you through that process.

What else keeps people from getting help? One important obstacle is what others might think. We know that the stigma of mental disorder is a barrier to seeking help,[8] and this is particularly true for older adults.[9] Unfortunately, stigmatizing attitudes about depression still exist in developed countries,[10, 11] including the United States.[12, 13] Another barrier to seeking help is not recognizing that one is suffering from depression.[14] You'll remember that Ann didn't recognize her depression for what it was. She remembers feeling unhappy but just didn't realize it was depression. Beliefs related to one's gender can also inhibit seeking treatment;[15] that is, perceptions about one's gender might be in conflict with getting treatment. For example, some men might have a belief that seeking treatment isn't manly. I hope that the knowledge you gain from reading this book will put these kinds of issues to rest in your mind once and for all and encourage you to seek treatment if you have not already done so.

I want to end this section with a few words about where people with mood disorders seek help. One study found that for people who have major depression, about 20% were receiving treatment from a psychiatrist and 33% were seeing some type of mental health specialist.[2] In contrast, about 33% were getting care in a general medical setting. So, the research suggests that for those who get help, less than half actually get treatment from a mental health professional. The implications are discussed in the next section.

Misdiagnosis and inadequate treatment

In this book, I use the word *misdiagnosis* to mean either that a disorder was not diagnosed at all or that the wrong diagnosis was given. Studies indicate that both of these problems occur for people who have mood disorders. One study found that among a group of individuals with major depression who were receiving primary care treatment, about a third did not receive a timely diagnosis.[5] With regard to a wrong diagnosis, there is evidence that 10%–15% of those initially diagnosed with unipolar depression will eventually have their diagnosis revised to bipolar disorder.[1] This likely means that a depressive episode was not recognized as bipolar depression. Misdiagnosis can occur if a person's first mood episode is depressive because currently there is no way to diagnose bipolar disorder until an episode of mood elevation occurs. However, misdiagnosis may also occur because previous episodes of mood elevation were not recognized.

Inadequate treatment is also a problem. A study found that among individuals with any mood disorder, only about 38% were receiving minimally adequate treatment.[2] For those receiving treatment in a general medical setting, however, only 14% were receiving minimally adequate treatment as compared to about 50% for those receiving mental health specialty treatment. With regard to specific mood disorders, the same study found that for people with major depression, dysthymia, or bipolar disorder, only about 37%, 40%, and 39%, respectively, were receiving minimally adequate treatment. For all three groups, among those receiving mental health specialty treatment, the percentages increased to the 52%–54% range. Other studies suggest additional concerns. For example, antidepressants are often discontinued too soon, which leads to a relapse of the illness.[16, 17] Another problem is infrequent appointments with health care providers,[2] which can limit the effectiveness of treatment. Finally, there is evidence that bipolar depression is often treated with antidepressants alone, which may result in the illness becoming worse.[18] See Chapter 8 for more details about this issue.

The research cited above indicates that far too many individuals with mood disorders do not receive a correct diagnosis or optimal treatment. Yet another problem is taking medication correctly. Studies suggest that individuals with both depression[19] and bipolar disorder[20] often do not take medications as prescribed. There are many reasons why these problems may occur. The aim of this book is not to cast blame but rather to offer solutions. The solution I propose is that you must have the knowledge to take charge of your recovery. This book provides the information you need to accomplish that goal.

Who will find this book useful

I have written this book for adults who are suffering from mood disorders. It will also be very helpful to those who have a friend or family member suffering from one of these conditions. Finally, it will be a useful tool for mental health clinicians. By having patients use this guide, professionals can help ensure that they are providing the best possible treatment for each person.

This book does not cover mood disorders among children and adolescents. It also provides limited information that is specific to issues related to mood disorders in the elderly. Both topics are complex and beyond the scope of a general guide. That said, much of the information is applicable to adults of any age. There may be some instances in which recommendations may be different for older individuals, particularly in regard to medication dosing.

different for older individuals, particularly in regard to medication dosing. This is not true for children and adolescents. THE INFORMATION PROVIDED HEREIN IS NOT INTENDED FOR AND SHOULD NOT BE USED FOR PERSONS UNDER THE AGE OF 18.

How to use this book

This book may be read in two ways. One is to start at the beginning and read it all the way through to the end. The chapters follow a logical progression to aid your understanding. The second way is to read the chapters that are most relevant to your situation first. Each chapter is written so that it is completely understandable by itself. So, you can read the chapters in any order, with one exception. Please read Chapter 1 first. The purpose of the first chapter is to guide you through the process of developing a safety and crisis management plan. Please read Chapter 1 and use Form 1.1 to develop your personal plan. The other thing to know is that some chapters are designed specifically to help you figure out how to get better. Other chapters provide additional information that will be helpful but is not as critical to your recovery. Table I.2 on pages 8 and 9 will help you decide how to best use this book to meet the needs of your specific situation.

One of the unique and perhaps most helpful features of this book is the inclusion of forms and checklists that have been specifically designed to help you maximize the effectiveness of your treatment and get well. These forms are reproduced in the book and are also available as PDF files that can be downloaded free from our website (http://www.bullpub.com/downloads). You will need more than one copy of some forms. Some are also designed for you to take with you to appointments or to keep as a ready reference. Thus in most cases, it may be more convenient for you to download forms rather than complete those in the book (of course, downloading will be necessary if you have purchased an electronic version of this book).

Finally, you can also use this book as a handy reference. For example, if you are prescribed an antidepressant, you can quickly look up information about it. Also, a glossary of words and terms is located at the end of the book. Items included in the glossary are indicated by bold type in the text.

Table I.2   Overview of chapters

Chapter	What you will learn about	Specific barrier(s) to recovery addressed or purpose of chapter	When reading may be especially helpful
1	Developing a safety and crisis management plan	Safety, stress management	Before reading any other chapters
2	Diagnosing mood disorders	Incorrect diagnosis	Before a diagnostic evaluation
3	Deciding on your most likely diagnosis and whether you should seek professional treatment	Not getting treatment, incorrect diagnosis, inadequate treatment	When deciding whether you should seek help or before a diagnostic evaluation
4	Understanding the causes of mood disorders	Background information	Any time
5	Finding professional help	Not getting treatment	When seeking professional help
6	Taking charge of your recovery and working with your team	Inadequate treatment	Before starting treatment
7	Preparing for a diagnostic evaluation	Incorrect diagnosis	Before a diagnostic evaluation

Chapter	What you will learn about	Specific barrier(s) to recovery addressed or purpose of chapter	When reading may be especially helpful
8	Choosing medication and other biological treatments	Inadequate treatment	Before starting medication treatment
9	Choosing psychotherapy treatments	Inadequate treatment	Before starting psychotherapy treatment
10	Using complementary approaches to recovery	Inadequate treatment	Before starting complementary strategies
11	Starting treatment	Inadequate treatment	Before starting any treatment
12	Making decisions about treatment during pregnancy and breastfeeding	Information for women of childbearing age	Before starting treatment (for women)
13	Using strategies to help you make the most of treatment and get well	Inadequate treatment	When starting any treatment
14	Making decisions about maintenance treatment and staying well	Inadequate treatment	When your symptoms are in remission

9

This book provides a lot of information. It may take you some time to read it all and to digest the many facts I have included. Thus, I want to make some suggestions. First, if you have symptoms of a mood disorder, please do not delay seeking treatment in order to read this entire book. If professional treatment is appropriate for your situation, the most important thing is to get that process started. Another suggestion is to feel free to skip the sections that do not apply to you or those that contain more information than you want to take in right now. You can always come back to those sections later. You might want to read some of the sections that provide more complex information with a loved one. It's sort of like studying with a friend in school. Having a partner to work through the complicated sections may help prevent a feeling of information overload. A close friend or family member may also be able to help you in another way: Sometimes, we aren't able to recognize certain things about ourselves. This can happen for a variety of reasons, but it frequently occurs when the information is uncomfortable for one reason or another. For example, some people with depression might find that the idea of having a mood disorder brings on negative thoughts or feelings. In that case, it might be easy for the person to fail to notice symptoms that are much more obvious to her or his loved ones. Asking for another person's honest opinion can often help us see what's hidden by our blind spots. So, please consider having a loved one read this book with you.

About the author

Two important questions for prospective readers are:

- Who wrote this book?

- Why should I believe him?

Right now, you may be considering buying this book. Or maybe you have already purchased it and are wondering whether it was money well spent. Either way, you need to know who I am and whether you can trust what I say.

So—a little about me. I am a board-certified academic psychiatrist. Board certification means that I completed specialty training in psychiatry after medical school and passed exams demonstrating my knowledge and skills. An academic psychiatrist is one who is on the faculty of a medical school. In my case, I am an Associate Professor of Psychiatry (Clinical) at the University of Utah School of Medicine. I also have an adjunct faculty appointment in the University of Utah Department of Psychology. Most academic psychiatrists spend their days doing a combination of clinical work and teaching. Many also do research. I do all three. In regard to teaching, I am one of many faculty members at our school of medicine involved with training psychiatry residents (physicians who are completing specialty training). My research is aimed at better understanding the causes of mood and anxiety disorders as well as normal brain function. I use a method known as functional neuroimaging. This technology allows us to see what areas of a person's brain become active during completion of a task (such as doing a math problem). Thus, we can learn what areas of the brain are required for specific functions, such as math. Most of my work involves comparing the brain activation of individuals with mood or anxiety disorders to those who do not have these conditions. This comparison helps us understand the causes of these conditions.

Figure I.1 (in the color section on page 97) shows an example of results from one of my studies. The red and yellow areas indicate regions of brain activation. In this particular study,[21] we found areas where brain activation was associated with severity of depression among individuals with bipolar disorder. This is useful information because it indicates which brain areas may be directly involved with the experience of mood symptoms. I will say more about what we have learned from these kinds of studies in Chapter 4, where I explain what we know about the causes of mood disorders.

I went to medical school at West Virginia University and completed my residency training in psychiatry at the University of Utah. I have been in practice for more than twenty years. Over the course of the last two decades I have helped many hundreds of patients recover from mood disorders. In this book, I combine my personal experience as a practicing psychiatrist and neuroscientist with the scientific literature to provide a guide for you to follow.

What this book can't do

The purpose of this book is to serve as a guide. It cannot replace treatment by qualified medical and mental health professionals. The information given here should not in any way be considered to provide final diagnoses or outline standards of medical or mental health care. While this book can help individuals determine their likely diagnoses, it cannot assess all of the complex information that is required to establish a final diagnosis. Similarly, standards of medical care can be determined only on the basis of all the clinical data available for an individual. It is not possible for a book to collect and evaluate that data. Further, standards of care may change over time as medical and psychiatric knowledge advances. Finally, following the treatment approaches discussed in this book will not ensure a successful outcome for every individual, and approaches not reviewed in this book may be appropriate and effective. The definitive assessment and treatment recommendation for any person must be made by a mental health or medical professional considering all the clinical information as well as the specific treatment options available. You, armed with all the relevant information, must make the final decision about treatment. The ultimate goal of this book is to provide information to help you make the best possible informed choices about treatment and the overall recovery process. The book will also help you develop a comprehensive plan that can give you the best chance of getting better.

Evidence-based information and the bibliography

A key feature of the information provided in this book is that most of it is evidence-based. "Evidence-based" means the information is based on scientific studies that have been completed and published in peer-reviewed psychiatric, mental health, or medical journals. Publication in peer-reviewed journals is the standard for communicating results of all kinds of scientific studies, from archeology to medicine to zoology. The fact that a journal is peer-reviewed means that experts in the field review the information to be sure the scientific methodology used was appropriate and the conclusions are justified. Manuscripts that fail to meet the standard are not published. This ensures the validity of the information provided.

In addition to publishing original research reports, many scientific journals publish review articles. These articles are also peer-reviewed and provide an overview of the current state of knowledge about a specific topic. Review articles are very helpful to clinicians and other readers because they give an overview and summary of many different research articles. Finally, some articles or other publications contain expert consensus treatment guidelines. These are statements of the consensus of experts in regard to the treatment of specific conditions based on the research available as interpreted by individuals who have extensive clinical experience. An example is the *Treatment Guideline* series published by the American Psychiatric Association.

The information in this book comes from three sources: (1) direct from articles that report peer-reviewed research; (2) from psychiatric textbooks, treatment guidelines, and peer-reviewed reviews; and (3) from my own clinical and scientific experience. I have used a reference system to identify the information sources for this book. Each sentence containing information from a published source—an original research article, a review article, or a treatment guideline—is followed by a superscript numeral. In the bibliography, the article or articles cited are listed by number. The result is a fairly extensive bibliography. Many of you will not want to look up the specific articles, however you have that option if you desire. Nevertheless, you will clearly know where the information I provide came from. What if information is given with no references provided? Sometimes this is explanatory material rather than specific facts. In other cases, it means I am giving you my opinion. I have tried to make it clear when I am giving specific information that is based on my clinical experience rather than research. I do this sometimes because the research doesn't definitively answer the question. Other times, I give my interpretation of the literature. Finally, please know that I have attempted to provide the most complete and current information possible. That said, new studies are published every day and a huge scientific literature about mood disorders exists. It is not possible to cover everything in a book of reasonable size. As a compromise, I have tried to focus on the information that is likely to be the most relevant for readers. But, please see your mental health providers for the latest information.

A message of hope

You can expect to get well. Sometimes it takes a little time, but almost everyone with a mood disorder can get better and stay well for life. This book provides information, guidance, and specific strategies to help you achieve full recovery. I strongly encourage you to use as many of these approaches as possible.

Managing Emotional Distress and Thoughts of Self-Harm

THIS IS THE MOST IMPORTANT CHAPTER IN THE BOOK. One goal is to help you stay safe if you have thoughts of committing suicide or harming yourself, either now or in the future. This chapter will also help you to manage times of emotional crisis and stress. Please read this chapter now. If you are currently in crisis or have suicidal thoughts, the next section provides options for getting help immediately. If you are not experiencing severe emotional distress right now, please read this chapter and complete the stress and crisis management plan (Form 1.1). We all have times of high stress and can feel overwhelmed by emotion. Ann, whom you met in the Introduction, put it like this: "Depression can feel like getting kicked in the stomach. Sometimes I feel hopeless and helpless." Having a plan prepared ahead of time can help you get through those times. It's like having a fire escape plan in place before a fire. It's hard to come up with a good plan when the building is burning. It will take you only a few minutes to develop a plan.

You might want to read this chapter and develop your stress and crisis management plan with a loved one. Others who know you well may be

Table 1.1   Options for seeking immediate help
◆ Call the National Suicide Prevention Lifeline: 1-800-273-TALK (8255).
◆ Call 911.
◆ Have a family member or friend take you to the nearest emergency room (do not go alone or drive yourself).
◆ Call your mental health or medical provider (if you have one). But if a provider is not immediately available to help, then take one of the above actions.

able to make suggestions for the plan that you might not immediately think of. Please read this chapter and make your plan now.

Options for receiving help immediately

If you are having thoughts of harming yourself (or others) or are in crisis, please take action immediately. Options for getting help immediately are listed in Table 1.1. One source of help is the National Suicide Prevention Lifeline (www.suicidepreventionlifeline.org). This is a free, 24-hour hotline available to anyone who is experiencing emotional crisis or having thoughts of harming self or others. The telephone number is 1-800-273-TALK (8255). Please consider programming that number into your phone now, so that it will be immediately available if you ever need it.

Suicide risk factors

The lifetime risk of suicide for people with **mood disorders** is thought to be 10%–15%.[1] This means that from a statistical perspective, one in every ten individuals with a mood disorder will commit suicide. Please do not be one of those. No matter how bad you may feel right now, you can get well and live a happy life. This book can help you get better and stay that way. So, please do whatever it takes to stay safe. This chapter provides some

Table 1.2   Factors that may increase suicide risk among those with mood disorders[1, 22, 34–37]

- ◆ An anxiety disorder in addition to a mood disorder
- ◆ A substance use disorder in addition to a mood disorder
- ◆ Birth in spring or summer
- ◆ Increased body mass index
- ◆ A serious medical illness in addition to a mood disorder
- ◆ Prior self-harm attempts
- ◆ Access to means to harm self
- ◆ Psychotic symptoms
- ◆ Significant stress
- ◆ Not enough emotional support
- ◆ Months of May and June

options to assist you. Even if you have never had thoughts of harming yourself, please complete Form 1.1. I hope that you, or those you care about, will never experience thoughts of suicide, but it could happen, so please be prepared.

A number of factors can increase the risk of suicide among those with mood disorders. Some of these risk factors are listed in Table 1.2. Many of these factors are not difficult to understand. For example, it makes intuitive sense that someone who is experiencing both a mood disorder and a serious medical illness might have increased stress and thus an increased risk of thinking about suicide. For other factors, such as having been born in spring or summer,[22] the relationship to suicide risk is not well understood.

In addition to the risk factors listed in Table 1.2, there is evidence of a vulnerability to suicide that is independent of having a mood disorder. What does that mean? Evidence indicates that a trait-related predisposition to suicide exists[23–26] that has a significant heritable component.[27] A primary candidate for this susceptibility is the trait of impulsivity.[28–32] In addition to suicide risk, this trait may be associated with risk of nonsuicidal self-injury.[33] *Impulsivity* means a tendency to do things or make decisions rapidly without thinking through the possible consequences. We all can be impulsive at times, but some people tend to be impulsive more frequently than others. Impulsivity may cause someone who is having thoughts of suicide to be more likely to act on those thoughts than a person who is less impulsive. If you or a loved one with a mood disorder tends to be impulsive, there could be a higher risk of suicide. If so, please complete the stress and crisis management plan (in the next section) now and discuss prevention strategies with your treatment team.

I want to be sure that one thing is clear. Having a mood disorder along with one or more of these risk factors does not mean that any individual will have thoughts of suicide or attempt self-harm. It just means that statistically there is some increase in risk. From a practical standpoint, if you have risk factors, then it is imperative that you do everything in your power to stay safe. Part of that process is seeking professional treatment. However, the following section provides an exercise to guide you in the process of developing a stress and crisis management plan.

Developing a stress and crisis management plan

Please complete Form 1.1 to develop your personal plan. It is a suicide and self-harm prevention plan as well as a stress and crisis management plan. You may also think of it as a "safety" plan. It can help you stay safe if you develop thoughts of suicide or self-harm. I use the words *suicide* and *self-harm* because some individuals engage in self-harm behaviors without the intent to commit suicide. Some also develop thoughts of harming others. The plan you develop here can be used in any of these situations as well as any time you are experiencing an emotional crisis or are in distress.

Form 1.1 has two parts. Part 1 is a list of some general responses that you can implement any time you feel unsafe or are in distress. I have listed the first four options. Please add as many others as you can think of. Some possibilities are talking with loved ones, contacting your clergyperson, engaging in meditation, and doing exercises or any activity that typically helps you feel better. If you feel unsafe, however, then please seek help immediately using one of the first four options (already listed on the form).

In Part 2 you list specific triggers that might cause you to develop thoughts of self-harm or feel emotional distress. Once you have developed a list of triggers, please list one or more responses to each. Triggers can be stresses that have led to suicidal thoughts in the past. Other triggers may be any type of event or experience that you typically perceive as stressful or that leads to negative emotions. I recommend being sure to list those stressors that you expect to encounter again in your life. In particular, please list any stressful situations that you anticipate encountering in the near future. The responses may be anything that you find helpful and that is not self-destructive or harmful to others. Members of your mental health treatment team or loved ones may be able to help you think of ideas. Please go ahead and list some options now, and then you can also add to the list later. If possible, try to list more than one response for each trigger. It is fine to use the same response for more than one trigger. Chapter 14 discusses developing plans in response to mood disorder relapse triggers. You will likely find that some of the same strategies are useful for both this plan and mood disorder relapse prevention. Form 1.1 is presented in this section and it is also available as a PDF file that can be downloaded free from our website (http://www.bullpub.com /downloads). Please download and complete Form 1.1 and then keep it with you at all times.

I strongly encourage you to make the stress and crisis management plan a "living" document. By that I mean update it on a regular basis. Reasons to update could include adding new response strategies that you have learned. If you become aware of new stressors in your life, then that is also a reason to do an update.

In addition to your stress and crisis management plan, please consider cultivating other protective factors. One of the most important is seeking treatment for your mood disorder if you have not already done so. Also, many of the complementary strategies listed in Chapter 11 may be helpful. Please use as many of the options suggested in this book as you possibly can—not only to stay safe and manage stress but also to maximize your chances of achieving a full recovery.

Finally, I think having a stress management plan is useful for everyone, whether they have a mood disorder or not. However, this plan is not intended to replace the safety planning that you may do with your treatment team. If you have a mood disorder, please seek treatment and discuss safety and stress management planning with your team.

Form 1.1   Your stress and crisis management plan

Part 1: General prevention actions when in distress or experiencing suicidal thoughts [Implement one of the first four options if you currently feel unsafe.]

1. Call the National Suicide Prevention Lifeline: 1-800-273-TALK (8255).

2. Call 911.

3. Have a family member or friend take you to the nearest emergency room (do not go alone or drive yourself).

4. Call your mental health or medical provider (if you have one). But if a provider is not immediately available to help, then take one of the above actions.

    a. Provider name and number:

    _____

    b. Provider name and number:

    _____

    c. Provider name and number:

5. _____

6. _____

7. _____

8. _____

9. _____

10. _____

Part 2: Potential triggers and specific responses

Trigger   Response

_____   _____

                                     _____

                                     _____

_____   _____

                                     _____

                                     _____

_____   _____

                                     _____

                                     _____

_____   _____

                                     _____

                                     _____

_____   _____

                                     _____

2

Mood Disorders and
the Diagnostic Process

As THE TITLE SUGGESTS, THIS CHAPTER EXPLAINS what **mood disorders** are and how these conditions are diagnosed. I have included a lot of information about the diagnostic criteria for mood disorders. My goal is to provide this material as a ready reference for you. For example, if a member of your treatment team says she thinks you have dysthymic disorder, you can quickly look it up. I certainly don't think you need to commit any of this to memory or even read the information that doesn't apply to you. In contrast, the description of how mood disorders are diagnosed is very important. As you will see, an accurate diagnosis requires good communication between you and the person doing the evaluation. Understanding how the diagnostic process works can help you provide the right information.

The term **mood** refers to one's emotional state, and mood disorders are primarily disorders of emotion. However, mood disorders also cause other symptoms, such as changes in energy level, appetite, and sleep. They can also dramatically affect how we think and even what we think about. But the defining characteristic of a mood disorder is a disturbance of emotional functioning. So, we'll start there.

We all experience a range of emotions every day. Roughly speaking, we can categorize our feelings as generally being either positive or negative. Obvious positive emotions are happiness, hope, and compassion. Negative feelings include anger, disappointment, and embarrassment. Being human means experiencing positive and negative mood states. But what distinguishes a normal mood from a disorder? Broadly speaking, a mood disorder exists when two basic conditions are met: (1) the mood state is abnormal and (2) the symptoms of the mood state are causing significant distress or impairment.

Although actually determining whether someone has a mood disorder is a bit more complicated (much more on that later in this chapter), it is important to start with these two basic criteria. So, what is an abnormal mood state? This is defined as either too much or too little emotion. "Too much" (or "too little") can refer to either intensity or duration. For example, the term **depression**, as used in the context of psychiatric disorder, means either excessive sadness or sadness that lasts for too long. Both intensity and duration are excessive in persons who have mood disorders. The other basic criterion is that some (or all) of the symptoms are causing significant distress or impairment. Before I move on, it is important to note that mood disorders are sometimes called "affective" disorders. The terms *mood disorder* and *affective disorder* are used interchangeably. **Affect** also refers to one's current experience of emotion. Technically speaking, *affect* refers to one's immediate emotional state, while *mood* means a more sustained period of a particular mood. A good analogy is that affect is like weather while mood is like climate.

The most accepted definitions of mood disorders are those listed in the *Diagnostic and Statistical Manual of Mental Disorders* published by the American Psychiatric Association.[38] Those definitions are used in this book unless otherwise noted. More about this manual later—for now just know that is the reference for the following discussion.

Mood disorders come in two basic varieties: unipolar and bipolar. Bipolar disorders are sometimes referred to as **manic-depressive disorders**; however, this terminology is used less frequently nowadays. **Unipolar** disorders cause abnormalities of mood intensity in only one direction or toward one "pole" of the emotional continuum. The depressive disorders are unipolar because they cause abnormalities only on the depressive end of the emotional range. In contrast, bipolar disorders result in both mood elevations and depressions and are thus "bi"-polar. You may notice that I used the plural word *disorders* for both conditions. This is because there is more than one disorder in each general category. These disorders are thought to represent a range from more to less severe (for example, from mild to severe depression) expressions of the same basic condition along the continuum. Thus, mood disorders are commonly referred to collectively as "bipolar spectrum" or "unipolar spectrum." That convention is used in this book, and disorders are generally referred to as either bipolar spectrum or unipolar spectrum.

Individuals with depressive disorders experience one or more episodes of depressed mood. Those with bipolar disorders have episodes of both mood depressions and elevations. So, what exactly are mood depressions and elevations anyway? The concept of depressed mood is straightforward. Feeling depressed is simply another way to say that one is sad, down, or blue. This is easy to understand because we all feel sadness as a normal life experience whether we have had a depressive disorder or not. The feeling may be the same, but the intensity and duration are greater for depression than for normal sadness. You may remember Ann from earlier in this book. She is fifty-five and has had depression since she was a child. Ann described the intense sadness of depression as feeling like she has been kicked in the stomach.

Mood elevations are bit trickier to understand because most people who do not have a bipolar disorder don't experience an abnormally elevated mood to any appreciable extent. The closest most people come is likely to be feeling very excited or giddy from time to time. Episodes of elevated mood associated with the bipolar spectrum disorders are referred to as **mania** or, if a milder form, **hypomania**. Manic and hypomanic episodes are generally characterized by excessive elation, known as **euphoria**. However, please be aware that mania and hypomania can cause irritability rather than euphoria. Since the concept of mania may be unfamiliar, some additional reading may be informative. For an authentic and courageous personal account of

---

Table 2.1   Symptoms that can be caused by depressive episodes[38]

+ Depressed mood

+ Loss of interest in, or the ability to experience pleasure from, activities that are normally enjoyed (the technical name for this is **anhedonia**)

+ Change in appetite (increase or decrease) or weight gain or loss

+ Insomnia or increased sleeping

+ Increase or decrease of motor activity

+ Fatigue or loss of energy

+ Feelings of worthlessness or inappropriate guilt

+ Difficulty thinking or concentrating or trouble making decisions

+ Thoughts of death or committing suicide

---

the experience of living with bipolar disorder, I strongly recommend *An Unquiet Mind: A Memoir of Moods and Madness* by Kay Redfield Jamison (see Appendix C, Recommended Reading). Dr. Jamison is a Professor of Psychiatry at the Johns Hopkins University School of Medicine. She also has bipolar disorder. She tells a compelling and highly intimate story from the unique perspective of a mental health professional who suffers from a mood disorder.

In addition to causing problems with emotion, **mood episodes** cause other kinds of symptoms as well. These are outlined in Tables 2.1 and 2.2.

Many depressive episodes don't result in all of the symptoms described in Table 2.1, but a minimum number is required to make the diagnosis (more about this later). There are also other symptoms commonly associated with depression, such as anxiety, that are not listed in Table 2.1. Those symptoms that are listed constitute the "official" criteria in the *Diagnostic and Statistical Manual of Mental Disorders*.[38]

Symptoms associated with mood elevations are listed in Table 2.2. As with depressive episodes, most people don't experience all of the listed

---

Table 2.2 Symptoms that can be caused by manic or hypomanic episodes[38]

- Elevated, expansive, or irritable mood

- Abnormally increased self-esteem (known as *grandiosity*)

- Decreased need for sleep

- Talkativeness

- Thoughts going faster than usual

- Easy distractibility

- Increased activity or agitation

- Excessive involvement in pleasurable activities that have a high potential to lead to painful consequences

---

symptoms during each manic or hypomanic episode. However, all mood episodes have a minimum number of symptoms that must be experienced during an episode in order to meet the "official" criteria.[38] Additionally, symptoms must persist for at least a minimum specified time period. These details are covered in the next section. The limitations of the "official criteria" are also discussed later in this book.

How psychiatric disorders are diagnosed

One definition of *diagnosis* is the identification of the nature and cause of an illness. In this book, I use the word *diagnose* to mean determining what disorder or disorders you may have, and I use *diagnosis* to mean the specific name of the disorder, such as major depression. The plural of diagnosis is *diagnoses*, referring to more than one disorder. One more word about terminology: A variety of medical and mental health professionals are trained to diagnose psychiatric disorders (see Chapter 5). So, I use the terms *diagnostic evaluation* and *initial evaluation* to mean a diagnostic assessment conducted

Table 2.3 Three categories of information used to make diagnoses

+ History: In medical terminology, the clinical history (or more commonly just "history") is used much the same as in everyday language. It is a patient's report of her or his illness. For example, "I have had pain in my left shoulder for about a week."

+ Physical examination: The "physical" or "physical exam" refers to the hands-on examination of the patient by the doctor or other health care professional. This may be a complete physical or a limited exam that is focused on a few areas that are relevant to the current problem.

+ Laboratory and other diagnostic procedures: These procedures can include lab work, such as a complete blood count or thyroid function tests, X-rays, or more invasive procedures, such as a biopsy.

by any qualified professional. These evaluations are also sometimes called "psychiatric evaluations" or "intake evaluations." In all areas of medicine, diagnoses are based on three general types of information, which are listed in Table 2.3.

The importance of the different categories of information varies greatly with the illness or disease process. For an injured arm, the most important information may be an X-ray to determine whether there is a fracture. For possible diabetes, blood glucose tests may be most important. For mood and all psychiatric disorders, the clinical history is most important.

The ideal diagnostic method is one that is objective (that is, not subject to different interpretations by different people) and definitive (gives a definite yes or no answer). In our example of an arm injury, an X-ray may provide both objective and definitive evidence of a fracture. In fact, it may be so obvious that anyone would be able to make the diagnosis—no medical training required! Unfortunately, many diagnostic tests are not so precise. Still, for most medical conditions some diagnostic tests can be helpful.

In contrast, there are currently no objective laboratory diagnostic tests or procedures that can be used to diagnose mood disorders. Therefore, the diagnostic process must be based almost entirely on history. In this case, *history* means your mood disorder history. That is why it is so critical to provide accurate and detailed information during a diagnostic evaluation to prevent misdiagnosis. In most cases, that requires some preparation, and this is especially true if the history is complicated. Part of this book is about gathering that information and helping you prepare for a diagnostic evaluation.

Before moving on, you need to know that diagnostic tests and a physical examination can be critical components of a diagnostic evaluation and in many cases are necessary (more about this later). However, the purpose is not to diagnose a psychiatric disorder, but rather to rule out other conditions that might be causing the symptoms. For example, hypothyroidism can cause symptoms that are similar to depression, and it may need to be ruled out. A physical exam and laboratory tests may also be useful to monitor treatment in some cases (see Chapter 8). Finally, psychological testing is often an important component of any assessment process.

Now you may be wondering why there are no laboratory diagnostic tests for mood disorders. Why can't we just draw some blood or do a brain scan and say, "Oh, that is definitely bipolar disorder"? The answer has to do with the complexity of the human brain. One great thing about being a member of the human race is our amazing intellectual and language capabilities. Our ability as a species to accomplish so many things is a direct result of our complex brains. However, our brains are so complex that it is very challenging to understand human brain function. It is even more difficult to understand many brain disorders, such as psychiatric conditions. We do know a lot and that information is presented in detail in Chapter 4. But, for now, the key point is that mood disorders are diagnosed based on what you tell your mental health or medical provider. So, it is essential that you get it right.

You now know that the history is the main component of a diagnostic evaluation. But how do we take that information and decide whether it means that you have a disorder and, if so, then which disorder? Mood disorders are defined by a set of criteria. Most criteria are symptoms. A symptom is something you experience, like chest pain or a toothache or sadness. Other criteria can be such things as how long you have experienced the symptoms and how much distress the symptoms cause. We'll take a detailed tour through the diagnostic criteria for mood disorders in a few pages. But first some more background information.

As mentioned above, the diagnostic criteria for psychiatric disorders are defined in a book known as the *Diagnostic and Statistical Manual of Mental Disorders*[38] or, as it's commonly known, the DSM. The current version is the fourth revision, so it is referred to as the DSM-IV. Another tidbit—this version has a minor text revision, so it is also called the DSM-IV-TR, with "TR" standing for text revision. I refer to the DSM-IV frequently in this book, so it will be helpful for you to know a bit about it. Before we move on, though, it is important to note that there are other classification systems, such as the International Statistical Classification of Diseases and Related Health Problems, 10th Revision. The ICD-10, as its commonly known, is a classification system of the World Health Organization. I refer to the DSM in this book because it is most commonly used in the United States.

First of all, the DSM isn't some kind of secret manual available to only psychiatrists and other mental health professionals. It is readily available to the public, and you can find it for sale in many bookstores and online. I'm not recommending that you purchase the DSM; my point is to make you aware that it is readily available. The American Psychiatric Association, the national organization for physicians specializing in psychiatry, publishes the DSM-IV. It outlines the diagnostic criteria for all psychiatric disorders. Additionally, it provides supplementary information about disorders, such as familial pattern or inheritability, other disorders that may be similar, and the prevalence and course of illness. The DSM is written by prominent psychiatrists and other mental health professionals based on the evidence suggesting how psychiatric disorders should be defined. It is updated periodically as new information becomes available. The DSM is the gold standard for defining mood disorders. However, it is important for you to know about its limitations.

The main problem with the DSM is that it is not based on the biological causes of disorders. In medicine, almost all disorders are defined, at least in part, by the underlying pathology. As discussed above, we do not yet understand the causes of psychiatric conditions well enough to use pathology as a part of the definition. As science advances, this will likely be possible in the future. For now, we are limited to definitions based on the existence of symptoms. The problem is that more than one pathological process may lead to the same set of symptoms. Further, one process may respond to a particular treatment while another does not. Thus, in the future, defining disorders by their **neurobiology**, or biological cause, may lead to more specifically targeted, and therefore more effective, treatment approaches.

Another limitation of the DSM-IV is that the criteria are, to a certain extent, arbitrary. For example, to meet the criteria for a major depressive disorder, one must experience one or more major depressive episodes that last at least two weeks. But what if someone has had many episodes of serious depression but the longest lasted twelve days? It would be illogical to say that person doesn't suffer from major depressive disorder, but technically she or he would not meet the DSM-IV criteria. So, it is important to keep in mind that the DSM-IV is very useful but someone may suffer from a disorder without completely meeting the diagnostic criteria as outlined in that manual. In this book, the DSM-IV criteria will be used to help you determine your most likely diagnosis; however, please keep in mind that the DSM definitions are imperfect and will likely change as we learn more.

Rather than strictly sticking to the DSM criteria, I think a more practical approach is to decide whether the criteria for a disorder are met for treatment purposes. Defining whether a disorder exists for "treatment purposes" means simply deciding whether a person has a condition that should be treated. Someone might, for example, have symptoms that meet the criteria for an episode of major depression but then those symptoms go away after just a few weeks and don't come back. Obviously, that person would not need immediate treatment, although the person should be on the lookout for a return of the symptoms. On the other hand, a person may have symptoms that don't meet all of the criteria for an "official diagnosis" but the condition persists and causes distress. In that case, treatment would likely be warranted. Mental health professionals generally make diagnoses for treatment purposes. There is one exception that you should know about: diagnoses made for "research purposes." That is the method my colleagues and I use for functional imaging studies of mood disorders. In research, we need to use precise definitions of psychiatric conditions. I mention this because some of you may have volunteered for a mood disorder study. Perhaps you were told you did not meet study criteria. Many potential volunteers for our studies have that experience. It is important to know that even if you didn't meet the research criteria, you may still have a disorder that warrants treatment.

One final point about the DSM: A new version, the DSM-V, is currently being developed. It is expected to be available in spring 2013. Some changes have been proposed to the mood disorder diagnostic criteria. These changes will not make the current criteria used in this book less useful. You can visit the DSM-V website (http://www.dsm5.org/) to see the recommended changes as well as follow the progress of the development of the new manual.

The disorders

This section provides the details of the criteria for the diagnosis of mood disorders according to the DSM-IV. Why do you need this information? It can help you collaborate more effectively with your treatment team during the assessment process. I certainly don't think you need to memorize anything, but an understanding of the diagnostic process can help prevent miscommunications and assist you in preparing for an evaluation. Remember, an accurate diagnosis depends on your providing an accurate history of your illness. The better you understand the process and definitions, the more effective the communication with your provider will be.

Mood episodes

Mood disorder diagnoses are based on the existence of periods of abnormal mood states, known as mood episodes. So, let's start with the definition of a mood episode. Mood episodes are discrete periods of a continuous mood state with a definite beginning and end. Episodes can last for days,

---

Table 2.4   Definitions of mood episodes[38]

+ **Dysthymic episode:** At least two years of depressive symptoms that do not meet the criteria for a major depressive episode

+ **Hypomanic episode:** A period of abnormally elevated mood and associated symptoms, but less severe than a manic episode

+ **Major depressive episode:** At least two weeks (usually more) of depressed mood and associated symptoms

+ **Manic episode:** A period of abnormally elevated mood and associated symptoms

+ **Mixed episode:** Manic and depressive symptoms that occur at the same time

+ **Normal mood:** Our day-to-day emotional state during which we experience a range of positive and negative emotions, also known as "euthymic mood" or "full remission" if one has previously had a period of abnormal mood

+ **Partial remission:** Incomplete symptom recovery from either an abnormally elevated or a depressed mood episode, typically used when one is starting to respond to treatment but is not yet completely better

---

months, or years; however, a minimum duration is often required to distinguish an episode of abnormal mood from the normal ups and downs we all experience. For example, two weeks of feeling sad is the minimum time required for the diagnosis of a depressive episode. Specific mood episodes are required for a diagnosis of a mood disorder. However, particular mood episodes can also serve to rule out a diagnosis. This information is summarized in Table 2.4. You need to know the definition of each type of mood episode. The general definitions are provided in Table 2.4 as a quick reference, and then detailed explanations follow.

This can all be a bit confusing because a lot of terminology is involved. An example of a mood episode is "I experienced three weeks of depression last month." A mood disorder is based on mood episodes. For example, "I was diagnosed with major depression because of my mood episode last month."

In addition to the general definitions listed in Table 2.4, the DSM-IV provides a list of criteria that have to be met in order for a diagnosis of a mood episode to be made. These criteria are outlined in Table 2.5. Let me point out that in most situations only one mood disorder is diagnosed at a time. For example, if someone meets the criteria for a diagnosis of an adjustment disorder but then symptoms worsen such that a diagnosis of major depression is warranted, the diagnosis is changed. The individual is not given both diagnoses. One exception is someone who develops an episode of major depression superimposed upon dysthymic disorder; then both diagnoses are given.

Depressive spectrum disorders

Three types of primary depressive disorders are currently recognized by the DSM-IV: **major depressive disorder, dysthymic disorder,** and **depressive disorder not otherwise specified.** Depressive symptoms can also be diagnosed as adjustment disorders with depressive symptoms, normal grief, and depressive disorders secondary to substance abuse or medical illness. The depressive disorders are listed in Table 2.6. See Table 2.8 for the defining characteristics of all the mood disorders.

Bipolar spectrum disorders

Four bipolar spectrum disorders are outlined in the DSM-IV. As with the depressive disorders, bipolar disorders secondary to substance abuse or medical illness are also described. Unlike with the depressive illnesses, however, there are no adjustment disorders with elevated mood and normal grief obviously does not cause mood elevation. The bipolar disorders are listed in Table 2.7. See Table 2.8 for the defining characteristics of all the mood disorders.

You now have a good idea of what mood disorders are. The next chapter will help you determine whether you are likely to have a mood disorder.

Table 2.5 Detailed criteria for the diagnosis of mood episodes according to the DSM-IV[38]

Mood episode type	Minimum duration	Required symptoms	Distress or impairment	Symptoms are not caused by
Major depressive episode	2 weeks	Must have at least 5. One must experience either (or both): • Depressed mood • Anhedonia Associated symptoms: • Change in appetite or weight • Insomnia or increased sleeping • Change of motor activity • Fatigue or loss of energy • Feelings of worthlessness or inappropriate guilt • Difficulty thinking, concentrating, or making decisions • Thoughts of death or suicide	Must cause significant distress and/or impairment in social, occupational, or other areas of functioning	Medication, medical condition, substance use, or bereavement

Continues ▶

Table 2.5 Detailed criteria for the diagnosis of mood episodes according to the DSM-IV[38] (*continued*)

Mood episode type	Minimum duration	Required symptoms	Distress or impairment	Symptoms are not caused by

Dysthymic episode	2 years	Must have at least 3. One must be:
		• Depressed mood
		Associated symptoms:
		  ♦ Change in appetite or weight
		  ♦ Insomnia or increased sleeping
		  ♦ Fatigue or loss of energy
		  ♦ Low self-esteem
		  ♦ Difficulty concentrating or making decisions
		  ♦ Feelings of hopelessness
			Same as for major depressive episode	Same as for major depressive episode

Manic episode	1 week (or any duration if hospitalized)	Must have at least 4 (or 5 if irritable mood). One must be:
		• Elevated or irritable mood
		Associated symptoms:
		  ♦ Elevated self-esteem or grandiosity
		  ♦ Decreased need for sleep
		  ♦ Talkativeness
		  ♦ Flight of ideas or racing thoughts
		  ♦ Distractibility
		  ♦ Increased goal-directed activity
		  ♦ Excessive involvement in pleasurable activities
			Must cause at least one:
			♦ Marked impairment
			♦ Hospitalization
			♦ Psychosis
				Same as for major depressive episode

Table 2.5 Detailed criteria for the diagnosis of mood episodes according to the DSM-IV[38] (*continued*)

Mood episode type	Minimum duration	Required symptoms	Distress or impairment	Symptoms are not caused by
Hypomanic episode	4 days	Same as for manic episode	Must cause: ◆ Change in functioning that is observable by others Does not cause: ◆ Marked impairment ◆ Hospitalization ◆ Psychosis	Same as for major depressive episode
Mixed episode	1 week	Must meet criteria for both a major depressive and a manic episode nearly every day	Must cause at least one: ◆ Marked impairment ◆ Hospitalization ◆ Psychosis	Same as for major depressive episode

Table 2.6   Depressive disorders[38]

- **Major depressive disorder:** The diagnosis given when someone has experienced one or more episodes of major depression

- **Dysthymic disorder:** At least two years of continuous depressive symptoms that do not meet the criteria for an episode of major depression

- **Adjustment disorder with depressed mood:** Depressive symptoms that develop in response to a specific stressor that do not meet the criteria for an episode of major depression and are not caused by bereavement

- **Adjustment disorder with mixed anxiety and depressed mood:** Both anxiety and depressive symptoms that develop in response to a specific stressor that do not meet the criteria for an episode of major depression and are not caused by bereavement

- **Bereavement:** Normal sadness in response to the death of a loved one

- **Substance-induced mood disorder:** Depression that occurs as a result of substance abuse or dependence

- **Mood disorder due to a medical condition:** Symptoms similar to depression that are known to be caused by a nonpsychiatric medical illness

- **Depressive disorder not otherwise specified:** Also known as "depressive disorder NOS," a catchall category for depressive symptoms that do not meet the criteria for any of the specific disorders

Table 2.7   Bipolar spectrum disorders[38]

+ **Bipolar I disorder:** At least one manic or mixed episode; usually multiple episodes of mood elevation and depression

+ **Bipolar II disorder:** One or more major depressive and one or more hypomanic episodes, but no manic or mixed episodes

+ **Cyclothymic disorder:** Hypomanic episodes as well as depressive episodes that do not meet the criteria for a major depressive episode

+ **Substance-induced mood disorder:** Manic or hypomanic symptoms that occur as a result of substance abuse or dependence

+ **Mood disorder due to a medical condition:** Symptoms similar to mania or hypomania caused by a nonpsychiatric medical illness

+ **Bipolar disorder NOS:** Bipolar features that do not meet the criteria for any specific bipolar disorder

Table 2.8 DSM-IV defining characteristics of all mood disorders

Disorder	Mood episodes required	Other possible mood episodes	Mood episodes not allowed
Major depressive disorder	One or more major depressive episodes	Depressive episodes that do not meet the criteria for an episode of major depression or dysthymic disorder	Any manic, hypomanic, or mixed episode
Dysthymic disorder	One or more dysthymic episodes	Same as for major depressive disorder	Any manic, hypomanic, or mixed episode
Adjustment disorder with depressed mood	Depressive symptoms in response to a specific stressor that do not meet the criteria for either major depression or dysthymic disorder	Any, but symptoms cannot be the result of a preexisting mood disorder	None, but symptoms cannot be the result of a preexisting mood disorder
Bipolar I disorder	One or more manic or mixed episodes	Major depressive, hypomanic, and mood episodes that do not meet the criteria for a manic, hypomanic, or major depressive episode	None
Bipolar II disorder	One or more major depressive and one or more hypomanic episodes	Major depressive, hypomanic, and mood episodes that do not meet the criteria for a hypomanic or major depressive episode	Any manic or mixed episode

Disorder	Mood episodes required	Other possible mood episodes	Mood episodes not allowed
Cyclothymic disorder	One or more hypomanic episodes and one or more depressive episodes that do not meet the criteria for a major depressive episode	Elevated mood episodes that do not meet the criteria for a hypomanic episode	Any major depressive, manic, or mixed episode
Substance-induced mood disorder	One or more depressed or elevated mood episodes that occur as a result of use of a substance	Any, but symptoms cannot be the result of a primary mood disorder	None, but symptoms cannot be the result of a primary mood disorder
Mood disorder due to a medical condition	One or more depressed or elevated mood episodes that occur as a result of a medical condition	Any, but symptoms cannot be the result of a primary mood disorder	None, but symptoms cannot be the result of a primary mood disorder
Depressive disorder NOS	One or more depressive episodes that do not meet the criteria for a specific mood disorder	Any, but symptoms cannot be the result of a primary mood disorder	None, but symptoms cannot be the result of a primary mood disorder
Bipolar disorder NOS	One or more episodes suggestive of bipolar illness that do not meet the criteria for a specific mood disorder	Any, but symptoms cannot be the result of a primary mood disorder	None, but symptoms cannot be the result of a primary mood disorder

3

Do You Have a Mood Disorder?

THE FIRST AIM OF THIS CHAPTER is to help you determine whether it is likely that you have a **mood disorder.** This information can help you decide if you should seek treatment. The second aim is to help you determine which disorder or disorders you most likely are suffering from.

Please note that I used the word *likely* twice sentences above. Any process for self-assessment, such as used in this book, has limitations. Specifically, it is not possible to interpret all of the variables that may exist in your situation. So the results of your self-assessment should be considered only as a guide to your diagnosis, not the final word. As I have said elsewhere, this book is not a substitute for an evaluation by a medical or mental health professional. However, knowing your *likely* diagnosis can be very beneficial. Potential advantages for you are listed in Table 3.1.

Before we move on, I want to make one very important point about what the exercise in this chapter cannot do: THE EXERCISE IN THIS CHAPTER CANNOT RULE OUT ANY DISORDER OR DISORDERS. Many people experience symptoms that don't exactly meet the diagnostic criteria for a disorder, but they still may benefit from some type of

---

Table 3.1   Advantages to knowing your most likely diagnosis

Knowing your most likely diagnosis will:

- ◆ Help you decide if you should seek treatment

- ◆ Assist you to prepare for a diagnostic evaluation

- ◆ Help you be sure that you are receiving the optimal treatment

- ◆ Help you collaborate with the members of your clinical team

- ◆ Aid you in determining whether a diagnosis you may have already been given is likely to be correct

- ◆ Prevent misdiagnosis of a bipolar spectrum disorder as unipolar illness

- ◆ Ensure that any comorbid conditions (for example, both a mood and an anxiety disorder) are identified

---

intervention. Also, as I discussed in Chapter 2, our diagnostic criteria are imperfect. Finally, a certain amount of interpretation often needs to be done to decide whether any symptom should be counted toward a diagnosis. That is because most symptoms represent our subjective experience. Energy level is a good example. What seems like high or low energy to me might seem to be in the normal range for you. That's because we have different baseline levels of energy. Thus, the determination of whether an experience represents a symptom is not as straightforward as this book might make it seem. A book cannot sort out these kinds of nuances. IF YOU HAVE SYMPTOMS THAT ARE BOTHERSOME, PLEASE HAVE A PROFESSIONAL DO AN EVALUATION, REGARDLESS OF THE RESULTS OF COMPLETING THE EXERCISE IN THIS CHAPTER.

Most of this chapter consists of an exercise for you to complete to determine your probable diagnosis or diagnoses. First, please download and print Form 3.1. It is available as a PDF file that can be downloaded from our website (http://www.bullpub.com /downloads). You will use that form along with the exercise in this chapter to complete the self-evaluation process. The sections of the form are also reproduced in this chapter, but it will be much more efficient if you use a separate printed copy as you work through the assessment.

One of the most important goals of the following exercise is to help you determine whether you most likely have unipolar or bipolar spectrum illness. This distinction is critical because bipolar depression is often mistaken for unipolar illness and treated incorrectly. So, please pay special attention to the questions about mood elevations.

We will start this process with reviewing your mood episode history, and then we will progress to determining your most likely diagnosis. See Chapter 2 for a detailed explanation of mood episodes and how disorders are diagnosed.

Mood episodes

The purpose of the first part of this exercise is to define the types of mood episodes that you have experienced. Section 1 of Form 3.1 on page 54 is a mood episode summary. You will be instructed to check boxes on the mood episode summary as a result of some of your answers to the questions on the following pages. Answer all questions unless you are specifically instructed to skip an item.

For each type of episode (depressive, manic, etc.), try to answer the questions for one specific episode that you have experienced. THE QUESTIONS FOR EACH EPISODE SHOULD BE ANSWERED FOR THE WORST EPISODE OF THAT TYPE THAT YOU HAVE EVER EXPERIENCED. This can be a current or previous episode. If you can't clearly define a "worst" episode, then use an episode that is representative of your usual or average episode of that type.

Depressive episodes

Answer the following questions to determine whether you may have (or have had in the past) a depressive episode. *Cardinal symptoms* are fundamental or essential symptoms required for a diagnosis.

Cardinal symptoms: Depression and anhedonia

The two fundamental symptoms of *depression* are sadness and *anhedonia* (difficulty experiencing pleasure).

Question 1. Some sadness is normal. Have you ever (either now or in the past) experienced periods of feeling sad, down, or blue that lasted two weeks or longer?

   ☒ Yes.

   ☐ No.

Question 2. If you answered yes to question 1, was the sadness caused by grief or a loss that would cause depression in most people?

   ☒ Yes.

   ☐ No.

   ☐ Not applicable.

Question 3. If you answered yes to question 2, was the sadness so severe that it interfered with your life and/or did it last longer than two months?

   ☒ Yes.

   ☐ No.

   ☐ Not applicable.

Question 4. Did you answer either yes to question 1 and no to question 2 OR yes to questions 1, 2, and 3?

   ☒ Yes. Check the depression box (a) on the mood episode summary (Form 3.1).

   ☐ No.

Question 5. Have you had periods of time lasting at least two weeks during which you lost interest in or were unable to experience pleasure from most activities that you normally enjoy?

   ☒ Yes. Check the anhedonia box (b) on the mood episode summary (Form 3.1).

   ☐ No.

Other depressive symptoms

In addition to the fundamental (or cardinal) symptoms, many individuals with depression also experience a number of other symptoms. Answer the following questions for a time (now or in the past) when you were experiencing depressed mood, anhedonia, or both. Please answer yes if you experienced the symptom most of the time while you were having depression and/or anhedonia. Respond no if the symptom was only occasional or rare.

Question 6. When you were experiencing depressed mood and/or anhedonia, did you also notice a change (increase or decrease) in your appetite or weight?

   ☒ Yes. Check the appetite/weight box (c) on the mood episode summary (Form 3.1).

   ☐ No.

Question 7. When you were experiencing depressed mood and/or anhedonia, did you also notice increased or decreased sleep on many or most nights?

   ☒ Yes. Check the sleep box (d) on the mood episode summary (Form 3.1).

   ☐ No.

Question 8. When you were experiencing depressed mood and/or anhedonia, did you also notice either that you were restless and had difficulty sitting still OR that your movements or levels of motor activities were decreased or slowed down?

   ☐ Yes. Check the psychomotor box (e) on the mood episode summary (Form 3.1).

   ☒ No.

Question 9. When you were experiencing depressed mood and/or anhedonia, did you also notice that you felt fatigue or low energy most days?

   ☒ Yes. Check the fatigue box (f) on the mood episode summary (Form 3.1).

   ☐ No.

Question 10. When you were experiencing depressed mood and/or anhedonia, did you also experience thoughts or feelings of worthlessness or inappropriate guilt on most days?

☑ Yes. Check the worthlessness/guilt box (g) on the mood episode summary (Form 3.1).

☐ No.

Question 11. When you were experiencing depressed mood and/or anhedonia, did you also experience either difficulty thinking and concentrating OR indecisiveness on most days?

☑ Yes. Check the thinking/concentrating/indecisive box (h) on the mood episode summary (Form 3.1).

☐ No.

Question 12. When you were experiencing depressed mood and/or anhedonia, did you also experience persistent thoughts of death or suicide OR have a suicide plan OR attempt suicide?

☑ Yes. Check the thoughts of death/suicide box (i) on the mood episode summary (Form 3.1).

☐ No.

Distress/impairment and medical causes

In order to meet the criteria for a major depressive episode, the symptoms should cause either distress or impairment. Impairment means that symptoms interfered with your work, relationships, or pleasurable activities. Also, it is important to know whether your symptoms might have been caused by a medical problem, such as thyroid disease.

Question 13. When you were experiencing depressed mood and/or anhedonia, did your symptoms cause you distress or interfere with your life in any way OR were you hospitalized because of your symptoms?

☐ Yes. Check the distress/impairment box (j) on the mood episode summary (Form 3.1).

☐ No.

Question 14. When you were experiencing depressed mood and/or anhedonia, were you told by a medical professional that your symptoms were caused by another medical illness?

☐ Yes. Check the medical cause box (k) on the mood episode summary (Form 3.1).

☐ No.

Dysthymic disorder

Chronic (long lasting) but milder symptoms are diagnosed as dysthymic disorder.

Question 15. Have you ever experienced depressive symptoms consistently on most days for two years or longer (with no more than a two-month period without symptoms during that time)?

☐ Yes. Check the episode lasting two years or longer box (l) on the mood episode summary (Form 3.1) AND answer questions 16 and 17 below.

☐ No. Skip to question 18.

Question 16. When you were experiencing depression, did you also experience low self-esteem?

☐ Yes. Check the low self-esteem box (m) on the mood episode summary (Form 3.1).

☐ No.

Question 17. When you were experiencing depression, did you also experience hopelessness?

☐ Yes. Check the hopelessness box (n) on the mood episode summary (Form 3.1).

☐ No.

Manic, hypomanic, and mixed episodes

The following questions will help you determine whether you have experienced either a manic or hypomanic episode.

Mood elevation

The cardinal symptom of *mania* and *hypomania* is elevated mood, which means several days in a row of being too "high." The elevated mood may be either too happy or irritable or a combination of both. PLEASE ANSWER THE FOLLOWING QUESTION YES ONLY IF THE MOOD EPISODE IS CLEARLY HIGHER THAN YOUR NORMAL BASELINE MOOD (WHEN YOU ARE NOT DEPRESSED).

Question 18. Have you ever experienced a period of time when your mood was abnormally elevated on a constant basis for several days in a row?

☐ Yes. Check the mood elevation box (o) on the mood episode summary (Form 3.1).

☐ No. Skip to the mood episode summary (Form 3.1).

Other mood elevation symptoms

In addition to mood elevation, a number of other symptoms accompany manic and hypomanic episodes. PLEASE ANSWER THE FOLLOWING QUESTIONS YES ONLY IF THE SYMPTOMS OCCURRED DURING THE TIME YOUR MOOD WAS ELEVATED AND PERSISTED FOR ALMOST ALL DAY EACH DAY OF THE MOOD ELEVATION.

Question 19. During the time your mood was elevated, did you also experience grandiosity (too high an opinion of your skills or abilities) or abnormally elevated self-esteem?

☐ Yes. Check the grandiosity/elevated self-esteem box (p) on the mood episode summary (Form 3.1).

☐ No.

Question 20. During the time your mood was elevated, did you also experience a decreased need for sleep? PLEASE ANSWER THE QUESTION YES ONLY IF YOU COULD GET BY ON MUCH LESS SLEEP THAN YOU NORMALLY NEED WITHOUT FEELING TIRED THE NEXT DAY. ANSWER NO IF YOU JUST HAD TROUBLE SLEEPING BUT FELT TIRED THE NEXT DAY.

☐ Yes. Check the decreased need for sleep box (q) on the mood episode summary (Form 3.1).

☐ No.

Question 21. During the time your mood was elevated, did you also experience increased talkativeness or feel an internal pressure to keep talking?

☐ Yes. Check the increased talkativeness box (r) on the mood episode summary (Form 3.1).

☐ No.

Question 22. During the time your mood was elevated, did you also experience the sense that your thoughts were racing or that your mind jumped rapidly from one thing to another?

☐ Yes. Check the racing thoughts box (s) on the mood episode summary (Form 3.1).

☐ No.

Question 23. During the time your mood was elevated, did you also experience problems with being easily distracted?

☐ Yes. Check the distractibility box (t) on the mood episode summary (Form 3.1).

☐ No.

Question 24. During the time your mood was elevated, did you also notice that you were much more active (socially, at work or school, or sexually) than normal or had trouble sitting still?

- ☐ Yes. Check the increased activity box (u) on the mood episode summary (Form 3.1).
- ☐ No.

Question 25. During the time your mood was elevated, did you also notice that you were much more involved in pleasurable activities with the potential for negative consequences (shopping sprees, sexual indiscretions, gambling, poor business investments)?

- ☐ Yes. Check the increased pleasurable activity box (v) on the mood episode summary (Form 3.1).
- ☐ No.

Question 26. During the time your mood was elevated, did you also experience psychotic symptoms? PSYCHOTIC SYMPTOMS ARE HALLUCINATIONS (HEARING OR SEEING THINGS THAT AREN'T REALLY THERE) OR DELUSIONS (BELIEVING THINGS THAT AREN'T REAL).

- ☐ Yes. Check the psychotic symptoms box (w) on the mood episode summary (Form 3.1).
- ☐ No.

Impairment and medical causes

In order to meet the criteria for a manic or hypomanic episode, the symptoms should cause impairment. Impairment means that symptoms interfered with your work, relationships or pleasurable activities. Also, it is important to know if your symptoms might have been caused by a medical problem, such as thyroid disease.

Question 27. When you were experiencing elevated mood, did your symptoms interfere with your life in any way?

- ☐ Yes. Check the interference with your life box (x) on the mood episode summary (Form 3.1).
- ☐ No.

Question 28. When you were experiencing elevated mood, were you hospitalized because of your symptoms?

☐ Yes. Check the hospitalization box (y) on the mood episode summary (Form 3.1).

☐ No.

Question 29. When you were experiencing elevated mood, were you told by a medical professional that your symptoms were caused by another medical illness?

☐ Yes. Check the medical cause box (z) on the mood episode summary (Form 3.1).

☐ No.

Mixed episodes

Some individuals with bipolar spectrum disorders have episodes during which they experience mania and depression at the same time. These are known as mixed episodes.

Question 30. When you were experiencing elevated mood, did you also experience depressive symptoms every day for at least one week?

☐ Yes. Check the mixed episode box (aa) on the mood episode summary (Form 3.1).

☐ No.

Episode duration

Determining the duration of episodes of mood elevation is important for diagnosis.

Question 31. Have you ever experienced AT LEAST ONE episode of elevated mood during which you experienced symptoms every day for at least seven days in a row?

☐ Yes. Check the one-week duration box (bb) on the mood episode summary (Form 3.1).

☐ No.

Question 32. Have you ever experienced AT LEAST ONE episode of elevated mood during which you experienced symptoms every day for at least four days in a row?

☐ Yes. Check the four-day duration box (cc) on the mood episode summary (Form 3.1).

☐ No.

Form 3.1, Section 1: Mood episode summary

The mood episode summary is the first section of Form 3.1. Section 1 is also reproduced below. However, it will likely be more convenient to download (http://www.bullpub.com/downloads) and print the form and complete it as you work through this assessment. You should have marked each of the following boxes (here or on Form 3.1) for which you checked yes to the corresponding question. If you have not yet done so, please answer the questions on the preceding pages and check the following boxes as instructed.

Depression and anhedonia

☐ a. Depressed mood (question 4)

☐ b. Anhedonia (question 5)

Other depressive symptoms

☐ c. Appetite/weight (question 6)

☐ d. Sleep (question 7)

☐ e. Psychomotor (question 8)

☐ f. Fatigue (question 9)

☐ g. Worthlessness/guilt (question 10)

☐ h. Thinking/concentrating/indecisive (question 11)

☐ i. Thoughts of death/suicide (question 12)

Distress/impairment and medical causes

☐ j. Distress/impairment (question 13)

☐ k. Medical cause (question 14)

Dysthymic disorder

☐ l. Episode lasting two years or longer (question 15)

☐ m. Low self-esteem (question 16)

☐ n. Hopelessness (question 17)

Mood elevation episodes

☐ o. Mood elevation (question 18)

☐ p. Grandiosity/elevated self-esteem (question 19)

☐ q. Decreased need for sleep (question 20)

☐ r. Increased talkativeness (question 21)

☐ s. Racing thoughts (question 22)

☐ t. Distractibility (question 23)

☐ u. Increased activity (question 24)

☐ v. Increased pleasurable activity (question 25)

☐ w. Psychotic symptoms (question 26)

☐ x. Interference with your life (question 27)

☐ y. Hospitalization (question 28)

☐ z. Medical cause (question 29)

☐ aa. Mixed episode (question 30)

☐ bb. One-week duration (question 31)

☐ cc. Four-day duration (question 32)

Interpreting your results

Form 3.1, Section 2: Mood episodes you have experienced

In section 2 of Form 3.1 (reproduced below), we will use information from the mood episode summary form to determine whether you have met the criteria for one or more specific types of mood episodes. First, put a check in each circle as instructed by taking information from the mood episode summary form on pages 54–55. Next, check the box on the left for any mood episodes for which you have ever met the criteria (as defined by the items listed below each). YOU MAY MEET (OR HAVE MET IN THE PAST) THE CRITERIA FOR MORE THAN ONE TYPE OF EPISODE.

☐ Major depressive episode. It is likely that you are now experiencing (or have experienced in the past) an episode of major depression if you:

  o Checked item (a) and/or (b), and

  o Checked at least five total symptoms from items (a) through (i), and

  o Checked item (j), and

  o Did not check item (k).

☐ Dysthymic episode. It is likely that you are now experiencing (or have experienced in the past) an episode of dysthymic disorder if you:

  o Checked item (a), and

  o Checked at least two other depressive symptoms from items (c) through (i) and (m) through (n), and

  o Checked item (l), and

  o Checked item (j), and

  o Did not check item (k).

☐ Other depressive episode. You may have (or have had in the past) a milder form of depressive episode if you:

  o Checked any item or items (a) through (i) and (m) through (n), and

  o Checked item (j), and

  o Did not check item (k).

☐ Manic episode. It is likely that you are now experiencing (or have experienced in the past) a manic episode if you:

- o Checked item (o), and
- o Checked at least three of items (p) through (v), and
- o Checked item (x), and
- o Checked item (bb), and
- o Did not check item (z).

☐ Hypomanic episode. It is likely that you are now experiencing (or have experienced in the past) a hypomanic episode if you:

- o Checked item (o), and
- o Checked at least three of items (p) through (v), and
- o Checked item (x), and
- o Checked item (cc), and
- o Did not check item (w), (y), (z), or (aa).

☐ Mixed episode. It is likely that you are now experiencing (or have experienced in the past) a mixed episode if you:

- o Checked item (aa), and
- o Met the criteria for a manic episode at least once in your life.

☐ Other mood elevation episode. It is possible that you are now experiencing (or have experienced in the past) a milder form of mood elevation episode if you:

- o Checked item (o), and
- o Checked any items (p) through (v), and
- o Did not check item (w), (y), (z), or (aa).

☐ Mood episode due to a medical condition. It is possible that you are now experiencing (or have experienced in the past) a mood episode due to a medical condition if you:

- o Checked item (k) and/or (z), and
- o Met the criteria for any mood episode listed above.

Form 3.1, Section 3: Your likely mood disorder diagnosis

Complete section 3 of Form 3.1 (reproduced below) to determine your most likely diagnosis. First put a check in each circle for which you meet the criteria from the section above. Then put a check in each box for which you meet (or have met) the required criteria. Below some disorders you will find listings for associated episodes, recurrence, and clinical status. The "associated episodes" bullet points provide information about the types of episodes you may have experienced in addition to those required for diagnosis. The recurrence and clinical status bullet points allow you to further characterize your disorder. Some individuals may have met the criteria for more than one disorder.

☐ **Major depressive disorder.** You most likely have major depressive disorder if you:

    ○ Met the criteria for a major depressive episode that was NOT due to a medical condition at least once in your life

    ○ Have never met the criteria for a manic, hypomanic, mixed, or other mood elevation episode

Associated episodes

    ○ You may have met the criteria for one or more episodes of dysthymic disorder and/or other depressive episode

Recurrence

    ○ Classify as single episode if you have had only one major depressive episode in your life

    ○ Classify as recurrent if you have had more than one major depressive episode

Clinical status

    ○ Classify as major depression, current if you are currently experiencing symptoms

    ○ Classify as major depression, partial remission if you have improved from treatment but are still having some symptoms o Classify as major depression, full remission if you are no longer having any symptoms as a result of either treatment or spontaneous remission

☐ **Dysthymic disorder.** You most likely have dysthymic disorder if you:

o Currently meet (or have met in the past) the criteria for a dysthymic episode that is NOT due to a medical condition

o Have never met the criteria for a manic, hypomanic, mixed, or other mood elevation episode

Associated episodes

o You may also have met the criteria for one or more previous episodes of dysthymic disorder and/or other depressive episode

o You may also have previously met the criteria for a major depressive episode as long as the most recent episode was in full remission for at least two months before the onset of your current symptoms

☐ **Depressive disorder not otherwise specified.** You may have depressive disorder not otherwise specified if you:

o Have currently (or have in the past) met the criteria for an "other depressive episode"

o Have never met the criteria for a major depressive, dysthymic, manic, hypomanic, mixed, or other mood elevation episode

☐ **Adjustment disorder with depressed mood.** You may have adjustment disorder with depressed mood if you:

o Have currently (or have in the past) met the criteria for an "other depressive episode"

o Have experienced symptom onset within three months of a specific stressor (other than grief)

o Have never met the criteria for a major depressive, dysthymic, manic, hypomanic, mixed, or other mood elevation episode

☐ **Bipolar I disorder.** You most likely have bipolar I disorder if you:

o Have met the criteria for a manic or mixed episode that was NOT due to a medical condition at least once in your life

Associated episodes

o You may also have met the criteria for one or more episodes of major depressive disorder, dysthymic disorder, other depressive episode, hypomanic episode, and other elevation mood episode

Clinical status

o Classify as bipolar I disorder, manic if you are currently experiencing a manic episode

o Classify as bipolar I disorder, hypomanic if you are currently experiencing a hypomanic episode

o Classify as bipolar I disorder, depressed if you are currently experiencing a depressive episode

o Classify as bipolar I disorder, mixed if you are currently experiencing a mixed episode

o Classify as bipolar I disorder, full remission if you are no longer having any symptoms

o Classify as bipolar I disorder, partial remission if you have improved from treatment but are still having some symptoms

☐ **Bipolar II disorder.** You most likely have bipolar II disorder if you:

o Have met the criteria for a hypomanic episode that was NOT due to a medical condition at least once in your life

o Have met the criteria for a major depressive episode that was NOT due to a medical condition at least once in your life

o Have never met the criteria for a manic or mixed episode

o Have never experienced psychotic symptoms or required hospitalization during an episode of mood elevation

Associated episodes

o   You may also have met the criteria for one or more episodes of dysthymic disorder, other depressive episode, and other elevation mood episode

Clinical status

o   Classify as bipolar II disorder, hypomanic if you are currently experiencing a hypomanic episode

o   Classify as bipolar II disorder, depressed if you are currently experiencing a depressive episode

o   Classify as bipolar II disorder, full remission if you are no longer having any symptoms

o   Classify as bipolar II disorder, partial remission if you have improved but are still having some symptoms

☐   **Cyclothymic disorder.** You most likely have cyclothymic disorder if you:

o   Have met the criteria for multiple hypomanic episodes that were NOT due to a medical condition over a two-year period or longer

o   Have met the criteria for multiple other depressive episodes that were NOT due to a medical condition over the same two-year period or longer

o   Have never met the criteria for a major depressive, manic, or mixed episode

o   Have never experienced psychotic symptoms or required hospitalization during an episode of mood elevation

☐   **Bipolar disorder not otherwise specified.** You might have bipolar disorder not otherwise specified if you:

o   Have ever met the criteria for hypomanic episodes that were NOT due to a medical condition but have NEVER experienced any depressive episodes

    ○ Have met the criteria for both other depressive episodes and other mood elevation episodes that were NOT due to a medical condition

    ○ Have never met the criteria for a major depressive, manic, or mixed episode

    ○ Have never experienced psychotic symptoms or required hospitalization during an episode of mood elevation

☐ **Mood disorder due to a medical condition.** You might have mood disorder due to a medical condition if you:

    ○ Have met the criteria for one or more mood episodes that were due to a medical condition

    ○ Have never met the criteria for a mood episode that was not due to a medical condition

You should now have a good idea of whether it is likely that you have a mood disorder and, if so, what your most probable diagnosis is. The next topic we need to consider is differential diagnosis.

Differential diagnosis

Medical and mental health care professionals use the term differential diagnosis to mean a list of all the possible causes of a set of symptoms. For example, if a person is experiencing depressive symptoms, there are a number of possible causes. Some of these causes are listed in Table 3.2.

The important point here is that a thorough diagnostic evaluation conducted by a mental health professional is necessary to reach a mood disorder diagnosis. Not only must the correct diagnosis be established, but other possible causes must also be ruled out (excluded). This process can be complicated and requires verbal discussion. In some cases, medical tests or a physical examination may be required. Therefore, the purpose of this section is to help you determine whether you should seek help and, if so, then empower you to be able to communicate effectively with your provider about your symptoms. ANY DIAGNOSIS DERIVED FROM THIS BOOK CAN ONLY BE CONSIDERED A POSSIBILITY AND

Table 3.2   Differential diagnosis of depressive symptoms

- Major depressive disorder
- Dysthymic disorder
- Bipolar I disorder
- Bipolar II disorder
- Mood disorder due to a medical condition
- Substance-induced mood disorder

MUST BE CONFIRMED BY A MEDICAL OR MENTAL HEALTH PROFESSIONAL.

With that in mind, we can move to the next section, which focuses on other psychiatric conditions that may coexist with mood disorders.

Coexisting conditions

Some people suffer from mood disorder and do not have any other psychiatric illness. Unfortunately, many individuals experience more than one psychiatric disorder at the same time. For example, one study reported that 79% of those with major depression suffered from one or more additional psychiatric disorders.[39] The medical term for having more than one condition is **comorbidity**. Table 3.3 lists some psychiatric illnesses that frequently coexist with mood disorders.

As Table 3.3 shows, a large percentage of individuals with mood disorders have other psychiatric conditions as well. Substance abuse and anxiety disorders are particularly common. This is a very important issue because there is considerable evidence that comorbid psychiatric conditions can worsen the course or outcome of some mood disorders.[40–43] For example, there is some evidence that comorbid panic disorder can increase the risk of suicide in persons with bipolar disorder.[44] Even if a coexisting condition does not worsen the mood disorder, it still requires treatment.

Table 3.3   Psychiatric disorders that frequently coexist with mood disorders[39, 45–52]

Mood disorder	Coexisting condition	Approximate percentage with comorbid condition
Major depression	Any substance use disorder	12%–28%
	Alcohol use disorder	25%
	Any anxiety disorder	57%
	Social phobia	18%
	Panic disorder	13%
Bipolar I disorder	Substance use disorders	50%
	Any anxiety disorder	41%
	Social anxiety disorder	13%
Bipolar II disorder	Substance use disorders	21%
	Any anxiety disorder	41%
	Generalized anxiety disorder	21%
	Panic disorder	13%
	Adult ADHD	16%

Thus, it is critical that coexisting psychiatric conditions be identified and then treated appropriately.

Do you have a coexisting (comorbid) psychiatric condition?

In this section, we will work through a process that will help you evaluate whether you might have some of the most common coexisting conditions.

The approach of this section is a little different from the method we used in the mood disorder diagnosis section. Here, we are going to use a screening approach for most disorders. Instead of taking you through a review of all the symptoms associated with a disorder, I will start by asking you to answer a screening question or two. Your responses will help you determine if you can most likely rule out a condition or if you need to further explore the possibility of having the disorder by seeking a professional evaluation. We will start with substance use disorders.

Work through this section as you did in the sections above. Check the boxes in section 4 of Form 3.1 as instructed.

Substance use disorders

As described above, substance use disorders frequently coexist with mood disorders. Please be completely honest as you answer the following three questions.

Question 1. Have you ever used alcohol, illegal drugs, or potentially addictive medications (prescribed or unprescribed)?

- ☐ Yes. Answer questions 2 and 3.
- ☐ No. Skip to the next section on psychotic disorders.

Question 2. Have you ever thought that you might be addicted to or dependent on (experienced tolerance or withdrawal) alcohol, illegal drugs, or any prescribed medication?

- ☐ Yes.
- ☐ No.

Question 3. Has the use of alcohol, illegal drugs, or prescribed medications ever caused problems for your work or relationships or has substance use ever interfered with your life in any way (e.g., substance-related legal problems, substance use in hazardous situations, such as driving, or failure to meet role obligations) on an ongoing basis?

- ☐ Yes.
- ☐ No.

If you answered yes to either question 2 or 3 or both, you may have a substance use disorder. Please check the substance use disorder box in the comorbidity summary (Form 3.1).

Psychotic disorders

Psychotic disorders include conditions such as **schizophrenia, schizoaffective disorder,** and delusional disorder. These conditions are characterized by distortions of perception, including **hallucinations** and **delusions**. However, some individuals also experience psychotic symptoms as a result of a mood disorder. Please note that the following questions use the words *recurrent* and *persistent*. This is because many people can experience unusual but infrequent perceptual experiences that are considered normal—for example, thinking that you heard your name being called when no one else is around. Answer a question yes only if you experienced the symptom on a consistent basis (e.g., multiple times over a two-week period) AND it caused you significant distress and/or interfered with your life.

Question 4. Have you experienced recurrent thoughts (delusions) that others may think are strange or odd (e.g., having an unfounded belief that others are conspiring against you or thinking that someone is inserting thoughts into your head)?

☐ Yes.

☐ No.

Question 5. Have you experienced persistent auditory hallucinations (hearing voices that others cannot hear)?

☐ Yes.

☐ No.

Question 6. Have you experienced recurrent visual hallucinations (seeing things that others cannot see)?

☐ Yes.

☐ No.

Question 7. If you answered yes to any question 4 through 6, have these symptoms ever occurred consistently when you were NOT experiencing an episode of depression or mania?

☐ Yes.

☐ No. Skip to the next section on obsessive-compulsive disorder.

If you answered yes to any question 4 through 6 AND yes to question 7, you may have a psychotic disorder. Please check the psychotic disorder box in the comorbidity summary (Form 3.1).

Obsessive-compulsive disorder

Obsessive-compulsive disorder (**OCD**) is a psychiatric illness that causes either recurrent *obsessions* or *compulsions* or both. Obsessions are recurrent and persistent thoughts, impulses, or images that are experienced as intrusive and cause anxiety or distress. Frequently obsessions cause distress because they are inconsistent with an individual's belief system—for example, someone with strong religious convictions experiencing blasphemous thoughts. Compulsions are repetitive behaviors or mental acts that the person feels driven to perform. Examples include excessive hand washing, checking, counting, and repeating words. Please answer yes to the following questions only if you experience PERSISTENT symptoms that cause distress or interfere with your life. Many people experience mild obsessions or compulsions that are not indicative of a disorder. For example, some people may double check to be sure their door is locked when they leave the house. This would not be considered a symptom of OCD unless the checking created a problem, such as the person being frequently late for work.

Question 8. Have you experienced persistent compulsive behaviors, such as excessive hand washing, double-checking, or counting, that seem difficult or impossible to control?

☐ Yes.

☐ No.

Question 9. Have you experienced recurrent bothersome or disturbing thoughts (other than worry) that seem difficult or impossible to control?

☐ Yes.

☐ No.

Question 10. If you answered yes to question 8 or 9, do these symptoms cause you distress and/or negatively affect your work, recreation, or relationships?

☐ Yes.

☐ No. Skip to the next section on generalized anxiety disorder.

Question 11. If you answered yes to question 8 or 9, have these symptoms occurred consistently when you were NOT experiencing an episode of depression or mania?

☐ Yes.

☐ No. Skip to the next section on generalized anxiety disorder.

If you answered yes to question 8 and/or 9 AND yes to BOTH questions 10 and 11, you may have OCD. Please check the obsessive-compulsive disorder box in the comorbidity summary (Form 3.1).

Generalized anxiety disorder

Generalized anxiety disorder (GAD) is an illness that causes excessive worry and/or anxiety accompanied by physical symptoms. We all worry from time to time; however, persons with GAD experience worry that is persistent and excessive and causes distress. Further, to meet the diagnostic criteria for GAD, the symptoms must be continuous (occurring more days than not) for a period of at least six months.

Question 12. Do you feel like you constantly worry much more than most other people do?

☐ Yes.

☐ No.

Question 13. When you worry, do you notice that you also consistently experience at least three of the following? Symptoms associated with GAD: (1) restlessness, (2) easy fatigue, (3) difficulty concentrating, (4) irritability, (5) muscle tension, (6) trouble sleeping.

☐ Yes.

☐ No. Skip to the next section on panic disorder.

Question 14. If you answered yes to both questions 12 and 13, do these symptoms cause you significant distress and/or negatively affect your work, recreation, or relationships?

□ Yes.

□ No. Skip to the next section on panic disorder.

Question 15. If you answered yes to questions 12, 13, and 14, have these symptoms occurred consistently when you were NOT experiencing an episode of depression or mania?

□ Yes.

□ No.

If you answered yes to all questions 12 through 15, you may have GAD. Please check the generalized anxiety disorder box in the comorbidity summary (Form 3.1).

Panic disorder

Recurrent attacks of intense fear (panic) that come on out of the blue are characteristic of *panic disorder*. To meet the criteria for panic disorder, the attacks must also cause recurrent concern about having additional attacks, worry about the implications of the attacks, or a significant behavior change.

Question 16. Have you ever experienced recurrent "out-of-the-blue" attacks of panic or intense anxiety?

□ Yes.

□ No. Skip to the next section on specific phobias.

Question 17. If you answered yes to question 16, have you consistently experienced at least four of the following during panic attacks? Symptoms associated with panic attacks: (1) sweating, (2) chest pain, (3) nausea or abdominal distress, (4) a sense that things aren't real, (5) trembling or shaking, (6) shortness of breath or a sense of smothering, (7) rapid heart rate or palpitations, (8) a choking sensation, (9) nausea, (10) dizziness or feeling faint, (11) numbness or a tingling sensation, (12) hot flushes or chills, (13) fear of dying, (14) fear of going crazy or losing control.

☐ Yes.

☐ No. Skip to the next section on specific phobias.

Question 18. If you answered yes to questions 16 and 17, have panic attacks ever caused any of the following for at least one month? Additional symptoms associated with panic disorder: (1) persistent worry about having additional attacks; (2) worry that you might die, have a heart attack, or go crazy because of the attacks; (3) significant change in behavior because of the attacks.

☐ Yes.

☐ No. Skip to the next section on specific phobias.

Question 19. If you answered yes to questions 16, 17, and 18, have these symptoms occurred consistently when you were NOT experiencing an episode of depression or mania?

☐ Yes.

☐ No.

   If you answered yes to all questions 16 through 19, you may have panic disorder. Please check the panic disorder box in the comorbidity summary (Form 3.1).

Specific phobias

A *specific phobia* is a persistent fear of a specific object or situation (e.g., spiders, blood, heights, flying) that is excessive or unreasonable. Some people may have more than one specific phobia.

Question 20. Do you experience irrational fears of objects, animals, or situations that significantly interfere with your life, such as fear of flying, fear of heights, or fear of certain kinds of animals?

☐ Yes.

☐ No. Skip to the next section on social phobia.

Question 21. If you answered yes to question 20, have these symptoms occurred consistently when you were NOT experiencing an episode of depression or mania?

☐ Yes.

☐ No.

If you answered yes to questions 20 and 21, you may have a specific phobia. Please check the specific phobia box in the comorbidity summary (Form 3.1).

Social phobia

Individuals with *social phobia* experience a persistent fear of one or more social or performance situations (e.g., speaking in public, attending parties, dating, eating in public). The anxiety is secondary to a concern that one's actions will result in significant embarrassment or humiliation.

Question 22. Do you experience excessive fears of being embarrassed or humiliated in social or performance situations that significantly interfere with your life?

☐ Yes.

☐ No. Skip to the next section on posttraumatic stress disorder.

Question 23. If you answered yes to question 22, have these symptoms occurred consistently when you were NOT experiencing an episode of depression or mania?

☐ Yes.

☐ No.

If you answered yes to questions 22 and 23, you may have a social phobia. Please check the social phobia box in the comorbidity summary (Form 3.1).

Posttraumatic stress disorder

Posttraumatic stress disorder (PTSD) is a constellation of persistent fear symptoms that occur in some people who have experienced traumatic events. What is a traumatic event? Traumatic events can be either a single experience or an enduring or repeating event or events. Examples include events that affect many people, such as war and natural disasters like earthquakes. Traumatic events can also affect only one or a few people, such as being a victim of violence or abuse.

Question 24. Have you ever experienced one or more traumatic events that involved the possibility of your own or someone else's death or serious injury?

☐ Yes.

☐ No. Skip to the next section on ADHD.

Question 25. If you answered yes to question 24, does that traumatic event still affect your life in any way (e.g., persistent memories or nightmares about the event, avoidance of things that remind you of the event, or problems with insomnia)?

☐ Yes.

☐ No. Skip to the next section on ADHD.

Question 26. Do you frequently reexperience the traumatic event(s) in one or more of the following ways? Reexperiencing symptoms: (1) distressing memories, (2) dreams or nightmares, (3) flashbacks or feelings of reliving the event, (4) distress when exposed to reminders of the event.

☐ Yes.

☐ No.

Question 27. Do you frequently experience at least three of the following avoidance and emotional numbing symptoms? Avoidance and numbing symptoms: (1) efforts to avoid thoughts, feelings, and conversations associated with the trauma; (2) efforts to avoid activities, places, or people that remind you of the trauma; (3) loss of memory about aspects of the trauma; (4) loss of interest in activities that you previously enjoyed; (5) feeling detached or estranged from others; (6) difficulty experiencing emotion; (7) a sense of a foreshortened future.

☐ Yes.

☐ No.

Question 28. Do you frequently experience at least two of the following symptoms of increased arousal that you did not experience before the trauma? Symptoms of increased arousal: (1) trouble sleeping, (2) irritability or anger, (3) trouble concentrating, (4) hypervigilance, (5) exaggerated startle response.

☐ Yes.

☐ No.

Question 29. Do the symptoms from questions 26, 27, and 28 significantly interfere with your life AND have these symptoms persisted for at least one month?

☐ Yes.

☐ No. Skip to the next section on ADHD.

If you answered yes to all questions 24 through 29, you may have PTSD. Please check the PTSD box in the comorbidity summary (Form 3.1).

Attention-deficit/hyperactivity disorder (ADHD)

Attention-deficit/hyperactivity disorder **(ADHD)** is a condition that causes problems with attention and concentration (inattentive type) or difficulties related to hyperactivity and impulsiveness (hyperactive-impulsive type) or both (combined type). To meet the diagnostic criteria, the onset of symptoms must occur prior to age seven. Also, the symptoms must cause impairment in social, academic, or occupational functioning. Some people who had ADHD as a child continue to experience symptoms as an adult.

Question 30. When you were a child, did you have difficulties in school or at home either because of trouble with hyperactivity/impulsivity or because of problems with attention/concentration?

☐ Yes.

☐ No. Skip to the next section on eating disorders.

Question 31. As an adult have you continued to have problems with either hyperactivity/impulsivity or attention/concentration that consistently interfere with your life?

☐ Yes.

☐ No. Skip to the next section on eating disorders.

Question 32. Do you consistently experience at least six of the following symptoms of inattention? Symptoms of inattention: (1) difficulty paying attention to details/making careless mistakes, (2) difficulty sustaining attention, (3) problems listening when spoken to directly, (4) trouble completing tasks, (5) lack of organization, (6) avoidance of tasks requiring sustained mental effort, (7) problems because of losing things, (8) easy distractibility, (9) forgetfulness.

☐ Yes.

☐ No.

Question 33. Do you consistently experience at least six of the following symptoms of hyperactivity-impulsivity? Symptoms of hyperactivity-impulsivity: (1) fidgetiness, (2) trouble sitting still, (3) restlessness, (4) difficulty engaging in quiet leisure activities, (5) needing to be "on the go," (6) excessive talking, (7) blurting out answers before others have finished asking a question, (8) trouble waiting your turn, (9) tendency to interrupt others.

Question 34. Do the symptoms from questions 32 and 33 significantly interfere with your life?

☐ Yes.

☐ No. Skip to the next section on eating disorders.

Question 35. If you answered yes to question 34, have these symptoms occurred consistently when you were NOT experiencing an episode of depression or mania?

☐ Yes.

☐ No.

If you answered yes to questions 30, 31, 34, and 35 AND yes to questions 32 and/or 33, you may have adult ADHD. Please check the ADHD box in the comorbidity summary (Form 3.1).

Eating disorders

There are two general types of eating disorders. *Anorexia nervosa* is a condition that leads to an intense fear of gaining weight and results in consistently maintaining a body weight lower than the minimum required for health. ***Bulimia nervosa*** involves episodes of binge eating and compensatory processes to avoid weight gain, such as self-induced vomiting, fasting, or excessive exercise.

Question 36. Do you experience intense concerns about body weight/shape that result in your maintaining an excessively low body weight and/or binge eating with compensatory behaviors?

☐ Yes.

☐ No.

If you answered yes to question 36, you may have an eating disorder. Please check the eating disorder box in the comorbidity summary (Form 3.1).

Form 3.1, Section 4: Summary of possible comorbid conditions

Please check the box to the left of all disorders that you screened positively for in the section above in section 4 of Form 3.1 (reproduced below).

☐ Substance use disorder

☐ Psychotic disorder

☐ Obsessive-compulsive disorder

☐ Generalized anxiety disorder

☐ Panic disorder

☐ Specific phobia

☐ Social phobia

☐ PTSD

☐ ADHD

☐ Eating disorder

Now that you have completed the process of determining possible diagnoses, we can use that information to help you determine whether you should seek further evaluation from a mental health professional.

Table 3.4 Symptoms that require emergency evaluation

- Thoughts of suicide
- Thoughts of harming others
- Symptoms of a psychotic disorder
- Symptoms of a manic episode
- In crisis (regardless of symptoms)

Should you seek further evaluation from a mental health or medical professional?

One aim of this section is to help you decide whether you should seek a professional evaluation. However, a more important goal is to help you decide whether you should seek help immediately. Some symptoms can be potentially life threatening. Symptoms for which you should seek help immediately are listed in Table 3.4. Options for emergency assistance are listed in Table 3.5. Also, see Chapter 1 for more information.

The recommendations listed in the tables are straightforward but may warrant some explanation. If you are having thoughts of harming yourself or others, please seek help to prevent acting on those thoughts. For those experiencing either mania or psychotic symptoms, the recommendation to seek help immediately is given because both can lead to behavior that is potentially self-destructive (e.g., doing things one might later regret, such as going on a spending spree) or even the inability to care for oneself. Thus, these symptoms must be treated immediately and may require hospitalization.

In addition, I strongly encourage you to obtain a professional evaluation if the diagnostic exercise in this chapter suggests that you likely have a psychiatric condition. Why do I recommend a professional evaluation if this book suggests you have any psychiatric disorder? WORKING THROUGH THIS CHAPTER CAN ONLY SUGGEST THE POS-

---

Table 3.5   Options for seeking immediate help

◆   Call the National Suicide Prevention Lifeline: 1-800-273-TALK (8255).

◆   Call 911.

◆   Have a family member or friend take you to the nearest emergency room (do not go alone or drive yourself).

◆   Call your mental health or medical provider (if you have one). But if a provider is not immediately available to help, then take one of the above actions.

SIBILITY OF A DISORDER; A PROFESSIONAL EVALUATION IS REQUIRED TO BE SURE. It is critical that you know for sure. If you know, then you can make good decisions about whether you need treatment and what approach would be best. You might meet the criteria for a diagnosis but experience symptoms are that mild, and therefore a complementary approach might be reasonable (see Chapter 10). Getting an evaluation doesn't automatically mean that you need treatment; it just means that you will have the information to make good decisions about what to do.

What if you have some symptoms that bother you, but you don't meet the criteria for any specific disorder? Well, as I said earlier in this chapter, only a professional evaluation can sort this out. The exercise in this chapter cannot be used to rule out any disorder or disorders. So, please consider getting a professional opinion.

I want to close the chapter by repeating and expanding on what I said above and at the beginning of this chapter. THE EXERCISE IN THIS CHAPTER CANNOT BE USED TO RULE OUT ANY DISORDER OR DISORDERS. By that I mean that the exercise can help you determine whether it is likely that you have a disorder and which disorder, but it is not designed to exclude the possibility of a disorder (see the introduction to this chapter for more information). IF YOU ARE HAVING SYMPTOMS THAT ARE BOTHERSOME, PLEASE SEEK A PROFESSIONAL EVALUATION.

4

Mood Disorders:
Facts and Causes

This chapter provides more information about **mood disorders**. In the first section, I will provide some general background information, such as how common these conditions are. After that, we will take a look at what we currently know about causes.

How common are mood disorders?

Many people experience a mood disorder at some point in their lives. For example, one study found that almost 10% of the U.S. population suffers from a mood disorder at any given time.[53] This means that if you are in a room with nine other people, statistically speaking, one of you will have a mood disorder. Of course, because of chance, small groups may have none or more than one person, but it is a way to think about how common these conditions really are. The lifetime risk of developing a mood disorder is thought to be around 8% in the United States.[1] The take-home message is that if you are reading this book because you or a loved one has a mood disorder, then you are not alone. These conditions are very widespread.

Depressive disorders are more common than bipolar spectrum illness. In regard to major depression, a recent report by the Substance Abuse and Mental Health Services Administration indicated that one in twelve adults (7.5% of the population) experienced a major depressive episode during the previous year.[3] Overall, it is thought that 14 to 16 million people experience a major depressive episode each year in the United States.[3, 54] For reasons that we don't understand, **depression** is about twice as common among women as in men.[1] The prevalence range of major depression is about 3%–5% for men and 6%–12% for women. So, around one in every ten women experience depression sometime in their life as compared to about one in twenty men. For **dysthymic disorder**, the prevalence is 3%–4%,[1] and thus about one in twenty-five individuals suffer from dysthymic disorder. Finally, postpartum depression is also frequent and occurs in about one in ten mothers (see Chapter 12 for much more about this).[1]

As mentioned above, bipolar spectrum disorders occur much less frequently than **unipolar** illness. One study reported that slightly more than 2% of the U.S. population suffers from a bipolar disorder at any given time.[53] In regard to the subtypes of bipolar illness, studies suggest that the lifetime prevalence may be about 1%–3% for **bipolar I disorder** and about 1% for **bipolar II disorder**.[55, 56] However, compared to unipolar illness, there is less agreement among experts regarding how frequently bipolar illness occurs, and some research suggests a prevalence rate as high as 7%.[1] The discrepancies between studies may have to do with the fact that bipolar disorders can be difficult to diagnose. Nonetheless, it is reasonable to conclude that at least one in every hundred people, and probably more, suffers from a bipolar spectrum illness.

Course of illness for mood disorders

Some of the most important facts for you to have at your disposal relate to the course of illness for mood disorders. What is "course of illness"? This term refers to how a disorder progresses over time, including the typical age of onset and the typical progression. For example, the common cold can come on at any time in life. In contrast, mood disorders are more likely to develop during a certain age range (see below). The common cold typically goes away within a week or so. Mood disorders often persist and recur. Thus, mood disorders have a very different pattern of progression from conditions that are of short duration, like the common cold. This kind of information is critical for making informed treatment decisions. Let's start by discussing depressive disorders.

The average age of onset for a first episode of depression is between 25 and 35.[4] What is important for you to know is that depressive episodes can get better without treatment, but this tends to occur within the first six months of the onset of symptoms. During the first months of symptoms, the possibility of spontaneous (without treatment) remission is thought to be around 50%.[4] Unfortunately, the chances of getting well without treatment decrease dramatically the longer the episode lasts. During the second six months of illness, the odds of spontaneous remission are only around 5%. Finally, studies indicate that more than 10% are still experiencing symptoms even after five years.[4] These studies indicate that the longer an episode of depression goes on, the less likely it is to get better without treatment. Further, they suggest that symptoms persist for years for some of those who experience an episode of depression.

How can you use this information? If you have been experiencing depressive symptoms (see Chapter 3) for more than a few weeks and they are not getting significantly better, then please seek help. Many people have a tendency to wait and see if symptoms will get better on their own. This is understandable, but it is not a good idea with mood disorders. The research suggests that the longer a person has symptoms, the more likely the disorder is to become a **chronic illness** (or long lasting).

Another highly relevant fact that you need to know about is the high risk of **recurrent illness**. Whether depression is treated or gets better spontaneously, the chances of recurrence are very high. After a person has one episode of major depression, the risk of having another is about 50% within the following two years and may be as high as 90% within the next six years.[4] Also the more episodes one experiences, the greater the likelihood of recurrence. After one episode the recurrence rate is at least 50%, after two episodes the risk of another goes up to 70%, and after a third episode the risk of **relapse** goes up to 90%.[1]

These studies indicate that major depression is most often a chronic (persistent or recurrent) illness. Overall, between 75% and 95% of individuals who have one major depressive episode will have at least one more at some time.[4] One of the major predictors of relapse is thought to be failure to achieve full remission.[4] Persistence of symptoms can increase the risk of having another episode fourfold.[4] Thus, any depressive episode should be treated to full remission if possible. These facts are why I encourage you to do absolutely everything you can to achieve full remission. Please use this book to develop a comprehensive recovery plan that will give you the best chance of getting completely well and staying that way.

Dysthymic disorder (see Chapters 2 and 3 for more information) frequently coexists with major depression. Studies indicate that 68%–90% of those who have dysthymic disorder also have at least one major depressive episode during their lifetime.[1] In fact, major depressive episodes are often superimposed on dysthymia; this phenomenon is known as "double depression." Research indicates that one-quarter to one-half of those with major depression have coexisting dysthymic disorder.[1] Unfortunately, there is also considerable evidence that double depression tends to be more severe and difficult to treat than major depressive episodes without dysthymic disorder and is also more likely to recur.[1] Thus, if you have episodes of more severe depression that are superimposed on long-lasting mild depression (dysthymia), please be especially diligent in developing your recovery plan and try to implement as many strategies as possible.

Bipolar disorders tend to come on at a younger age than unipolar illness.[4] Both bipolar I and II disorders are thought to always have a chronic course. We know much less about the course of illness for **cyclothymic disorder** and **bipolar disorder NOS**.

In summary, research indicates that major depression often becomes a chronic illness. The risk is significantly increased for those who have both major depression and dysthymic disorder. One of the most important actions you can take to prevent chronic depression is to do everything possible to achieve full remission. The same is true for bipolar spectrum disorders. Please consider using all of the strategies outlined in this book to maximize your chances of staying well for life.

Additional features of mood disorders

A detailed description of the basic features of mood disorders was provided in Chapters 2 and 3. In this section, I will discuss some additional characteristics that can be associated with affective illness. Some of these symptoms have important treatment implications.

Psychotic symptoms

The psychotic symptoms most associated with mood disorders are **hallucinations** and **delusions**. Hallucinations are perceptions in the absence of a stimulus—for example, hearing a voice when no one is speaking. Further, hallucinations are defined as perceptions that occur in a conscious and awake state; they are not the result of a dream. Finally, hallucinations seem real. Hallucinations can occur in any sensory modality, but auditory and visual are the most likely to be associated with a mood disorder. Delusions are false beliefs held with absolute conviction despite strong evidence to the contrary. An example is a belief that one is being conspired against in the absence of any evidence to support that belief. Psychotic symptoms can accompany episodes of major depression (associated with unipolar and bipolar spectrum disorders) as well as mixed and manic episodes of bipolar disorder. The existence of psychotic symptoms has important implications for treatment (see Chapter 11) and requires an emergency evaluation. If you or a loved one is experiencing psychotic symptoms, then please seek an emergency evaluation (see Chapter 1 for more information).

Rapid cycling bipolar illness

Rapid cycling is formally defined as four or more **mood episodes** (depressed, manic, or hypomanic) per year in individuals who have either bipolar I or II disorder. However, some individuals have very rapid cycling, known as "ultradian" or "ultrarapid" cycling. Persons with ultrarapid cycling may experience multiple brief occurrences of **mania** and depression over the course of days or sometimes even hours.

The cause of rapid cycling is unknown. However, hypothyroidism may contribute to this phenomenon, even in very mild cases that do not cause medical symptoms.[1] There is also some evidence that antidepressant use may contribute to the development of rapid cycling, although this correlation has not been absolutely proven.[1] Finally, there is evidence that rapid cycling illness can be less responsive to **lithium**.[1] So, if you think you may have a rapid cycling variety of bipolar spectrum illness, then please discuss this with your treatment team.

Seasonal symptoms

Individuals who do not have mood disorders but live in regions with seasonal shifts in the length of daylight may have associated variations in energy levels and **mood**. Further, seasonal variation is common in mood disorders.[1] For example, unipolar depression is more common in spring, bipolar depression in fall, and mania during summer.

Mood disorders with a specific seasonal pattern are known as **seasonal affective disorder** (SAD). This diagnosis according to the DSM-IV requires that: (1) depression onset as well as remission (or switch to **mania/hypomania** in bipolar spectrum illness) tends to occur at a specific time of year, (2) the mood episodes are not related to season-specific stressors (e.g., the winter holidays), (3) at least two major depressive episodes have met seasonal criteria during the previous two years and no nonseasonal episodes have occurred, and (4) the total number of seasonal depressive episodes is greater than the number of nonseasonal episodes.

SAD tends to be more common in women than men. Some symptoms are particularly associated with this condition: irritability, anxiety, decreased activity, increased appetite, carbohydrate craving, weight gain, and increased sleep.[1] In regard to treatment, SAD may be responsive to light therapy either alone or in combination with other treatment approaches (see Chapters 8 and 11).

Mood episodes caused or worsened by other disorders, medications, or substances

The goal of this section is to provide information about nonpsychiatric causes of mood episodes. Some clinicians use the term **secondary mood disorder** to indicate that the cause of an episode was another disorder, a medication, or a

---

Table 4.1   Medical disorders that may cause or worsen mood episodes[1]

Cancer	Hypothyroidism	Parkinson's disease
Crohn's disease	Irritable bowl syndrome	Rheumatoid arthritis
Diabetes		Stroke
Fibromyalgia	Kidney disease	Systemic lupus erythematosus
Heart disease	Liver disease	
Huntington's disease	Lung disease	Traumatic brain injury
Hyperthyroidism	Multiple sclerosis	Wilson's disease

---

substance. Please also see Chapters 2 and 3 for more information on the diagnosis of mood disorders. Additionally, some medical conditions as well as prescribed medications and substances of abuse can worsen preexisting mood disorders. Some of these medical conditions are listed in Table 4.1, and medications are listed in Table 4.2. It is very important to point out that if you have one or more of these conditions or take one of the listed medications, that does NOT mean there is a causal relationship with your mood disorder. For many of the items listed in Tables 4.1 and 4.2, only a small number of individuals develop a mood disorder as a result of one of these conditions or medications. Also, in any given person, the association may be difficult to sort out. For example, Parkinson's disease is a very disabling condition that causes significant stress. Thus, the stress of coping with the disorder may contribute to mood symptoms. However, Parkinson's disease is thought to also directly contribute to the development of mood symptoms because it damages certain structures in the brain. For any given person, there isn't currently a way to tell whether either or both potential causes are contributing to affective disturbance. Finally, even if there is thought to be an association for a specific person, knowing this may not change the recommended treatment. As an example, a medication that you are taking for another disorder and that is thought to be contributing to mood symptoms might be the only treatment option. In that situation, the solution would be to treat the secondary mood

Table 4.2   Some medications that may cause or worsen
mood episodes[1]

Medications or substances	Used to treat	Mood symptoms
Acyclovir	Herpes zoster, genital herpes, chickenpox	Depression, psychosis
Amantadine	Influenza A, parkinsonism	Mania, psychosis
Amphetamines	ADHD	Mania, depression, anxiety on discontinuation
Anticonvulsants	Seizures, bipolar disorder	Mania, depression
Asparaginase	Lymphoblastic leukemia	Depression, psychosis
Baclofen	Muscle spasticity	Mania, depression, psychosis
Benzodiazepines	Anxiety	Depression
Beta-blockers	High blood pressure, cardiac arrhythmias	Mania, depression
Bromocriptine	Parkinson's disease, elevated prolactin	Mania, depression, psychosis
Buspirone	Anxiety	Mania
Captopril	High blood pressure, congestive heart failure	Mania, psychosis, anxiety
Carbidopa/levodopa	Parkinson's disease	Psychosis
Clonidine	High blood pressure	Depression

symptoms. Of course, if it is possible to change the medication, that would be the first choice in most cases.

So, you may be thinking, how is this information useful? First of all, in some cases this knowledge may affect your treatment. As I said above, if a medication you are taking for another disorder is likely to be causing mood symptoms, it may be possible to change to a different drug. If you have any of the conditions or are taking of the medications that can cause mood symptoms (see Tables 4.1 and 4.2), then I strongly recommend that you discuss the possibility of a causal relationship with your treatment team.

Table 4.2 Some medications that may cause or worsen
mood episodes[1] (*continued*)

Medications or substances	Used to treat	Mood symptoms
Cyclobenzaprine	Muscle spasm	Mania, psychosis
Cycloserine	Tuberculosis	Depression, psychosis, anxiety
Dapsone	Dermatitis herpetiformis, leprosy	Mania, depression, psychosis
Disulfiram	Alcoholism	Depression, psychosis
Hydrochlorothiazide	High blood pressure	Depression
Interferon-alpha	Hepatitis, leukemia, melanoma	Mania, depression, psychosis
Methyldopa	High blood pressure	Depression, psychosis
Metoclopramide	Gastroesophageal reflux disease	Mania, depression
Narcotics	Pain	Depression, psychosis
Norfloxacin	Urinary tract infection	Depression
Oral contraceptives	Birth control	Depression
Theophylline	Asthma, chronic bronchitis	Mania, depression
Vinblastine	Hodgkin's disease, lymphoma	Depression
Vincristine	Leukemia, lymphoma	Depression

If there is a chance of a causal relationship, it may be reasonable to explore the possibility of making changes in your treatment. Often the only way to know whether a medication is causing mood symptoms is to stop the medication and see if the affective disturbance gets better. Please don't do this on your own. Always discuss medication changes with your treating prescriber.

Finally, most substances that can be abused, including alcohol, have the potential to cause mood symptoms. This is particularly likely with greater use. Some people may also attempt to control mood disorder symptoms by using substances to "self-medicate." Self-medication almost always makes things worse, sometimes much worse by progressing to a substance use disorder. One thing you can do to facilitate your recovery is to avoid misusing any substances.

The biology and psychology of mood disorders

Mood disorders are both biological and psychological. Sometimes this dual classification can be confusing, so I will discuss one way to think about it.

Psychology is often defined as the study of the human mind and behavior. Other definitions include the study of animal behavior and the mental characteristics of a particular individual. All of these definitions apply to mood disorders except animal behavior. That applies too, just less directly. Studies of animal behavior have added to our understanding of human psychology and emotion. A definition that I like is that psychology refers to our thoughts, feelings, and unconscious mental processes as well as our behaviors that occur as a result of these. I will use that definition in this book. Mood disorders clearly affect our thoughts, emotions, and behaviors. The other side of the coin is that our emotional characteristics and behaviors have a great influence on mood disorders. Our psychological disposition and the way we behave can make us more vulnerable to mood disorders. Also, psychological and behavioral change can play a major role in the recovery process. Most psychotherapy and self-help strategies focus on treating mood disorders by changing the way we think and act (see Chapters 9 and 10). Making these changes is often critical to achieving full remission, and these are sometimes the only treatments necessary.

In contrast to *psychology*, I will use the word *biology* to mean the chemical, electrical, and other processes that occur unconsciously in our brains and underlie our thoughts and emotions. As we understand the brain today, all of mental life is the result of the biological machinery that is constantly working away in our heads. So, biology and psychology are really just different aspects of the same thing. Still, the distinction is useful because approaches to recovery are divided into the broad general categories of biological and psychological. In this book, the term *biological* is also used to define treatments, such as antidepressants, that are aimed at changing the underlying brain mechanisms causing the disorder. One analogy is to think about computer hardware versus software. Biological treatments try to correct the hardware—think of replacing a defective hard drive. We can think of psychological treatments as fixing software programs. The aim is to change the "program" that causes thoughts, feelings, or behaviors.

Before moving on, I want to make one important point. While I use the hardware/software analogy as way to think about our complicated brains, it is not completely accurate. Biological treatments change our thoughts, feelings, and behaviors (as a result of changing the underlying biology), and psychological treatments change our brain function and perhaps even brain structure in some cases.

In the next section, we'll take a tour of our emotional machinery. The final two sections of this chapter will discuss our current understanding of the biology and psychology of mood disorders.

The neurobiology of emotion

Neurobiology simply means the biology of the nervous system. Before we jump into a discussion of our emotion-generating machinery, let's take a quick look at how our brain is put together. The most fundamental component of the brain is the nerve cell, or **neuron**. Neurons are electrically excitable cells that transmit information from one point to another in the brain. A good analogy is electric or telephone transmission lines. The human brain is thought to contain about 100 billion of these cells, which connect with one another to form circuits or networks. Again, think about a network of phone lines connecting multiple buildings in a city. Each neuron has, on average, connections with about 7000 other nerve cells. I mention these facts because the magnitude of both the numbers of neurons and their connections is a major reason it has been so difficult to understand how our brains work. The complexity of the brain makes it very difficult for us to comprehend how it functions. In fact, some have called the human brain the most complex structure in the universe. Whether that is true is impossible to know, but it is certainly the most complicated organ in the human body. The take-home point is that because we don't completely understand how the healthy brain works, it has been very challenging to figure out the abnormalities underlying mood disorders. It's like trying to sort out an automobile electrical problem without having a wiring diagram. But there is a lot that we do know, and I'll discuss that later in the chapter.

Neurons communicate with each other by way of **synapses**. Synapses are specialized regions that allow the passage of information from one neuron to another. The most important way this works is through chemical synapses. Messages are transmitted along individual nerve cells by way of an electrical impulse. When the impulse reaches the end of the nerve cell (the presynaptic neuron), a chemical is released into the gap between neurons (the gap is synaptic cleft). These chemicals, known generally as **neurotransmitters**, cross the synapse and are taken up by the nerve cell (postsynaptic neuron) across the gap (see Figure 4.1 on page 98). The neurotransmitters can cause a variety of actions, but the most basic function is to cause the electrical signal to be sent along the postsynaptic neuron. Thus, many neurons can participate in complex circuits.

There are a number of neurotransmitters in the human brain. Those most relevant to mood disorders are **serotonin**, **norepinephrine**, **dopamine**, **glutamate**, acetylcholine, and gamma-aminobutyric acid, also known as **GABA**. We will come back to neurotransmitters, but first a few words about larger scale brain anatomy.

In adult humans, the brain weighs about 3 pounds. It is very soft, with a consistency similar to gelatin. The external surface of the brain is known as the cerebral cortex. The cortex is divided into left and right hemispheres, and each hemisphere is further divided into four regions: the frontal, temporal, parietal, and occipital lobes (see Figure 4.2 on page 98). Beneath the cortex are other regions, including the brain stem and cerebellum. For our purposes the most important brain areas are the frontal lobe, amygdala, hippocampus, basal ganglia, and thalamus (see Figure 4.3 on page 99). The frontal lobe is the cortical area most involved with what are known as executive functions. Executive functions represent our ability to think, solve problems, and make decisions. Additionally, the frontal cortex is thought to be involved in emotional control. The amygdala is located in the temporal lobe (one amygdala on each side) and is involved with the generation of the fear response. Hence, this structure is thought to play a key role in disorders of excess fear (anxiety disorders). The hippocampus is also located in the temporal lobe and, as with the amygdala, there is a hippocampal structure on each side of the brain. This brain area is important for memory functions. The two final brain areas important in mood disorders are the basal ganglia and thalamus. These are collections of nerve cell bodies located below the cortex near the thalamus but not shown in Figure 4.3 (again, one set on each side). The basal ganglia facilitate cognitive, emotional, and motor processing. They form a circuit that goes from the cortex to the basal ganglia and then on to the thalamus and ultimately back to the cortex. This network is known as the basal ganglia circuitry. Disruptions of networks involving the frontal cortex, amygdala, hippocampus, and basal ganglia circuitry are thought to contribute to the causes of mood disorders. One basal ganglia structure, known as the striatum, is thought to be particularly involved with the production of emotion and mood disorders. The role of the striatum is discussed below.

Now that we have an overview of brain organization, we can discuss how emotions are thought to be generated and regulated. Although humans have a large number of emotions, they can be roughly categorized as either positive or negative. Positive emotions include happiness, joy, hope, and wonder. In contrast, feelings such as sadness, fear, anger, worry, and disappointment are negative. It is believed that the underlying purpose of emotions is to motivate humans and animals. For example, fear motivates us to avoid dangerous situations. In contrast, positive emotions inspire us to meet our needs for survival. Illustrations of positive emotional drive include eating because we enjoy the taste of food and engaging in reproductive behaviors because of the pleasure associated with sex.

Though an oversimplification, one way to think of mood disorders is that these conditions represent either abnormal emotional production or regulation or both. Thus, depression can be thought of as a disorder of too much negative, and not enough positive, emotion. Using the analogy of a factory, we could say the excess negative emotion is the result of a problem on the production side causing too much to be manufactured. Another possibility is that the regulation process is not working correctly, resulting in failure to slow down the production at the right time. The lack of positive emotion could similarly occur as a result of either a problem with the production mechanism or an overactive control system turning the manufacturing process down or off.

The factory analogy is useful because brain regions implicated in both the production and regulation of emotion are thought to function abnormally in mood disorders. While we don't yet completely understand how emotions are created and regulated, there is evidence that emotional production occurs in the subcortical brain regions, such as the amygdala and basal ganglia. In contrast, regulation is likely a function of the frontal cortex. So, mood disorders are thought to be problems with either subcortical production machinery or cortical regulatory processes. Now, with that background information, we can discuss what is currently known about the neurobiology of mood disorders.

The biology of mood disorders

Let's start with a bit of history. The modern era of biological treatments for depression began in 1951. At that time, two new medications for tuberculosis (isoniazid and iproniazid) were being studied, and it was discovered that these agents had antidepressant effects. Both drugs were found to be **monoamine oxidase inhibitors (MAOIs)**. Monoamine oxidase functions in the breakdown of the monoamine neurotransmitters (dopamine, norepinephrine, and serotonin), and MAOIs limit the breakdown of these neurotransmitters, which makes more neurotransmitter available at the synapse. At about the same time, a medication called imipramine was developed for the treatment of **schizophrenia**. It was not effective for schizophrenia but turned out to be a good antidepressant. Imipramine is one medication in the class known as **tricyclic antidepressants (TCAs)** (see Chapter 8 for more about antidepressants). It works by blocking the recycling (or the reuptake into the nerve cell) of norepinephrine and serotonin (see Figure 4.4 on page 99). Because both iproniazid and imipramine resulted in increased availability of monoamines in the synaptic cleft, the **neurotransmitter hypothesis of depression** was born. The theory was that depression was the result of a deficiency of these molecules. Since the time that imipramine was discovered to be an antidepressant, many more medications have been developed to treat depression. These will be discussed in detail in Chapter 8. For now, I will just mention that all of the currently available antidepressant medications were designed to make more neurotransmitter available in the brain.

The idea that depression occurs as a result of a lack of available neurotransmitters is often referred to as a "chemical imbalance." So, if you hear someone speak of having depression because of a chemical imbalance, that is what he or she is talking about. In the decades since the neurotransmitter hypothesis was developed, extensive research has been conducted with the aim of expanding our understanding of what causes mood disorders. Unfortunately, we still do not completely understand the neurobiology of these conditions, but we have learned a lot. So now let's take a tour of what we currently know about the biological causes of mood disorders. Before we start, though, one final thought: There is probably not one single cause of any mood disorder.[1] It is most likely that complex interactions of brain function and environment lead to these disorders, and different combinations of these factors cause illness in different individuals.

Brain structure

One possibility is that mood disorders occur because of problems with the structure of the brain. For example, the physical composition of the brain can be damaged by head injury, brain tumors, stroke, or various disease processes. In fact, structural damage to some brain regions can result in depression, along with other symptoms. For example, individuals who experience brain injury secondary to trauma[57, 58] or stroke[59, 60] may develop depression. Mood disorders are also associated with very mild structural abnormalities: however, these abnormalities tend to be nonspecific—that is, not specifically related to a particular disorder.[61] This is why currently available brain imaging methods are not useful for the diagnosis of mood disorders.

Our current understanding is that mood disorders occur as a result of functional, rather than structural, causes. By "functional" I mean that the brain circuitry is not operating correctly. This could occur as a result of problems with the communication between two or more nodes in a circuit. Another possibility is that one specific brain region, or node, is not functioning properly and is disrupting the entire circuit. Let's begin by discussing genetic factors that could affect circuit function. I'll talk more about the actual circuits later in this chapter.

Genetic factors

Multiple studies have convincingly demonstrated that mood disorders are partly caused by genetic, or inherited, factors.[1] I use the word *partly* because the evidence indicates that what is inherited is a risk for developing a mood disorder, rather than the actual illness. We often use the term *vulnerability* to describe this risk. You met Ann in earlier chapters. She is a fifty-five-year-old professional woman who suffers from major depression. She has relatives who also have mood disorders. Thus, she most likely inherited a biological vulnerability to developing depression.

As stated above, it is likely a combination of biological and environmental factors that actually determines whether a specific person develops an illness. These biological factors are thought to be a result of genetic and perhaps other influences. Specifically, genetic factors may contribute to disruptions of the brain circuits involved in mood regulation.

Let's start with a brief discussion of genes and inheritance. A gene is a unit of inheritance information in a human or other living organism. One way to think about genes is as an instruction manual or recipe. The instructions involve development, such as building the brain prior to birth, as well as carrying out actions and behaviors throughout life. Our cells contain strands of deoxyribonucleic acid (DNA) known as chromosomes. Each chromosome is a single, long DNA helix on which thousands of genes are encoded. A gene, then, is a short piece or segment of DNA on a chromosome that carries specific inheritance information. Our DNA is copied and inherited across generations, thus providing the molecular basis for all inheritance. In regard to the language of the science of genetics, the total complement of genes in an organism is known as its genome. The region of the chromosome at which a particular gene is located is called its locus. Finally, the language used by DNA to carry and transmit information is called the genetic code.

Two main processes carry out gene instructions. First, genes direct or "code" for the construction of proteins. Proteins are the primary building blocks of our bodies and carry out many functions. Second, genes code for ribonucleic acid (RNA). RNA is similar to DNA and carries out many functions related to inheritance and gene expression.

Genes can transmit disorders from one generation to the next in a variety of ways. For example, some diseases can be caused by a mutation or abnormality associated with a single gene. In contrast, other illnesses have a much more complex pattern of inheritance. These conditions are known as "multifactorial" or "**polygenic**," meaning that they are likely associated with the effects of multiple genes in combination with lifestyle and environmental factors. Unfortunately, mood disorders fall into this latter category, which has made it much harder to understand the genetic factors associated with affective illness. Not only are many genes thought to be involved, but also different combinations of these genes acting in concert with various environmental factors likely lead to the development of a mood disorder in any given person. Because of this complexity, some studies aimed at determining which genes are associated with mood disorders have yielded conflicting results.[4]

Several types of studies have investigated the role of inheritance in the development of mood disorders. One approach is family studies, which have clearly shown that mood disorders run in families.[1] Further, these investigations have indicated that familial transmission is greater for bipolar than unipolar spectrum conditions. However, having either unipolar or bipolar illness in a family increases the risk of having either condition in other family members. First-degree (parent, child, sibling) relatives of individuals with bipolar disorder have about a 4%–14% likelihood of having either bipolar or unipolar illness.[1] In contrast, first-degree relatives of those with unipolar illness have a 5%–28% risk of having unipolar illness but only a 0.7%–8% risk of suffering from bipolar disorder.[1]

Twin studies are also used to study the role of genetics in mood disorders. Investigations of twins utilize the fact that monozygotic (identical) twins come from one egg and have the same genes. Dizygotic (fraternal) twins come from different eggs and share only 50% of their genes. A greater presence of the same trait, such as a mood disorder, in both members of a pair of identical twins (concordance) than in a pair of fraternal twins suggests a genetic component to an illness. These kinds of studies have confirmed that the overall risk of a mood disorder is three times greater among the identical twins than among the fraternal twins of individuals with an affective disorder.[1] Results of these studies also suggest a stronger genetic component for bipolar than unipolar disorders as well as a role for environment influences.

In addition to the studies described above, considerable research has focused on finding specific genes associated with mood disorders. Some progress has been made toward determining which genes may contribute to the causes of these conditions. These are mostly genes that are involved with the function of neurotransmitters or information transfer along the brain circuits. Thus, it is likely that genetic factors result in mood disorders by disrupting information transmission between brain areas and therefore disrupting one or more circuits. Specific neurotransmitters thought to be affected by genetic defects include serotonin, norepinephrine, GABA, and dopamine.[62–68] There is also evidence for a genetic influence on the function of monoamine oxidase,[69] which breaks down neurotransmitters, as well as neurotrophic factors,[70, 71] which support neuron survival and signaling.

In summary, there is no doubt that an increased risk for developing mood disorders can run in families. However, it is definitely possible for a person to develop a mood disorder in the absence of known genetic risk. Further, genetic factors appear to interact with environmental influences in the development of these conditions. Thus, what is passed on in families is an elevated vulnerability, not the disorder itself. From a practical standpoint, our understanding of the genetics of mood disorders suggests two implications related to treatment. First, if you have a mood disorder, your close relatives are at a higher risk than the general population for developing an affective disorder too. Thus, if someone in your family starts to experience symptoms, please consider suggesting that he or she receive a professional evaluation. Second, those who have relatives with mood disorders and develop depression may have more severe illness than individuals who do not have family members with the illness.[72] This possibility should be considered when you make treatment decisions; it may suggest more aggressive treatment and relapse prevention approaches.

Neurotransmitters

As mentioned above, one of the main explanations of the cause of depression has been the **monoamine hypothesis of depression**. This hypothesis, originally proposed in 1965, holds that two monoamine neurotransmitters

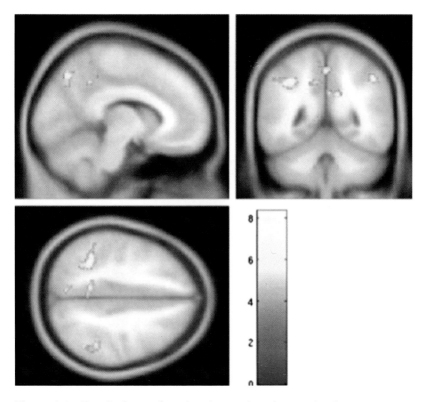

Figure I.1   Results from a functional neuroimaging study of
bipolar disorder

Reprinted from *Progress in Neuro-Psychopharmacology & Biological Psychiatry*,
Volume 35, William R. Marchand, James N. Lee, Cheryl Garn, John Thatcher, Phillip
Gale, Sebastian Kreitschitz, Susanna Johnson, Nicole Wood, Aberrant emotional
processing in posterior cortical midline structures in bipolar II depression, Pages
1729–1737, Copyright © 2011, with permission from Elsevier.

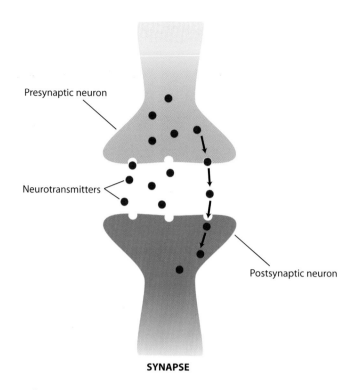

Figure 4.1   Chemical neurotransmission at the synapse

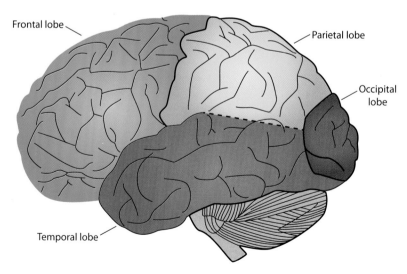

Figure 4.2   Cerebral cortex of the human brain

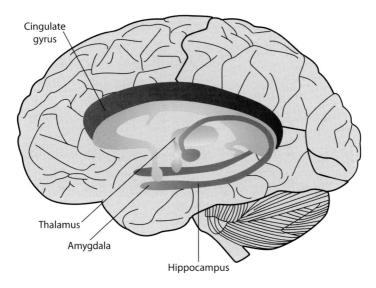

Figure 4.3   Amygdala, hippocampus, thalamus, and cingulate gyrus

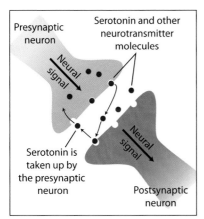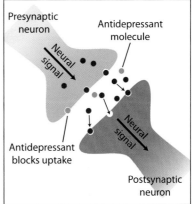

Figure 4.4   Inhibition of neurotransmitter reuptake by antidepressants

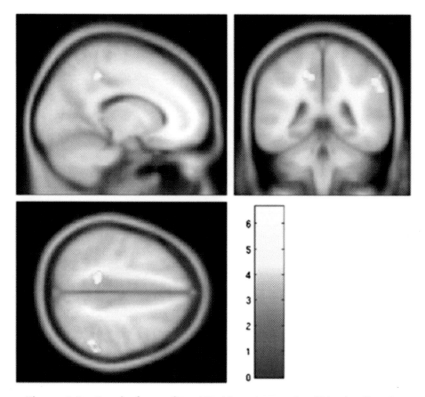

Figure 4.8   Results from a functional imaging study of bipolar disorder

The colored areas indicate regions of brain activation associated with depression in bipolar disorder. The top left image shows that part of the cortical midline region is involved in the expression of depressive symptoms.

(serotonin and norepinephrine) and possibly a third (dopamine) are deficient in unipolar depression. A related hypothesis is that elevations in dopamine levels contribute to mania. Extensive research over the years (including the genetic studies described above) clearly establishes a role for disruptions of neurotransmitter function in mood disorders. However, it is almost certainly more complicated than deficits or elevations of specific neurotransmitters.

One neurotransmitter that may play a role in mood disorders is **glutamate**. This chemical serves as the primary excitatory neurotransmitter in the brain. "Excitatory" means that when glutamate is released at the synapse, the postsynaptic neuron increases its firing rate. In contrast, inhibitory neurons cause the postsynaptic neuron to decrease its firing rate. Some structures in the middle section of the brain seem to be hyperactive in unipolar illness, and it is thought that increased excitatory neurotransmission by glutamate may contribute to this phenomenon.[73] In regard to bipolar spectrum illness, the evidence is inconclusive, but studies have suggested both increased and decreased glutamate signaling.[73]

The primary inhibitory neurotransmitter in the brain is gamma-aminobutyric acid, commonly known as GABA. There is some evidence of abnormal GABA signaling in unipolar but not bipolar spectrum disorders.[73] Glutamate and GABA have direct excitatory and inhibitory functions, but most other neurotransmitters are considered modulatory. These signaling molecules are involved in a variety of information transfer processes. Neurotransmitters in this category include serotonin, norepinephrine, acetylcholine, dopamine, and the endorphins.

Serotonin and norepinephrine have been previously mentioned, and abnormalities of signaling by these molecules undoubtedly play a role in mood disorders. However, it is likely much more complex than the notion of a deficit of these substances, as was originally thought. There is some evidence that acetylcholine signaling may be abnormal in both unipolar and bipolar illness, but the details are not completely understood.[73]

There is considerable evidence of problems with dopamine neurotransmission in both unipolar and bipolar spectrum disorders.[73] Evidence in support of this hypothesis includes the association of manic symptoms with drugs that cause an increase in the release of dopamine at the synapse, such as psychostimulants.[74] Also, antipsychotic medications, which inhibit dopamine function, are effective antimanic agents.[75–78] Finally, there is evidence that the mood stabilizers valproate and lithium may modulate dopamine neurotransmission.[79–82] These biological treatments are discussed in detail in Chapter 8. In contrast to mania, decreased dopamine neurotransmission may play a role in unipolar illness.[73]

Endorphins are opioid peptide compounds produced by the pituitary gland and the hypothalamus during strenuous exercise, excitement, and pain.[83] These substances resemble the opiates used in narcotic pain medications in their abilities to relieve pain and produce a sense of well-being. As discussed in Chapter 10, exercise is an effective treatment for depression. The "endorphin hypothesis" suggests that exercise releases endorphins, which results in the decrease of depressive symptoms. This hypothesis has been based on the idea that the so-called runner's high associated with long-distance running occurs as a result of endorphin release.

In summary, problems with neurotransmitters undoubtedly play a role in the causes of mood disorders. However, this system of information transfer is incredibly complex and we do not completely understand everything that neurotransmitters do in individuals who do not suffer from these conditions. Thus, it will likely be some time before we are able to completely define the role of these substances in affective disorders. Nonetheless, we know that treatments that affect neurotransmitter function (see Chapter 8) are effective treatments for mood disorders.

Inflammation

Inflammation is part of the body's response to harmful stimuli, such as bacteria, damaged tissue (e.g., from a wound), or irritants. The purpose of inflammation is to protect the body by removing the injurious stimuli and facilitating the healing process. While the aim of these processes is to help the body recover, in some cases inflammation can be harmful. For example, inflammatory processes are now thought to play a crucial role in a number of brain disorders, such as Alzheimer's disease, Parkinson's disease, and Huntington's disease.[84, 85] Considerable evidence also indicates that the inflammatory response may in some cases contribute to the causes of unipolar illness.[86–93]

Some of this evidence includes the fact that there are biological similarities among stress, depression, and inflammation.[94, 95] Immune system signaling molecules, known as cytokines, may provide the link between inflammation and depression. Cytokines (e.g., interleukins, interferons, and tumor necrosis factors) are released in response to injury, infection, and stress.[96] Elevated levels of cytokines can negatively affect processes that are required for neuron health.[97] Also the cytokine interferon-alpha, which is used to treat hepatitis and some cancers, frequently results in depressive symptoms as a side effect.[98] In animals, cytokines can lead to a phenomenon known as sickness behavior.[99] Sickness behavior is thought to optimize survival[100] by diverting metabolic resources away from goal-directed behaviors and toward recovery. Behavior changes are similar to those associated with depression in humans and include lethargy, depression, **anorexia nervosa**, reduction in grooming and sexual activity, increased sensitivity to pain, sleep disruption, and altered response to rewarding and affective stimuli. Thus, unipolar depression could in some cases represent aberrant and persistent sickness behavior as a result of inflammation and cytokines.

At this point, we do not know to what extent inflammation plays a role in depression. However, there is enough evidence to suggest that it may be a factor in some cases. Unfortunately, knowing this does not currently help us with making treatment choices. As more research is done, it may be that medications used to treat inflammation will have a role in the treatment of some cases of depression.

Neurocircuitry

Neurocircuitry refers to the networks of connected brain regions that function together in support of various processes, such as thinking, interpreting sensory information (hearing, vision, etc.), and controlling motor behavior. In the sections above, I described some of the possible causes of mood disorders that may affect various circuits. In this section, we will discuss some of the evidence for abnormalities of specific brain regions and circuits in mood disorders.

At the beginning of this chapter, I suggested that one way to think about affective illness is as disorders of emotional control. I also proposed that a simple way to conceptualize these conditions is to think of them as resulting from too much or not enough emotion. Depression lacks the positive emotions, such as happiness, joy, and contentment. Mania, on the other hand, is associated with an excess of such feelings. Deficits and excesses of emotion could occur as result of production or control problems, again using the analogy of an "emotional factory." Let's take a quick factory tour.

Emotions are thought to be generated by older parts of the brain located below the cortex. The two structures most involved are the amygdala and striatum. The amygdala is associated with the production of fear and anxiety, while the striatum and associated circuitry are involved with the manufacture of positive emotions, including reward and motivation. The striatum is one structure in the basal ganglia circuitry mentioned earlier.

The amygdala likely serves primarily as a threat detector.[101] It receives extensive sensory information and thus is able to perceive potential threatening situations.[102] In response to a threat, the amygdala sends signals to multiple areas. Together, these signals cause the "fight or flight" response that we are all familiar with.[102] However, we also need a "control" mechanism to evaluate the fear response in order to determine whether it is appropriate and adequate. For example, if we mistake a shadow for a monster, we need a process by which to discover our mistake and turn the fear off. In contrast, if the fear is appropriate, then we need to know that as well and decide whether our response is adequate. The frontal cortex, or thinking part of our brain, provides the control system for the emotional factory.[102] It is illustrated in Figure 4.5.

Figure 4.6 shows how excessive fear could occur because of too much output from the amygdala (thick arrow) or too little regulation from the frontal cortex (thin arrow). This mechanism likely plays a role in some anxiety disorders, which are essentially disorders of excessive fear. For example, it is thought that **panic attacks** occur as a result of hypersensitivity of the fear circuitry.[103] Abnormalities of this circuit likely also contribute to the anxiety symptoms often associated with mood disorders.

Similar circuitry accounts for the experiences of pleasure, motivation, and reward; however, in this case the subcortical structure is the striatum. The names of the structures aren't particularly important, but I think the general concept will be helpful for you: First of all, both positive and negative emotions are produced automatically and unconsciously by subcortical structures (amygdala and striatum). For example, if you get a surprise phone call from a dear friend with whom you haven't had contact for a

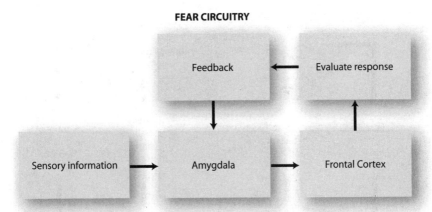

Figure 4.5   Brain circuitry responsible for fear generation and regulation

while, you will most likely experience a positive emotion. You don't have to decide that you want to feel that way; it just happens automatically. The same is true when you are in a scary situation. You don't have to decide to feel fear; it just comes on by itself. Sadness is another example. Once these emotions are perceived by the thinking part of your brain, the cortex, emotional regulation can occur by way of feedback to the subcortical structures. This circuitry is illustrated in Figure 4.7.

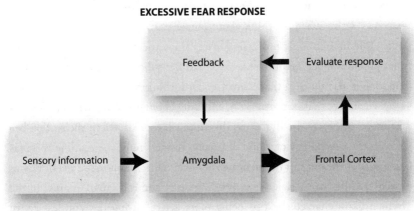

Figure 4.6   Excessive fear response

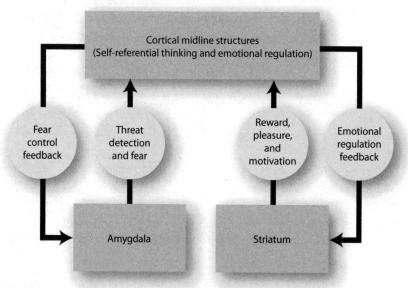

Figure 4.7   Human emotional control circuitry

One cortical region is particularly important for emotional regulation—the middle, or midline, surface of each cerebral hemisphere (the surface shown in Figure 4.3). Most of the midline cortex is thought to be a functional unit known as the **cortical midline structures (CMS)**.[104] The CMS are thought to be important in mood disorders because of anatomical connectivity with the two subcortical structures mentioned above, the amygdala and striatum.[105–110] Further, the CMS are the area of the brain that becomes active when we think about ourselves.[104, 111–115] This area also plays a key role in emotional processing.[116–118] Thus, the area of the frontal cortex that provides much emotional feedback to the subcortical areas that produce emotion is also the area that is involved with thinking about ourselves. This is why we believe that our patterns of thinking about ourselves are so important for mood disorders. I will discuss this in much more detail in the section below on the psychology of mood disorders. Interestingly, the midline cortex is also part of the **default mood network**.[119, 120] The default mood network was discovered by M. E. Raichle and colleagues[121] and is a group of areas in the human brain characterized by being more active during rest and less active during activity. This network has sparked a lot of scientific interest because it may underlie fundamental (or default) processes such as consciousness.

Studies of healthy subjects provide evidence that these regions contribute to mood. For example, functional imaging studies indicate that transient sadness is associated with activation of the CMS[122, 123] and striatum.[122] More important, there is extensive evidence that these regions function abnormally in mood disorders. Many studies demonstrate dysfunction of the striatum in both bipolar and unipolar spectrum illness.[73] Multiple studies also demonstrate abnormal functioning of the amygdala,[124–130] CMS,[131–137] and default mode network in unipolar illness.[116] CMS dysfunction is associated with bipolar spectrum disorders.[138–150] Finally, both medication[124, 136] and psychotherapy[151, 152] treatment of unipolar illness has been shown to affect the function of the CMS. Unipolar treatment has also been shown to change the functioning of the amygdala[124, 127, 151] and striatum.[125, 151] Figure 4.8 on page 100 is an example of one of my imaging studies.[21] In this study we found evidence that CMS function is associated with symptoms of depression in bipolar II disorder.

Summary of the neurobiology of mood disorders

Modern neuroscience methods are providing exciting insights into the neurobiology of human emotion and the causes of mood disorders. However, as this section has illustrated, many unanswered questions remain. Nonetheless, we are making progress that we hope will lead to more effective treatments in the near future.

Out of necessity, the information presented above is an overview of a very complicated topic. Further, it is only a summary of some key findings. Space constraints do not allow an exhaustive review of the literally thousands of research papers that have been published on this topic. With those limitations in mind, it is my hope that at the very least this information will convince you that mood disorders are biological disorders. These conditions are just like any other biological illness, such as heart disease or high blood pressure. I hope the information presented in this book will help decrease the stigma that is still unfortunately associated with these conditions.

The psychology of mood disorders

This section reviews psychological factors associated with mood disorders. There is no doubt that mood disorders are both biological and psychological conditions. Further, the distinction between the two is somewhat artificial,

as all psychological processes that occur in our brain depend on the biological mechanisms described previously. It is unlikely that we will ever be
able to completely explain the richness of human psychology in terms of
biological functions. Nonetheless, as I have mentioned, the distinction is
convenient for discussion purposes, since treatments can be categorized as
being either biological or psychological.

Two kinds of "psychological" processes contribute to mood disorders. One of these is psychological stress. By "psychological stress" I mean
the stresses, pressures, and hassles of life that we normally refer to simply
as "stress." Sometimes the term *psychosocial stress* is used when the stress involves our interactions with others and our social environment. Stress can
play a major role in mood disorders. For example, the onset of depression is
often associated with a variety of stresses, including those related to work,[153]
natural disasters,[154] perinatal loss,[155] humiliation,[156] and relationship loss.[157,
158] Job loss worsens depressive symptoms. Similarly, stress is associated with
the onset of mania.[159] Thus, psychological methods of stress management
(see Chapters 9 and 10) can be very important to the recovery process.

The other psychological process is "psychological vulnerability"; in
other words, some individuals may have a greater risk of developing a mood
episode based on their psychological makeup or traits. Some of us may be
more likely to develop a mood disorder because of either psychological or biological factors (discussed in the previous section) or both. Again, I want to
emphasize that "biological" and "psychological" are not necessarily different
causes. In many cases they are one and the same. We are just choosing to look
at them from either a biological or psychological perspective. Finally before
discussing some psychological traits that may contribute to mood disorders, I
want to tie together the concepts of vulnerability and stress.

We think this combination works as follows: Everyone likely has some
vulnerability to develop a mood disorder. For some, this may be very low. For
others, because of biological and/or psychological factors, it may be higher.
Stress can also be placed on a scale from high to low. The combination of
high stress and high vulnerability is more likely to lead to a mood episode
than the combination of low stress and low vulnerability. So, whether or not
any of us develops a mood episode at a given time is likely a result of where
we are on the two continua of stress and vulnerability. Since we don't have the

means to measure our biological vulnerability and we generally can't predict our future levels of stress, it is impossible to predict with certainty whether a given person will develop a mood disorder in the future. However, having a sense of where we are on the vulnerability and stress continua can be helpful. For example, if you have close relatives who have a mood disorder or if you have experienced mood symptoms in the past, then you may have a relatively high level of vulnerability. If you experience a period of high stress, it makes sense for you to watch carefully for the onset of mood symptoms. You might also want to consider preventive strategies, such as psychotherapy (Chapter 9) or complementary approaches (Chapter 10). Now, let's discuss psychological vulnerabilities to mood disorders.

A number of theories have been put forward to explain psychological causes or factors that contribute to the development of depression. Most theories focus on depression rather than bipolar spectrum illness because the latter is generally thought of as a primarily "biological" disorder. This section will be limited to psychological theories of depression; however, it is important to point out that psychological treatments are very important to the recovery process for bipolar spectrum disorders. Also, psychological factors undoubtedly contribute to bipolar disorder; we just don't understand them very well.

Before we talk about specific theories, I want to draw your attention to a relationship between how we see ourselves and depression. Studies going back several decades and investigating a variety of populations suggest complex relationships between self-concept and depression. These investigations generally indicate a relationship between low self-concept and depression.[160–178] As you will see in the following section, psychological theories of depression often involve multifaceted relationships between our self-concept and this disorder.

I also want to point out that this chapter does not attempt to cover all of the psychological theories of depression. It certainly does not address all of the psychological factors that may be relevant for you. We all have distinctive characteristics, personality traits, and experiences that contribute to our unique psychology. That said, the aim of this section is to discuss psychological elements that are relevant for many individuals with mood disorders. Further, I have focused on thinking patterns and behaviors that you can readily modify as part of your recovery.

One final point before we move on: We all have psychological characteristics that don't always serve us well. Some of these characteristics may need to be modified as part of a recovery plan. This is just part of being human. I have traits, habits, and behaviors that can cause problems just like you and everyone else on the planet. I am making this point because there is a tendency to beat ourselves up when we discover that aspects of our personality might be contributing to mood symptoms. Please don't do that. You didn't sign up for those characteristics. Our personalities, thinking patterns, and behaviors develop as a result of complex interactions between our inherited personality traits and life experiences. The remainder of this chapter and Chapter 9 (about psychotherapy) suggest that you begin to think about the psychological factors that may be causing your mood symptoms and/or preventing you from being happy. It is critical to begin this self-exploration process with an attitude of absolute compassion for yourself. Becoming more self-aware will reveal thinking patterns and behaviors that you may want to change. These do not mean anything negative about you. However, developing the ability to look at yourself in an accepting and objective way is crucial for your recovery. Compassion and love for yourself will help you to see what needs to be changed without feeling bad about what you discover. Practicing **mindfulness** (explained in detail in Chapter 9) can help you cultivate greater compassion for yourself and others. That is why I strongly recommend developing a mindfulness practice as part of your recovery plan. Options for doing this are outlined in Chapters 9 and 10.

Now let's take a short tour of some psychological theories of depression. Please do not think that these theories are mutually exclusive. As you will see, there are many commonalities among them. My take is that they are most likely all at least partially correct. Also, since each of us has a unique psychology, it is likely than some are more relevant for one person than another.

Freudian theory

To provide historical perspective, I will briefly mention Freudian theory, even though much of Freud's work has been heavily criticized. As mentioned above, various stresses are associated with depression, and most of these stresses involve some type of loss for the depressed person. Freud suggested that both grief and depression could occur in response to loss. However, he thought that grieving turned into depression when the bereaved felt ambivalent about the loss (as in ambivalence about the person in the lost relationship).[1] He further theorized that unresolved losses from early in life could result in more difficulty dealing with loss as an adult. Studies do suggest that early loss (e.g., of a parent) is associated with adult depression.[1] The issue of ambivalence is less clear, however, if for no other reason than we all have some degree of ambivalence about all of our relationships. In my view, the take-home point from Freud's thinking is that, in a general sense, depression is often linked to loss. Specifically, the losses often have to do with our self-identity and self-esteem. For example, loss of a love relationship may lead to the sense that our "self" is receiving less love or that we have in a way lost a part of our "self." Further, such a loss may lead us to question our self-concept—how we think about our "self." Did we do something wrong? Why can't we stay in a relationship? Aren't we lovable? These painful questions relate to our idea of who we are—that is, our concept of "self."

The rest of this chapter will focus primarily on the concept of self in relation to depression. This is an exciting area of current research, and there is considerable evidence that psychological treatments focused on issues of self are very effective. These approaches are effective because you can change the way you think about yourself (see Chapters 9 and 10).

Cognitive theory

Next, let's talk about cognitive theories of depression, which underlie the **cognitive therapy** treatments discussed in Chapter 9. As the name suggests, these theories posit that depression is a result of our thought processes. By extension, then, we can overcome depression by changing how we think. Cognitive theory and the associated cognitive therapy treatment are best thought of as a single entity and, therefore, I use the abbreviation CT to refer to both in this book. In regard to terminology, CT is also known as cognitive behavior therapy or CBT.

Aaron T. Beck proposed the cognitive approach to depression in the 1960s. The development of CT was influenced by the concepts of the Greek Stoic philosophers, Eastern schools of thought, such as Buddhism, as well as a variety of developments in the general field of psychotherapy.[1] Many individuals have contributed to the evolution and refinement of CT over the last 50 years.

CT is based on the idea that our brains process information inaccurately in mood, anxiety, and other psychiatric conditions. Beck specifically proposed that three major errors (or cognitive distortions) were associated with depression: a negative view of self, world, and future.[1] Further, these cognitive distortions lead to sadness as well as behaviors (or lack of behaviors) that fail to get our needs met. The result of these behaviors is then reinforcement of the cognitive distortions, creating a vicious cycle. It is important to note that CT does NOT state that the cognitive distortions are the "only cause" of depression but rather a phenomenon that can be treated and may come about as a result of a variety of psychological, environmental, and biological factors.[1]

Two levels of cognitive distortions have been proposed. The first level describes "automatic thoughts" and the second deeper level encompasses "basic beliefs." Automatic thoughts are cognitions that occur spontaneously in various situations and are not based on logic or subjected to rational analysis.[1] Examples are "I can't do anything right" and "I always forget something important." Basic beliefs are incorporated into "schemas," which are deeper cognitive organizing structures developed during childhood and influenced by our later experiences.[1] In general, schemas may have a useful purpose of facilitating rapid information processing. However, some are thought to lead to depression as well as behaviors that interfere with meeting our goals. Examples of such schemas are[1] "I must be perfect to be accepted," "No matter what I do, I won't succeed," and "Others can't be trusted." It is easy to see how such beliefs could result in our interpreting events as being more negative than they really are. Further, since our actions are guided by our thoughts, these interpretations could easily lead us to behave in ways that are not in our ultimate best interest. These behaviors could then lead to more depression.

That's the theory, but what about the evidence? Numerous studies indicate that alterations in self-referential thinking may be associated with a number of mood and anxiety spectrum disorders. First of all, as mentioned above, many investigations indicate an association between how we think about ourselves and both unipolar depression[160, 161, 167, 177, 178] and bipolar spectrum disorders.[179–184] Similar evidence also exists for **generalized anxiety disorder,**[185] **obsessive-compulsive disorder,**[186, 187] **PTSD,**[188–190] **social phobia,**[191, 192] and **panic disorder.**[193] Many studies also indicate that negative self-concept is associated with suicidal behavior.[194–204]

I will discuss cognitive therapy in more detail in Chapter 9; however, before moving on, I want to return to the topic of "self." As in Freudian theory, the central issue in CT is self. Schemas that cause problems for us involve how we perceive self ("No matter what I do, I won't succeed"), our expectations for self ("I must be perfect to be accepted"), or our self in relation to the world ("Others can't be trusted"). While it might seem like that schema is about "others," it is really about us. What is actually being said is "Others can't be trusted, because if I trust them, then self will be harmed." With that in mind, let's move on to another theory that focuses more directly on self in relation to others.

Interpersonal theory

As with cognitive therapy, interpersonal theory and the associated therapy are essentially indistinguishable, so I will use the abbreviation IPT to refer to both. IPT is based on the idea that depression is influenced by, and itself affects, the depressed individual's psychosocial environment.[205]

IPT was developed by Gerald Klerman and Myrna Weissman in the 1970s and built upon the work of Adolf Meyer, Harry Stack Sullivan, and John Bowlby.[205] IPT does not state that interpersonal factors "cause" depression but rather that addressing interpersonal problems can help treat depression.[205] Techniques of IPT are discussed in Chapter 10. One of the tasks of the early phase of treatment is to develop a perspective of one's depression in an interpersonal context. To do this, the depressed individual must consider factors such as relationship expectations, satisfying and unsatisfying aspects of relationships, and changes in relationships.[205] As with the other theories discussed, the central issue is again self. What does the self expect and want from relationships? Is the self getting what it needs from relationships? Is the self providing what the other person needs? So, again, our friend self is in the starring role. Let's talk about a theory that is more directly based on issues of self.

Mindfulness theory

The concept of mindfulness is very important for our understanding of mood disorders because there is compelling evidence that interventions based on mindfulness are effective treatments for depression and anxiety (see Chapter 9). Developing a mindfulness practice is also something that you can do on your own (see Chapter 10). Finally, this topic links together our understanding of the psychological and biological causes of mood disorders.

What is mindfulness? There are a number of definitions, but most descriptions include focusing attention in the present moment—that is, being aware of the sensations we are experiencing right now. See Chapter 9 for a much more detailed discussion of mindfulness.

What does mindfulness have to do with mood? It has to do with our patterns of thinking about ourselves. As I discussed in the section on biology, one particular brain region, known as the cortical midline structures, or CMS, is involved with both thinking about self and emotional control. Multiple studies indicate that functional alterations exist in the CMS in both unipolar[131-137, 151, 206-212] and bipolar[138-150] spectrum disorders. Further, evidence directly links the CMS with both self-referential processing (thinking about the self) and the emotional dysregulation associated with depression. For example, a study of healthy controls demonstrated that self-referential thinking activates the CMS and that this neural response is specifically associated with negative mood.[213] This finding suggests that the process of thinking about the self can be directly linked to negative emotion. Furthermore, it indicates that this link occurs at the CMS.

What about in depression? In unipolar illness, studies indicate that abnormal self-referential thinking is mediated by the CMS and other regions.[209, 214] Thus, CMS function appears to underlie the patterns of thinking about the self associated with depression. Studies of emotional processing in depression also have shown disruptions of CMS function.[116, 214] Finally, depressive symptoms are associated with the degree of CMS activity during a self-negative judgment task.[214] Thus, a large body of evidence indicates that CMS play a key role in mediating the relationship between self-referential thinking and negative **affect** in depression.

Now we know that the patterns of thinking about the self contribute to depression. We also know that these patterns and emotion are linked by the CMS. But, what thinking patterns contribute to depression?

This is where the concept of mindfulness comes in. Mindfulness is a state of awareness, including self-awareness and nonjudgmental awareness of one's thoughts, emotions, and sensations. Mindfulness may involve thinking about the self, but it is experiential thinking.[215] In other words, we are aware of our thoughts but view them from a distance; it's like watching ourselves think. We "experience" thoughts and other sensations, but we aren't carried away by them. We just watch them come and go.

In contrast to mindfulness, another type of thinking about the self is known as analytic self-referential thinking. This means thinking about the self in a methodical and usually judgmental way. When we analyze, we often ask questions—for example, "Why am I feeling bad today?" or "What did I do wrong?" We also compare—perhaps a comparison of how we feel today versus yesterday or last week. The main point is that analytical thinking about the self is the opposite of being mindful.[215] When we think analytically about ourselves, we are not experiencing what is going on right now; instead, our attention is focused on whatever we are analyzing. Sometimes thinking about the self analytically can be useful; however, often it is the opposite. This is particularly true when we ruminate. By "ruminate" I mean thinking about something for an extended period of time. We typically ruminate when we are worried or upset about something.

Why is this important? Analytical self-focused rumination is maladaptive.[215] Specifically, it is associated with misinterpretation of memories,[216] negative self-judgments,[217] negative thinking about the future,[218] and sadness.[219, 220] Most important, there is compelling evidence that ruminative self-focus is associated with both the severity and duration of depressive symptoms[221-227] as well as relapse of illness.[228] There is less research investigating the role of rumination in bipolar spectrum illness, but some evidence suggests that rumination is associated with these conditions as well,[229, 230] and one study[229] found that rumination predicted the number of depressive episodes.

The amount of time spent thinking about the self is also associated with depression. Individuals with unipolar illness have increased self-focused thinking.[231, 232] Excessive self-focus in general is associated with negative emotion,[233] and high levels of self-focus are thought to contribute to depressive pessimism.[234] Finally, cognitive impairment in depression may be associated with increased self-focus.[235]

The conclusion is that both the amount of time spent thinking about the self and the patterns of thinking about the self are likely major contributors to the development of depressive symptoms. Practicing mindfulness has the potential to prevent thinking patterns related to the self from leading to depression. I hope you find the idea of mindfulness intriguing and consider giving this practice a try. One way to do this is through meditation, which I discuss in Chapter 10. Another approach is specific evidence-based psychological treatments, discussed in detail in Chapter 9.

Summary of the biology and psychology of mood disorders

I hope this chapter has provided a helpful overview of some of what we currently know about mood disorders. One take-home point is that these are biological disorders, just like diabetes and high blood pressure. Another is that mood disorders are also psychological conditions. However, in regard to brain function, "biology" and "psychology" are best understood as different aspects of the same underlying processes. That said, we will likely never be able to completely reduce the complexity of human psychology to an equation describing the underlying biology. I think it is still important to recognize that biology and psychology are not opposites but rather interacting processes that cause mood symptoms.

How does having this information help to facilitate your recovery? It is my hope that knowledge of both the biological and psychological factors will put any ideas of stigma and blaming oneself to rest once and for all. I have been a psychiatrist for more than two decades and I have not met anyone yet who signed up for a mood disorder. If you have a mood disorder, it is because of a complex set of factors that put you at higher risk than the general population. Please do not blame yourself or think that you have any reason to be embarrassed or ashamed.

Another way that I hope this information will help you is by providing the rationale for biological, psychological, and complementary treatment approaches. Unfortunately, mood disorders are often chronic and can be difficult to treat. Thus, a comprehensive recovery plan including a combination of strategies is likely to give you the best chance of getting completely better and staying well for life. I encourage you to implement as many of the approaches outlined in this book as possible. This is especially important if you have already been in treatment and have had difficulty achieving full remission.

5

How and Where to Find Help

THIS CHAPTER IS ABOUT PICKING THE PROFESSIONAL members of your treatment team. It is critical to your recovery to have team members who are highly competent. Equally important is having members on your team whom you feel comfortable working with. Sometimes putting together your team can be challenging. The aim of this chapter is to provide information to make the process easier.

Our starting point will be reviewing the various professionals who typically treat **mood disorders**. There are two basic groups. One group is all of those who prescribe medications or other biological treatments. In this book, I use the word *prescribers* for these potential team members. The other group is those who provide psychotherapies and other treatments that do not require prescription privileges. Since this group encompasses a diverse group of professionals, I use the general term *therapists* for these individuals. There is no implication that one group is more important for your recovery than the other; I simple use this division to facilitate explaining who does what. In some cases, team members may provide both biological treatments and psychotherapy. Finally, I use the terms *provider* and *clinician* to encompass both groups. I will start by discussing prescribers.

Prescribers who treat mood disorders

There are several categories of prescribers who may provide treatment for mood disorders. For ease of discussion, I use three general groupings: (1) physicians other than psychiatrists, (2) psychiatrists, and (3) other prescribers.

Physicians other than psychiatrists

We typically think about physicians in terms of their specialty. Because the entire field of medicine and surgery is so extensive, it is not practical to obtain and maintain proficiency in all areas of medicine. Thus, almost all doctors focus their practice in one specific area—that is, their specialty. Of course, for primary care providers, the scope of practice is much broader than for some other specialists. In this and the following sections, we will be discussing physicians based on their specialty, so a brief explanation of specialty training and certification is warranted.

Physicians in the United States and many other countries complete postgraduate specialty training after medical school. This period of training lasts several years and is known as "residency." The first year of residency is sometimes called an "internship." Physicians in postgraduate training are referred to as "residents" or "interns." After residency, physicians are eligible to undergo testing to demonstrate competency in their chosen specialty. Successful completion of this testing process results in board certification. Physicians who have passed the "boards" are then board certified in their specialty. Nowadays, continued demonstration of competency is frequently required to maintain certification status. For more information about the board certification process, go to the American Board of Medical Specialties website (http://www.abms.org/).

Many, but not all, physicians in the United States are board certified in one or more specialties. While there are many outstanding physicians who are not board certified, having successfully completed the certification process does provide strong evidence of competency. To determine whether a physician is board certified, go to the American Board of Medical Specialties website (http://www.abms.org/) and choose "Is Your Doctor Certified?"

What about receiving treatment from a physician who is still in post-graduate (residency) training? This issue may come up if you receive care at an academic medical center that has residency training programs in one or more specialties. Residents have less experience, but they also almost invariably have the most up-to-date information about disorders and treatment. Further, they are supervised by another physician who has completed training, typically known as an "attending physician." Personally, I am fine with being treated by a resident, since I get my general medical care at the university where I teach. That said, it is a decision each person has to make for himself or herself. It is one of those decisions that is best made before you need care. So, if you are planning to seek treatment at an academic medical center (usually associated with a university), I recommend thinking this through before you schedule an appointment. If you have a preference one way or the other, it is absolutely appropriate to state whether or not you are willing to have treatment from a resident when you make the appointment. If you state that you would rather be treated by an attending physician, then that request should be honored.

With that background information, let's now talk about physicians who are not specialists in psychiatry but nonetheless may treat mood disorders. Primary care physicians frequently provide mental health treatment. The primary care specialties are family medicine and internal medicine for adults and pediatrics for children and adolescents. Primary care providers for women may also include gynecologists. Other specialists may provide treatment for mood disorders from time to time, but I will focus this discussion on primary care, as that is the setting in which you are most likely to receive treatment from a non-mental health specialist. Most of what I say applies, regardless of the specialty.

Why do some people receive treatment for mood disorders in primary care? There are a number of reasons. One reason is that many people have primary care providers and mood disorders are common; therefore, many individuals who receive primary care treatment for medical problems also have an affective disorder. For example, one study found about 20% of primary care patients suffered from **depression**.[236] Therefore, mood disorders are often diagnosed and treated in that setting.

Like almost everything in life, there are both pros and cons to receiving treatment for a mood disorder from a primary care provider. The main advantage is convenience. We all like "one-stop shopping." If we can receive treatment for all of our medical and psychiatric conditions in one spot, that can save a lot of time. Another advantage may be accessibility of treatment. In some places there is limited availability of mental health professionals and long wait times for initial and follow-up appointments. So, you may be thinking: Why even consider obtaining treatment from a mental health professional? In some cases there may be absolutely no reason. However, it is important to be aware of some possible pitfalls. While many primary care physicians provide outstanding treatment for mood disorders, there is evidence that this doesn't always happen. Some studies have indicated that depression is both underdiagnosed[237, 238] and undertreated in primary care.[236, 237] There are several reasons this can happen. One is the relatively short duration of appointments. The typical primary care appointment may be fine for an uncomplicated single episode of mild depression that responds well to treatment. However, more complicated depression and bipolar disorders usually require a fairly extensive evaluation and careful monitoring of treatment response. There often may not be adequate time in the usual primary care visit, especially if other medical conditions are also the focus of treatment. That said, appointments for medication management with mental health professionals are often short too (see Chapter 6 for time management strategies). Another, and perhaps more important, issue is the expertise of primary care physicians. Some are interested in mood disorders and are highly competent in their treatment; others aren't. It is absolutely appropriate to ask your primary care physician whether she or he feels comfortable treating you for your mood disorder. Another possible disadvantage is that treatment in primary care settings usually consists of pharmacology only. For most people, I recommend psychotherapy either alone or in combination with medication and/or complementary strategies (see Chapters 8, 9, and 10). It is certainly reasonable to receive medication treatment for a mood disorder in a primary care setting and also see a therapist elsewhere.

My recommendation is that, in most situations, mood disorder treatment in primary care may be a good option for those with a relatively uncomplicated depressive disorder that responds adequately to treatment.

To clarify, by "uncomplicated" I mean an episode of depression for which both of the following are true: (1) it is not complicated by multiple coexisting psychiatric disorders, and (2) there is no history of failure to respond to multiple treatments. Chapter 13 explains how you can judge whether your response to treatment is adequate. I also recommend STARTING treatment for more complicated depression or bipolar spectrum illness in primary care if that means initiating treatment sooner. This could occur because of a long wait time to get an appointment with a mental health specialist. In that situation, it is very appropriate to start treatment with your primary care doctor and consider switching to a mental health professional as soon as you can get an appointment. Of course, if you are getting better (see Chapter 13), then switching may not be necessary. The most important thing you can do is discuss the options with your primary care provider so that the two of you can make a decision together.

For those with uncomplicated depression who receive medication treatment in a primary care setting, I recommend that they consider adding psychotherapy or other recovery strategies (see Chapters 9 and 10). Most important, if you are not getting better, then please consider seeking treatment from a team of mental health professionals regardless of your type of illness or severity of symptoms. My suggestion is to first discuss this with your primary care provider. Ideally, the two of you will discuss the pros and cons of switching to specialty treatment and then decide together on the best course of action. If switching is the best option, she or he may be able to make a referral or recommendation for specialized mental health treatment. See Chapter 13 for details about how to evaluate your response to treatment. Table 5.1 provides an overview of the pros and cons of mood disorder treatment in primary care.

Psychiatrists

Psychiatrists are physicians who specialize in the treatment of psychiatric disorders. We go through the same medical school process as other physicians and then complete a four-year residency in psychiatry. Psychiatrists focus almost exclusively on the treatment of psychiatric illness, although some may also treat common, uncomplicated medical problems. Many psychiatrists provide primarily biological treatments, but some are also psychotherapists.

Table 5.1   Pros and cons of receiving treatment in a primary care
               setting

Possible advantages

+ Rapid and easy access to treatment

+ One-stop shopping for medical care

+ A provider you already know and trust

+ Less expensive

Possible disadvantages

+ Short duration of appointments

+ Variable physician expertise

+ Treatment with only pharmacotherapy

It is entirely appropriate to ask your psychiatrist whether she or he provides psychotherapy. If not, she will most likely know a number of good therapists in your area and will be happy to provide a referral. Many of us provide treatment for most or all psychiatric conditions, but some specialize in one or more disorders. This is important to find out before scheduling a first appointment if you have several psychiatrists to choose from in your area.

The main advantage of receiving treatment from a psychiatrist is that we specialize in the treatment of psychiatric illness. The possible disadvantages are limited treatment availability in some areas and inconvenience compared to primary care. We may also be more expensive. The pros and cons are summarized in Table 5.2. These pros and cons also apply to other prescribers (discussed in the next section) who specialize in the treatment of psychiatric disorders. If possible, I recommend obtaining treatment from a psychiatrist or other specialized mental health prescriber except in cases of relatively uncomplicated depressive disorders, as described above. However, if you start treatment in primary care and do not respond, then I strongly suggest that you discuss with your current provider whether seeking care from a prescriber

Table 5.2 Pros and cons of mental health specialty treatment

Possible advantages

◆ Expertise in the treatment of psychiatric illness

◆ Possibility of both pharmacotherapy and psychotherapy from one provider

Possible disadvantages

◆ Longer wait for initial and follow-up appointments

◆ Inconvenience compared to primary care

◆ More expensive

who specializes in mental health conditions is warranted. Another possible exception is for those who have more complicated conditions but who are in stable full remission. In that situation, primary care treatment may be very appropriate. Table 5.3 outlines my recommendations for when to seek treatment from a psychiatrist or other mental health specialist.

Table 5.3 When to seek treatment from a mental health specialist

Strongly recommended

◆ Any bipolar spectrum disorder

◆ Multiple psychiatric conditions

◆ Prior depression that has been difficult to treat

◆ Failure to respond to treatment

May not be necessary

◆ Uncomplicated depression

◆ Stable remission for more complicated conditions

For more information about the profession of psychiatry, go to the American Psychiatric Association website (http://www.psych.org/). To determine whether a psychiatrist is board certified, go to the American Board of Medical Specialties website (http://www.abms.org/) and choose "Is Your Doctor Certified?"

Other prescribers

In addition to physicians, other professionals may also prescribe medications. Physician assistants (PAs) and nurse practitioners (NPs) sometimes provide treatment for mood disorders.

PAs are licensed to practice medicine under the supervision of a licensed physician. All states as well as the District of Columbia have laws or regulations authorizing PAs to practice medicine and prescribe medications. For more information about PAs, go to the American Academy of Physician Assistants website (http://www.aapa.org/).

NPs also provide medication treatment for mood disorders. NPs are licensed in all states and the District of Columbia and practice under the rules and regulations of the state in which they are licensed. NPs have graduate education (usually a master's or doctoral degree) and clinical training beyond their registered nurse training. Many are nationally certified in their specialty area, and some specialize in mental health treatment. For more information about nurse practitioners, go to the American Academy of Nurse Practitioners website (http://www.aanp.org/AANPCMS2).

So, should you receive treatment from a PA or NP? My recommendation depends on the individual prescriber. If she or he is not a mental health specialty provider, then use the same recommendations as for primary care prescribers. If the PA or NP specializes in mental health, then please use the same general recommendation that I gave for psychiatrists. However, if you have very complicated illness and/or are not responding to treatment, then I recommend that you discuss with your current provider whether you should consider obtaining treatment from a psychiatrist.

Therapists who treat mood disorders

This category encompasses a diverse group of professionals who do not pre-scribe medications but provide psychotherapy and, in most cases, diagnostic assessments. The training, certifications, and licensing of psychotherapists depend on the specific discipline and the jurisdiction. Psychotherapy can be provided by psychologists, social workers, marriage and family therapists, mental health counselors, nurse psychotherapists, pastoral counselors, and other mental health disciplines. The following is a brief overview of some of the disciplines that provide psychotherapy. Please do not perceive that any specific discipline listed is "better" than one that is not listed here. Further, there is no implication intended that any listed discipline is "better" than any other. My aim is only to acquaint you with some of the categories of clinicians you may encounter.

Many psychologists provide psychotherapy. However, the field of **psychology** is broad and encompasses professionals who provide clini-cal care as well as those who teach and do research. Membership in the American Psychological Association requires a doctoral degree in psy-chology or a related field. Psychologists who do clinical work may provide psychological testing and diagnostic evaluations as well as psychotherapy. Psychological testing can be useful for diagnostic purposes for some indi-viduals with mood disorders. For more information about psychologists, go to the American Psychological Association website (http://www.apa.org/). To find a psychologist, click on "Find a Psychologist."

Social workers also provide psychotherapy. Like psychology, social work is a broad professional field involved with issues of social welfare, social change, and social justice. Thus, not all social workers are psycho-therapists. However, those who are psychotherapists have a master's degree with a focus on clinical work from an accredited graduate program and are trained to make diagnoses and provide individual and group counseling. For more information about social workers, go to the National Association of Social Workers website (http://www.naswdc.org/).

Marriage and family therapists (MFTs) are mental health professionals who are trained in psychotherapy and family systems and licensed to diagnose and treat mental disorders within the context of marriage, couples, and family systems. For more information about MFTs, go the American Association for Marriage and Family Therapy website (http://www.aamft.org/).

Recreational therapists utilize activity- and community-based interventions to address the physical, cognitive, emotional, social, and recreational needs of their clients. These professionals assist individuals to develop skills, knowledge, and behaviors that are important for daily living and community involvement. For more information about recreational therapy, go to the American Therapeutic Recreation Association website (http://www.atra-online.com/).

Other providers include nurse psychotherapists, who are registered nurses trained in the practice of psychiatric nursing, licensed professional counselors, and pastoral counselors.

Finding help

There are a number of approaches to finding treatment. A recommendation from friends or family is one possibility. Another option is to ask your primary care provider for a recommendation or referral. The following resources may also be helpful for locating appropriate providers in your area.

Getting help if you are in crisis

If you are currently having thoughts of harming yourself (or others) or are experiencing an emotional crisis, please take action immediately. Options for getting help immediately are listed in Table 5.4. One of these is the National Suicide Prevention Lifeline, a free, 24-hour hotline available to anyone in emotional crisis or having suicidal thoughts. The number is 1-800-273-TALK (8255). Please consider programming that number into your phone now, so that it will be immediately available if you ever need it.

Table 5.4   Options for seeking immediate help

♦   Call the National Suicide Prevention Lifeline: 1-800-273-TALK (8255).

♦   Call 911.

♦   Have a family member or friend take you to the nearest emergency room (do not go alone or drive yourself).

♦   Call your mental health or medical provider (if you have one). But if a provider is not immediately available to help, then take one of the above actions.

National resources for finding treatment

The following options may be helpful for finding professional members for your treatment team:

♦   American Association for Marriage and Family Therapy: To find a marriage and family therapist, go to the website http://www.aamft.org/ and click on "TherapistLocator.net."

♦   American Association of Pastoral Counselors: To find a pastoral counselor, go to the website http://aapc.org/ and click on "Find a Counselor."

♦   American Board of Medical Specialties: To find out whether a physician is board certified, go to the website http://www.abms.org/ and choose "Is Your Doctor Certified?"

♦   American Psychological Association: To find a psychologist, go to the website http://www.apa.org/ and click on "Find a Psychologist."

♦   Call 211: If the service is available in your area, dial 211 for help with food, housing, employment, health care, counseling, and more. You can look up information about your local 211 at http://www.211.org/. Learn more about 211 at http://www.211us.org.

- Department of Veterans Affairs: Find health care information for eligible veterans at http://www.va.gov/.

- Depression and Bipolar Support Alliance: Go to the DBSA "Find a Pro" page at http://findapro.dbsapages.org/ for peer-recommended mental health resources.

- Medicaid: The website http://www.cms.gov/ provides benefit information.

- Medicare: The website http://www.medicare.gov/ provides benefit information.

- Mental Health America: The website http://www.nmha.org/ provides helpful information about finding treatment.

- National Alliance on Mental Illness (NAMI) Information Help Line: This is an information and referral service. Call 1-800-950-NAMI (6264), Monday through Friday, 10 AM–6 PM, Eastern time. For more information about NAMI, visit the website http://www.nami.org/.

- *Psychology Today*'s Therapy Directory: To find mental health professionals in your area, go to the online source at http://therapists.psychologytoday.com/nmha/.

- Substance Abuse and Mental Health Services Administration (SAMHSA) Mental Health Treatment Locator: For information about mental health services and resources, go to http://store.samhsa.gov/mhlocator.

- Substance Abuse and Mental Health Services Administration (SAMHSA) Substance Abuse Treatment Facility Locator: For information about substance abuse treatment services, go to http://dasis3.samhsa.gov/.

- TRICARE: Treatment information for eligible uniformed service members, retirees, and their families may be found at http://tricare.mil/mybenefit/.

Local resources for finding treatment

The following are some resources to assist you with finding treatment that may be available in your area. Please use your phone book or an Internet search engine to find the contact information.

- Community mental health center

- Psychiatric hospital or general hospital with a psychiatric unit

- A friend or family member

- Your primary care physician

- The local chapter of one of the national organizations listed above

Support organizations

Though not treatment providers, support organizations can be very helpful to persons with mood disorders. The following organizations provide support and information to individuals suffering from affective illness:

- Depression and Bipolar Support Alliance (http://www.dbsalliance. org/): DBSA is a patient-directed organization focusing on the most prevalent mental illnesses. The organization provides up-to-date, scientifically based tools and information written in language the general public can understand.

- National Alliance on Mental Illness (http://www.nami.org/): NAMI is an organization dedicated to improving the lives of individuals and families affected by mental illness. NAMI's support and public education efforts are focused on educating Americans about mental illness as well as offering resources to those in need and advocating that mental illness become a high national priority.

- Mental Health America (http://www.nmha.org/): MHA is an advocacy organization that aims to inform, advocate, and provide access to quality behavioral health services for all Americans.

Costs of treatment

The cost of treatment is an important consideration. One goal of this book is to help you maximize the benefits of professional treatment. As a result, you can make the most of treatment and prevent unnecessary costs. But, even if your treatment is as cost-effective as possible, the potential impact on your budget will no doubt be an important consideration.

Unfortunately, the costs of treatment are highly variable, and it is difficult to even provide a rough estimate of what the costs will be in your specific situation. Thus, you will have to do some research. I will provide some suggestions to make that process as painless as possible for you.

The first step to take involves your insurance. Are you covered by a health insurance plan? If so, what type of plan do you have? Three general types of health plans are available to consumers. Private health plans are common. These are typically insurance plans offered by employers to their employees. Individuals, for example someone who is self-employed, can also purchase these plans. Medicaid is government-funded health care, typically provided for lower-income individuals and families. Finally, Medicare is also government-funded health care, typically provided for individuals aged sixty-five and over. In addition to those plans, eligible veterans can receive treatment through the Veterans Administration Healthcare System, and TRICARE is the health care program that serves uniformed service members, retirees, and their families.

If you are covered by a health insurance plan, the next step is to figure out what coverage you have for mental health treatment. If you have private insurance, this may mean reviewing any documentation you have, checking the plan website, and/or calling the plan or your employer. The websites listed above are good starting points for Medicaid, Medicare, TRICARE, and Veterans Administration benefit information.

A number of questions must be answered about your insurance coverage in order to determine how much mental health treatment may cost you out of pocket. Some critical questions are listed in Table 5.5. Be aware that treatment may not be covered or may be covered at a lower rate by

---

Table 5.5   Questions to ask about your health insurance coverage for mental health treatment

---

- Do you need a referral from your primary care provider to see a mental health specialist?
- Does your plan have a network of providers that you must see in order for your treatment to be covered?
- What is the yearly deductible (the yearly amount you pay for all or some services before the plan starts to pay)?
- Is there a separate deductible for different kinds of services?
- What costs or services apply toward the deductible?
- What is the yearly out-of-pocket-maximum?
- What is the co-pay when you have an office visit with a mental health specialist?
- What is the co-pay for a hospital stay?
- Does the plan have an approved list of psychiatric medications?

---

some policies if provided by an out-of-network provider. The same is true for nonapproved medications.

What if you don't have insurance or your insurance doesn't provide enough coverage? Some mental health professionals offer a fee service schedule known as a sliding scale. This means that the fee may "slide"; in other words it may go down based on your income. If you're making a middle-class salary, the discount may be minimal. However, for those who have a lower salary or are unemployed, the discount may be substantial.

Community mental health centers are another option to investigate. These are public resources available in hundreds of communities across the country. They are often funded and run by the local government. Like the sliding scale model in private practice, these clinics usually charge fees based on an individual's ability to pay.

Health care systems that train providers may also be a source of lower cost treatment. Often these systems are associated with university schools of various health care professions, such as medicine, nursing, psychology, and social work. Finally, many companies and organizations have employee assistance programs (EAPs). These may focus mainly on general life issues rather than mood disorders. But, if you have access to an EAP, they are worth checking out because at the least they will likely keep an updated listing of services and programs within your local community.

In regard to medication costs, many prescribers receive supplies of medications from pharmaceutical companies at no cost. These are typically referred to as "samples." The idea is that these medications can be given to individuals when medications are initially started, so that the consumer can try the medication before purchasing a prescription. If your prescriber is aware that the cost of medication is an issue for you, she or he may be able to provide at least some samples to help decrease your out-of-pocket expense. It is unlikely that he or she will be able to provide enough samples to cover an entire course of treatment for any one person, but any decrease of out-of-pocket expense can be helpful. Many pharmaceutical companies also have programs to help individuals who have difficulty affording their medication. Check the company website or ask your prescriber about this possibility.

I hope this section will be helpful as you negotiate the sometimes complex process of paying for treatment. My best advice is not to delay seeking treatment because of cost considerations. Mental health professionals want to help you get well. Please get help and let your treatment team know about your financial situation and insurance coverage. They will work with you to come up with the best options for your situation.

6

Collaborating with Your Team

THIS CHAPTER IS ABOUT TEAMWORK. Effective collaboration with your health care team and others is critical to ensure your full recovery. In order to have an effective partnership, it is necessary to first decide who is going to be on the team. Next, the roles and responsibilities of each team member must be agreed upon. This process includes clearly defining who is in the role of team leader. Finally, everyone needs to speak the same language and communicate effectively. By the end of this chapter, you will be ready to put together a championship team.

Before you read on, I want to make one more point: You don't have to put together your entire team all at once. If you are not already in treatment, then the most important thing is to get that process started. So go ahead and make your first appointment or appointments (see Chapter 5) if you have not already done so. Then you can work on deciding who the other team members will be.

Who's on your team?

Let's start with the most important person—the star player. That's you. This team is all about your recovery, so you are not only the most important individual but also the team captain. Now some of you might be thinking, But I don't want to be the captain. Or maybe you view one of your mental health providers as the "skipper." I hope that I can convince you to take charge. Other players have very important roles, but this is about you. One aim of this book is to empower those with **mood disorders** to take charge of their recovery. I hope you will accept this challenge.

What if you are too sick to be the captain? It is fine to delegate a family member, trusted friend, or provider for a short period of time if you need help. But, for the long run, I encourage you to take complete charge of your recovery. Of course, you will want lots of professional advice and feedback from those who care about you. Still, decisions will have to be made and you should be the one to make them whenever possible. After reading this book, you will have much of the information you need to make well-informed decisions about your treatment and the recovery process. Further, you will have the facts that you need to put together a comprehensive recovery plan that will give you the best chance of getting completely better and staying well.

Who else is on your lineup? There are many possibilities depending on your specific situation. Many teams include mental health or medical professionals (see Chapter 5). The most common scenario is to have a prescriber and an individual therapist; in some cases, these might be the same person. Other professionals might play a role as well, such as a case manager, group therapist, or recreational therapist. Your primary or specialty care providers might be involved in your recovery. This is especially likely if you have medical problems or take nonpsychiatric medications that may be contributing to your mood symptoms. When medical factors contribute to a mood disorder, good communication and collaboration between mental health and medical providers are critical. You may have to be the one to make sure this communication happens.

Other professionals may be involved in your healing process. Spiritual advisors frequently play a key role. You may also engage professionals who focus on specific stresses in your life, such as financial planners, attorneys, and the like.

Last, but absolutely not least, friends and family need to be on your team. Of course, you may not want to discuss your mood disorder with all of your friends and acquaintances. You may not want all of your relatives to know either. But having at least one, and preferably more than one, person who has a personal relationship with you on your team is very helpful.

Before we move on, now is a good time to pause and think about who your teammates will be.

Roles and responsibilities

Now that you have some ideas of who is going to be on your team, let's take a look at job descriptions.

Medical and mental health professionals

What are the job descriptions of the medical and mental health professionals who are on your team? These individuals have two possible roles: (1) to provide advice and (2) to perform procedures (including psychotherapy). These are highly trained, compassionate, and intelligent people, but their job is NOT to tell you what to do. This is such an important point that I'm going to repeat myself: Their job is not to tell you what to do.

Given all their training and other wonderful qualities, you may be wondering: Don't they know what's best for me? Maybe sometimes, but certainly not always. And even if they do know what's best in a given situation, it is still your decision. Professionals should give you their opinions about diagnosis and treatment options. It is fine for them to make a specific recommendation. In fact, that often happens and most of the time it is very helpful for those with mood disorders. That said, you must always be informed about all of the treatment options and the risks and benefits of each so that you can make an informed decision. The final choice has to take your specific needs and personal preferences into account. For example, say you have mild **depression** and psychotherapy is the recommended treatment. Therapy might be the best approach for many people with a similar diagnosis and clinical situation. But, if you don't have access to a qualified therapist or your insurance will not pay for therapy, then it's probably not the best option for you. This is why you have to make decisions based on all the information available.

I'm certainly not suggesting that you should not follow the recommendations of your treatment team. In most cases you should and, of course, if a professional makes a recommendation that works for you, then that is fine. Also, in some situations there really isn't much of a decision to make. To use a dental example, if the choice is to endure continued pain or to undergo a procedure to fix a decayed tooth, then the decision does not require a lot of thought. The point is to always have the mindset that you want to obtain as much information as possible, have all of your questions answered, and then make your decision based on all the pertinent facts. All of this is important because when it comes to the treatment of mood disorders, there are often several possible treatment approaches (many of these are discussed in subsequent chapters). Frequently, these options have different potential risks and benefits. Choosing the best approach for your given situation is not always straightforward. The purpose of this book is to help you sort out the options and decide what is best for you. This is particularly important if you are already in treatment and not getting better. As I have said throughout this book, please use as many strategies as possible to give yourself the best chance of getting completely better and staying well.

Now back to the roles of medical and mental health professionals. Table 6.1 summarizes the responsibilities of these team members.

Friends and family

What about friends and family? These team members often play a key role. Their specific job description will vary with each person and the specifics of your relationship. Of course, those who care about you can provide emotional support to aid your recovery. Another role is to provide a sounding board and second opinion. Treatment decisions can be complicated, and it is often useful to have someone who knows you on a personal level with whom you can talk over the pros and cons of different options.

Further, I encourage you to have a friend or family member go with you to at least some of your mental health care appointments. This can be

---

Table 6.1   What to expect from professionals on your team

Information and advise

- Your most likely diagnosis or diagnoses

- Evidence supporting the diagnostic impression

- If your diagnosis is uncertain, what additional steps can be taken to clarify it

- All reasonable treatment options, including no treatment

- Potential risks and benefits of all treatment options

- Adequate monitoring of your treatment and appropriate recommendations based on your response

- Answers to all of your questions

- Help if you are in a crisis situation

Prescriptions and procedures

- Prescriptions for medications

- Injections, electroconvulsive therapy, transcranial magnetic stimulation, and other interventions

- Psychotherapy

---

particularly helpful during evaluations and when important treatment decisions have to be made. Unfortunately, a lot of complicated information is frequently discussed in a short period of time. Having another set of ears can help prevent miscommunication. A friend or loved one may also come up with important questions or concerns that you don't think of during the appointment. Of course, it is not always appropriate or helpful to take someone with you to appointments, especially to group and some individual therapy sessions, where you discuss very personal information. My recommendation is to talk over the issue of bringing someone to some of your visits with your providers at the onset of treatment. If you want to bring a loved one to your initial appointment, discuss that possibility when you call to make the appointment. The person conducting your evaluation may want to spend some time with you alone, but in most cases it should be appropriate to have someone with you at least when treatment options are discussed.

The team captain

Now that we have reviewed the roles of the supporting cast, it is time to get back to the star of the show—you. What are your responsibilities as CEO of your recovery? Your number one job is to be the decider. Former President George W. Bush famously said, "I'm the decider." Regardless of your political leanings, I encourage you to take that statement as your personal mantra. What do you have to decide? Many decisions must be made during your recovery. One of the most important is whether to seek treatment. Equally important are choices about treatment approaches. There may be many possible treatments or only a few. Some decisions may be relatively minor and others very important. Regardless, I hope you will take your role as the decider very seriously. Your recovery may depend on it.

Besides being the decider, you have another very important job— information collection and analysis. Good decisions require good data. Just having the facts and figures isn't enough, however; the data must be understood and interpreted correctly. This can be tricky. The problem is that medical information can be difficult to understand and interpret by those who are not medical professionals. Understanding the data isn't always easy even for medical professionals. Today, medical treatment is highly specialized and each specialty has, to some extent, its own language and knowledge base. So, even medical professionals can get lost quickly when complex information from another specialty is being discussed.

My point is that you should not feel bad if you aren't following something you read or are told by a member of your treatment team. It happens to all of us. But, this information is often critical for decisions that you have to make, so you can't afford not to understand. The good news is that by reading this book you are taking a step toward solving that problem. Between the communication strategies and background information provided here, you should be able to obtain all the data you need to make well-informed decisions about your treatment and recovery.

Putting together a comprehensive recovery plan is also part of your job description. Of course, your treatment team can help you with this, but please be sure that this happens. A comprehensive plan is especially important if you have **recurrent unipolar** or bipolar spectrum illness. The more strategies for recovery that you can use, the better are your chances of getting well and staying that way.

You're not off the hook yet. You have one more very important role— to provide accurate information. This can be harder than it sounds. Let me give you two examples. Suppose you suffered from an episode of depression several years ago and were treated with two different antidepressants. Further, suppose the first one you tried caused bothersome side effects and was not effective. So, after a few weeks, your doctor prescribed a different medication. That one worked very well and caused no adverse effects. After a number of months of remission, the medication was stopped and you stayed well. Fast-forward to today. You have had a return of depression and your previous doctor has retired. You have sought help and are sitting in your new doctor's office. The problem is that you can't remember the names of the medications that you took before. Since you will most likely have the same response as when you were treated before, knowing the name of the antidepressant that worked can save weeks or months of trying medications that are ineffective or cause intolerable side effects. Here's another example: Suppose you and your new doctor decide on a medication to try and you start taking it. In about three weeks, you come back for a follow-up appointment. "So, are you feeling better," your doctor asks. You respond, "Uh, I'm not sure. Maybe a little. I really haven't thought about it that much." Knowing whether you are trending better is critical after a few weeks of treatment. This information is used to decide whether to continue treatment as is or consider making some adjustment. Getting this right can mean the difference between getting better quickly and enduring unnecessary extra weeks of symptoms.

Why do situations like these happen? A common reason is that many people don't know what information is important at any given point in treatment. I think most of us have a general idea, but we may not realize how critical the details are. In the first example, perhaps you knew that the doctor would ask about your past history of depression but you didn't spend a lot of time thinking about what information would be most important. Had you thought about it beforehand, you most likely could have obtained the information about your prior treatment. In the second example, no doubt most people would go in for a follow-up appointment expecting to be asked how they were doing. The problem is that improvement can be subtle and symptoms wax and wane. It is surprisingly easy to forget exactly how you felt before treatment and thus to be unsure whether you are really any better. The fix for this is very easy. There are multiple ways to easily track improvement. But, of course, you have to know what information is important at any given point in treatment to adequately prepare yourself for an appointment with your provider. I used medication treatment examples above, but the same idea applies to psychotherapy. Chapters 7 and 13 in this book prepare you for all of your appointments by clearly outlining the information that you need to collect and be ready to discuss.

Communication strategies

The goal of this section is to help you communicate effectively with your team members who are medical or mental health clinicians.

Learning the language

One thing you can do to facilitate communication is to learn the lingo. As I mentioned earlier, not only does medicine in general have a specialized language, but all specialties have their own jargon. Mental health is no different. I believe most clinicians genuinely try to speak English when interacting with patients, but, honestly, we forget sometimes. Further, we are so used to using certain terms and phrases that we forget that they are gobble-dygook to others. At least I have been guilty of that. Finally, specialized language developed because "regular" English doesn't have words to meet a particular need. Jargon does permit more precise communication—as long as everyone communicating has the same level of comprehension. For these reasons, I encourage you to learn at least some of the language of mood disorders. I have explained terms throughout this book and included a glossary at the end of the book to help you master the language. Words and terms included in the glossary are boldfaced throughout this book.

Managing time

Time management is important to an effective exchange of information. Always be sure you know how long your appointment is expected to last. This can be more complicated than it seems because the block of time clinicians schedule for any given patient often does not directly correspond to the amount of face-to-face time spent with that person. Appointments are usually scheduled for an hour, a half-hour, or even fifteen or twenty minutes. However, in many cases that block of time has to include everything related to your visit, not just the time spent with you. Other tasks that take away from face-to-face time are reviewing your record before meeting with you and updating it afterward. There may be laboratory studies or other tests to review before the visit. So, most appointments last about ten minutes less than the scheduled time. Is this a good system? Like everything in life it has pros and cons. Whether we like it or not, it is often the way appointments work. It is very appropriate for you to ask how much time you will have with your provider so that you can plan accordingly. Either ask the provider directly or ask the person you schedule with (if that's not directly with the clinician). A good time to ask is when you schedule your first appointment and when you schedule follow-up visits. Once you know how much time you have, you can plan to use the time to your best advantage.

This book provides management tools to help you. Please consider using the checklists and specific guidance for various kinds of appointments that I provide in the following chapters.

Avoiding intimidation

I want to discuss the issue of avoiding the feeling of intimidation. Some people tend to feel intimidated when they interact with medical or mental health professionals. This seems to be a somewhat natural human reaction that occurs when we are in situations in which we perceive that others know more about something than we do. Most of us don't like to look dumb, and we have an irrational fear that our lack of knowledge will make us look unintelligent. It can happen to anyone. The problem is that if we feel inferior, then we may be uncomfortable when we need to be assertive. For example, your doctor may say, "Well, that's all of our time for today," but you still have a crucial question to ask. It is very important for your recovery to be able to say, "Okay, but I really need to ask one more question."

I think the best cure for intimidation is to remind ourselves *before* the visit that we might have a tendency to feel that way. If we are ready for this possibility, we can usually dismiss those thoughts if they come up. Also, by reading this book, you will have an extensive amount of information going into your appointments. That knowledge should help you feel more comfortable.

Finally, please avoid putting your providers on a pedestal. We are all just imperfect people like everyone else. Perhaps we have spent a lot of our lives in school to get to where we are, but fundamentally we are still just folks like you. It is certainly appropriate to be respectful, but that is different from feeling inferior.

What to do if things aren't working out with your provider

The final section of this chapter discusses what to do if things aren't working out well with your professional team members. This can be an awkward situation, and it is important to think through how to deal with it. There can be a variety of reasons that a relationship with a provider doesn't work out. Sometimes it is related to personalities; often it is at least partly related to communication.

My recommendation is to start by being clear about what isn't working in the relationship. It is often helpful to write your ideas down. Writing often helps us clarify our thinking. A related step is to write down exactly how you would like things to be different. I also encourage you to honestly ask yourself whether you are contributing in any way to the problem. If you decide that you are, don't beat yourself up. We all do things that interfere with professional and personal relationships. Usually we don't recognize what we are doing. If we recognize that we are contributing to the problem, then we have the option of trying to change. Now that you have completed the assessment, it is time to decide what to do. If you think the relationship is salvageable and you want to save it, then make a plan to do that. If not, then be okay with that and start the search for a new provider.

If you want to try to fix the relationship with your provider, I recommend honest communication using "I" statements—for example, "I feel frustrated at the end of our sessions because it doesn't seem like there is enough time to get my questions answered." Further, I recommend following up with very specific requests, such as "Can we set aside five minutes at the end of each session for questions?" You may be pleasantly surprised at how well your provider responds to your requests. Most of us want to be helpful; after all, that's why we have chosen our particular profession. Feedback helps us provide better care by pointing out things we may not have realized. So, I encourage you to consider giving your provider honest feedback if you are unhappy with the relationship.

What if your feedback doesn't result in any improvement in the relationship? Then it may be time to change providers. Also, in some cases, there just may not be a good fit and making a change is your best course of action. If you feel that you need to change providers, please do so.

7

The Diagnostic Evaluation

THE DIAGNOSTIC EVALUATION IS THE PROCESS during which a clinician, or occasionally more than one provider, meets with you to determine your most likely diagnosis or diagnoses. The goal of this chapter is to prepare you for that assessment. Or, if you have already been evaluated, the information provided here can help you understand the process.

What to expect

Usually the diagnostic evaluation occurs during your first appointment with a mental health clinician. It could also occur at a subsequent visit if you are very distraught at the time of the first visit and it is more appropriate to spend that time helping you resolve immediate concerns. Sometimes initial psychotherapy appointments do not involve a diagnostic evaluation but instead focus on the initiation of therapy. If the assessment is completed by your primary care or specialty medical provider, the evaluation may well occur during a follow-up visit for other medical conditions. Finally, in some mental health clinics, the person who conducts the initial assessment may not be the person who ultimately provides either psychotherapy or psycho-pharmacology treatment for you. Some clinics have individuals who specialize in assessment. Another possibility is that clinicians take turns doing assessments and then refer their patients to the most appropriate providers for ongoing treatment.

The amount of time devoted to the assessment varies considerably. Mental health providers often schedule an hour for assessment sessions. However, as discussed in Chapter 6, this probably means about 45–50 minutes of face-to-face time. Occasionally, evaluations can take longer than an hour. A diagnostic appraisal may take considerably less than an hour, too, especially in primary or medical specialty care settings. The determining factor SHOULD be the complexity of your specific situation. For example, the assessment of an individual with a first episode of major **depression** who has not had prior treatment and has no coexisting conditions is not likely to be very time consuming. In contrast, someone who has had **bipolar disorder** for many years and has received treatment with a number of medications requires a much more detailed and longer evaluation. You may have noticed that I said the complexity of your situation *should* determine the length of your evaluation. Unfortunately, that does not always happen. The information in this book should help you deal with that situation if it occurs. Finally, a reassessment is sometimes indicated for those with more complicated clinical situations who are not getting better. This is especially true if a complete and thorough assessment has not been made recently.

I end this section with what may be a burning question: Will I be lying on a couch? The answer is no. Because of media stereotyping, one could get the impression that lying on a couch in a mental health provider's office is the norm. In fact, it is rare. Some psychotherapy approaches might involve lying on a couch, but today most people just sit in a regular chair during their evaluation and subsequent sessions.

Components of a diagnostic assessment

The aim of this section is to explain what kinds of information are needed for a psychiatric evaluation and how the data is used. You will be best able to collaborate with your provider if you understand why she or he is asking

---

Table 7.1 Categories of information collected during a diagnostic evaluation

---

◆ Current psychiatric history (also called "history of present illness")

◆ Past psychiatric history

◆ Psychiatric disorder and substance use screening

◆ Medical and surgical history

◆ Current medications

◆ Medication allergies

◆ Family history

◆ Social history

◆ Mental status examination

◆ Physical examination (not always required)

◆ Laboratory or diagnostic procedure results (not always required)

◆ Psychological testing (not always required)

◆ Diagnostic and symptom severity testing (not always required)

---

certain questions and if you know about them in advance so that you can prepare. I will discuss all the components of an extensive evaluation in this section. However, a less detailed assessment may be appropriate in some situations. Table 7.1 lists the types of information collected during a typical diagnostic evaluation.

Table 7.1 also indicates the organizational structure most mental health professionals use during an assessment and to record the results of an evaluation. The next section will provide more details about each category.

Current psychiatric history

What it is: The "history" of your current **mood episode** (or other psychiatric disorder)—also known as "history of present illness" or just "HPI." If you currently have more than one disorder (e.g., **major depressive disorder**

and **generalized anxiety disorder**), then a separate history is required for each condition. Elements include:

- When the episode began

- Duration of the episode (weeks, months, years)

- Specific symptoms

- Precipitating factors (if any)

- History of treatments (if any) for this episode and response

What it's used for: Diagnosing a mood episode that you are currently experiencing.

Past psychiatric history

What it is: The history of previous mood episodes (if any) or other psychiatric conditions. If you currently have more than one disorder, then a separate history is required for each condition. Elements are the same as for the current history.

What it's used for: Diagnosing a current mood episode. For example, if the current episode is depression but there is a past history of **mania,** then the diagnosis would be bipolar disorder. If there have been no prior mood episodes, or only episodes of depression, then the diagnosis would be major depression. This distinction is very important because the treatments for the two disorders are different. Past psychiatric history can also be important in another way: For example, if an individual previously suffered from generalized anxiety disorder but is now experiencing depressive symptoms, then the information about the earlier anxiety disorder is important. Knowing about the prior anxiety disorder would alert the clinician to screen carefully for current anxiety symptoms. It would also indicate the need to monitor for the future development of a **relapse** of anxiety. Finally, information about any treatments for prior episodes and response is key to deciding what the best approach may be for treating the current episode.

Psychiatric disorder and substance use screening

What it is: Additional information on the past psychiatric history. Often a few screening questions are asked about all of the major categories of psychiatric disorders and substance abuse (besides those already covered in the current and past psychiatric history). If any of the screening questions indicate the presence of symptoms, then additional information is required to determine whether one or more additional diagnoses should be given.

What it's used for: Determining whether you have another psychiatric or substance abuse disorder in addition to a **mood disorder**. Coexisting psychiatric conditions (sometimes called **comorbid** disorders) are common (see Chapter 4). In other words, many people have more than one psychiatric illness. The occurrence of more than one disorder has significant implications for treatment.

Medical and surgical history

What it is: A description of any nonpsychiatric medical or surgical conditions you have had during your lifetime.

What it's used for: Suggesting alternative causes of symptoms. For example, hypothyroidism can cause some symptoms similar to those of depression. The history may also help define the most appropriate treatment. For example, a seizure disorder may limit antidepressant choices.

Current medications

What it is: Information about any prescription and nonprescription medications you are currently taking as well as any supplements.

What it's used for: Suggesting alternative causes of symptoms. For example, many medications may cause fatigue or sleepiness, both of which can be symptoms of depression. Some medications cannot be taken with others. So, any medications you are taking for nonpsychiatric disorders must be considered when deciding on a psychiatric medication for a mood disorder.

Medication allergies

What it is: Information about any allergic reactions you may have had to any medication.

What it's used for: Making decisions about treatment, to be sure that you are not prescribed a medication that you are allergic to.

Family history

What it is: Information about any of your relatives who have psychiatric disorders.

What it's used for: Making a diagnosis. Psychiatric disorders are, to some degree, inherited (this is discussed in Chapter 4). If you have relatives with a specific disorder, then you may be more likely to experience the same condition and you may also be at risk for more serious illness.

Social history

What it is: Information about you as a person and your current life situation. Components include:

+ Relationship status—for example, married, divorced, and so on

+ Family relationships

+ Current work situation

+ Education

+ Recreation activities that you enjoy

+ Any current stressors

What it's used for: Making decisions about diagnosis and treatment. Some conditions, such as **adjustment disorders,** are specifically related to life stressors. In regard to treatment, an episode of depression worsened by marital conflict may warrant marital therapy as one component of treatment. Or, if you like to take walks, then daily walking might be included in the treatment plan.

Mental status examination

What it is: An evaluation of your current psychiatric symptoms and thought processes. Elements typically included, along with explanations and examples, are:

+ Appearance and hygiene: Some disorders can be associated with lack of attention to hygiene and appearance.

- Behavior: Unusual behaviors can be a feature of some psychiatric conditions, such as **schizophrenia**.

- Speech: Rapid speech is associated with mania, and slowed speech sometimes occurs during depression.

- **Mood**: The state of one's mood over an extended period, usually weeks to months, is important information.

- **Affect**: Current mood state is usually described as euthymic (normal), elevated, or dysphoric (depressed). Other descriptors, such as anxious or worried, may also be used. The term *flattened affect* is used when an individual displays little or no emotion.

- Form of thought: An evaluation is made of whether thought processes are logical and directed toward a goal. This is measured by one's ability to carry on a normal conversation.

- Content of thought: Is there evidence of unusual thinking, such as **hallucinations** or **delusions**? Also concerning thoughts, such as suicidal ideation, are noted.

- Cognition: Alertness, memory, judgment, and insight are evaluated.

What it's used for: Making a diagnosis. Your mental status may also influence decisions about treatment. For example, someone with suicidal thoughts might require hospitalization.

Physical examination

What it is: An examination of your body. This may not be required unless there is evidence that a nonpsychiatric medical condition may be the cause of your symptoms. Your primary care physician, rather than your mental health specialist, may conduct the physical examination, particularly if a more extensive examination is indicated. However, in some cases, a limited examination focusing on a particular area, such as checking blood pressure or weight, may be all that is required.

What it's used for: Ruling out medical conditions that might be contributing to your symptoms. Also, an examination may be used to monitor medication side effects, such as elevated blood pressure or weight gain. For some medications it is important to obtain baseline values in order to determine whether changes occur after starting medication (e.g., weight gain).

Laboratory or diagnostic procedure results

What it is: Such tests as blood work and brain scans. These tests may not be indicated unless there is evidence of a medical or neurological disorder that you should be monitored for possible medication side effects.

What it's used for: Ruling out medical conditions that might be contributing to your symptoms and evaluating for possible medication side effects. If you are monitored for medication side effects—for example, possible elevated level of blood glucose (sugar)—then a baseline value may be obtained at or near the time the medication is started.

Psychological testing

What it is: Tests administered by a licensed psychologist. A large number of psychological tests exist, including those that assess intelligence and achievement, attitude, personality, and cognitive function. These tests may not be indicated unless there is diagnostic uncertainty or concern about cognitive function.

What it's used for: Providing additional information about diagnosis, personality, or cognitive function.

Diagnostic and symptom severity testing

What it is: Short tests given to confirm either the diagnosis or the current severity of symptoms. These tests are much less formal than psychological testing and may be given by most providers. In some cases they may be paper-and-pencil tests that you complete, or the tests may be completed by the provider in response to your answers to questions. This testing may not be indicated unless there is uncertainty about a diagnosis. However, some systematic monitoring of symptom severity is strongly recommended to assess response to treatment. I recommend using mood charts as described in Chapter 13.

What it's used for: Providing additional information about diagnosis and symptom severity and monitoring response to treatment.

Getting ready for the appointment

Now that you know all about diagnostic evaluations, we are ready to talk about getting prepared. You have probably figured out by now that a lot of this book is about being prepared. There isn't any situation for which being ready is more critical than your diagnostic assessment. Your provider must have accurate information to make the best recommendations for treatment. In this section, I will guide you through the process of gathering and organizing all the relevant data.

I have designed Form 7.1 to help you collect all the pertinent information. The form is reproduced here and is also available as a PDF file that can be freely downloaded from our website (http://www.bullpub.com/downloads). This exercise will be most useful for you if you take the completed form with you to any psychiatric diagnostic evaluation. Thus, I suggest you download a copy from the website. Further, I strongly recommend that you keep a copy in a safe place for your records. It is useful to update the form any time you undergo a new treatment or any other information changes.

Completing Form 7.1 will take more of your time if you have a **chronic** (long lasting) mood disorder and have had previous treatment. However, this is also the situation for which completing this exercise can be most helpful. For example, it is critical to know what treatments you have tried before and whether or not they worked or caused side effects. That said, in some cases you may not have all the information. Many of us have taken medications in the past and don't remember what they were several years later. So, just do the best you can. Completing the form will help you organize the information for the evaluation even if you don't know the answer to some of the questions. Please consider taking the time to complete Form 7.1 before your evaluation.

Preparing your evaluation form

Let's start with some good news. If you have completed the self-assessment exercises in Chapter 3, you have already done much of the work for this section. If not, please work through Chapter 3 first and then come back here because we are going to use the information from the earlier exercises in this section. Form 7.1 may seem long, but you will be able to skip any portions that are not relevant.

As described above, other typical components of the evaluation are your social history and a mental status exam. There isn't any need to prepare for either of these, so you won't find either on Form 7.1. However, your last project is to prepare a list of questions to take to the evaluation.

In order to be an effective treatment team captain (see Chapter 6 for more about this), you need information. Reading this book is a great start; however, you also need the expert opinion of the professionals on your team. For most of us, it is helpful to have a list of questions prepared before we go to any kind of appointment where information will be provided. Please use the last section of Form 7.1 to jot down questions as you think of them. I have suggested some questions that are relevant for most people.

Form 7.1 Diagnostic evaluation form

Your current psychiatric history (mood disorder)

We will start with your current psychiatric history—in other words, the most likely mood disorder diagnosis from Chapter 3.

Check the box corresponding to your most likely mood disorder diagnosis from Chapter 3, Interpreting your results.

- ☐ Major depressive disorder
- ☐ Dysthymic disorder
- ☐ Depressive disorder not otherwise specified
- ☐ Adjustment disorder with depressed mood
- ☐ Bipolar type I disorder
- ☐ Bipolar type II disorder
- ☐ Cyclothymic disorder
- ☐ Bipolar disorder not otherwise specified
- ☐ Mood disorder due to a medical condition

Check the box corresponding to your current mood from Chapter 3, Mood episodes.

- ☐ Full remission (euthymic)
- ☐ Depressed
- ☐ Hypomanic
- ☐ Manic
- ☐ Mixed depression and mania

Check the boxes corresponding to the symptoms you are currently experiencing from Chapter 3, Mood episodes. Mark all that apply. If you are currently in full remission, then go on to next question.

- ☐ Depressed mood
- ☐ Anhedonia (lose of interest in/difficulty enjoying normally pleasurable activities)
- ☐ Appetite/weight change
  - o Increased
  - o Decreased
- ☐ Sleep change
  - o Increased
  - o Decreased
- ☐ Psychomotor change
  - o Increased
  - o Decreased
- ☐ Fatigue
- ☐ Thoughts/feelings of worthlessness and/or guilt
- ☐ Difficult with thinking and/or concentrating and problems with indecisiveness
- ☐ Thoughts of death or suicide
- ☐ Low self-esteem
- ☐ Hopelessness

☐ Mood elevation

☐ Excessively happy/euphoric

☐ Irritable/agitated

☐ Grandiosity/elevated self-esteem

☐ Decreased need for sleep

☐ Increased talkativeness

☐ Racing thoughts

☐ Distractibility

☐ Increased activity

☐ Increased involvement in pleasurable activity with potential for negative consequences

☐ Psychotic symptoms

    o Hallucinations

    o Delusions

Check the box corresponding to the severity of your current mood symptoms. Use an average over the last two weeks if your symptoms are waxing and waning.

☐ In full remission (you are not experiencing any symptoms)

☐ Mild (you are aware of your symptoms but they are mild and there is minimal impairment of your social and/or occupational functioning)

☐ Moderate (your symptoms are between mild and severe)

☐ Severe (your symptoms are very distressing and/or there is significant impairment of your social and/or occupational functioning)

Check the box corresponding to any statements that apply to you in regard to stress and your current mood episode.

☐ Current mood episode came on out of the blue (not related to any apparent stress).

☐ Current mood episode came on during a period of greater than normal stress.

    o List stressor(s) _____

☐ Current stress level is low or very low (go on to next section on treatment).

☐ Current stress level is moderate or higher.

    o List if different from above _____

Check the boxes corresponding to any treatment you have received for your current mood episode (treatment for previous episodes will be listed below).

☐ No treatment (go on to the next section)

☐ Psychotherapy (complete the psychotherapy table)

☐ Pharmacotherapy (complete the pharmacotherapy table)

☐ Hospitalization

☐ Other (please list):

☐ Self-help approaches (please list):

Psychotherapy you have received for this mood episode

Type of therapy	Frequency of sessions	Duration of treatment	Response (pick one)	Currently receiving this therapy?
			No response Partial response Full remission	
			No response Partial response Full remission	
			No response Partial response Full remission	

Pharmacotherapy you have received for this mood episode

Medication name	Maximum total daily dose in milligrams	Duration of treatment at maximum dose	Response (pick one)	Any side effects?	Currently taking?	Regularity of taking medication (pick one describing the doses missed)
			No response Partial response Full remission		Yes No	Few/none Occasional Many
			No response Partial response Full remission		Yes No	Few/none Occasional Many
			No response Partial response Full remission		Yes No	Few/none Occasional Many
			No response Partial response Full remission		Yes No	Few/none Occasional Many
			No response Partial response Full remission		Yes No	Few/none Occasional Many

Your current psychiatric history (other disorders)

In this section, you will provide information about possible coexisting conditions.

Check the box corresponding to all disorders that the exercises in Chapter 3 suggested you might be experiencing or have experienced in the past.

☐ None (skip to next section)

☐ Substance use disorder

☐ Psychotic disorder

☐ Obsessive-compulsive disorder

☐ Generalized anxiety disorder

☐ Panic disorder

☐ Specific phobia

☐ Social phobia

☐ PTSD

☐ ADHD

☐ Eating disorder

Complete the table for any conditions that you checked above

Disorder	How long have you suffered from this condition?	Currently experiencing symptoms?	Current symptoms (if any)	Treatments and responses (if any)

Your past mood episodes

In this section, you will provide information about all of your previous mood episodes.

Check the box corresponding to any mood episodes that you have previously experienced (from Chapter 3).

- ☐ No prior mood episodes (skip to next section)
- ☐ Major depressive episode
  - ○ Approximate lifetime number of episodes _____
  - ○ Approximate average duration of episodes _____
- ☐ Dysthymic episode
  - ○ Approximate lifetime number of episodes _____
  - ○ Approximate average duration of episodes _____
- ☐ Other depressive episode
  - ○ Approximate lifetime number of episodes _____
  - ○ Approximate average duration of episodes _____
- ☐ Manic episode
  - ○ Approximate lifetime number of episodes _____
  - ○ Approximate average duration of episodes _____
- ☐ Hypomanic episode
  - ○ Approximate lifetime number of episodes _____
  - ○ Approximate average duration of episodes _____
- ☐ Mixed episode
  - ○ Approximate lifetime number of episodes _____
  - ○ Approximate average duration of episodes _____
- ☐ Other mood elevation episode
  - ○ Approximate lifetime number of episodes _____
  - ○ Approximate average duration of episodes _____

☐ Mood episode due to a medical condition

    o Approximate lifetime number of episodes _____

    o Approximate average duration of episodes _____

Check the boxes corresponding to any treatment you have received for your previous mood episode (treatment for previous episodes will be listed below).

☐ No treatment (go on to the next section)

☐ Psychotherapy (complete the psychotherapy table)

☐ Pharmacotherapy (complete the pharmacotherapy table)

☐ Hospitalization

☐ Other (please list): _____

_____

☐ Self-help approaches (please list): _____

_____

Psychotherapy for previous mood episodes

Type of mood episode	Type of therapy	Frequency of sessions	Duration of treatment	Response (pick one)
				No response Partial response Full remission
				No response Partial response Full remission
				No response Partial response Full remission

Pharmacotherapy you have received for previous mood episodes

Type of mood episode	Medication name	Maximum total daily dose in milligrams	Duration of treatment at maximum dose	Response (pick one)	Currently taking?	Any side effects?
				No response Partial response Full remission		
				No response Partial response Full remission		
				No response Partial response Full remission		
				No response Partial response Full remission		
				No response Partial response Full remission		

Your medical and surgical history

In this section, you will have the opportunity to organize information about any medical or surgical conditions that you may have experienced as well as any nonpsychiatric medications you may be taking.

Current and previous medical illnesses

_____

_____

_____

_____

_____

Surgeries

_____

_____

_____

_____

Serious injuries

_____

_____

_____

_____

Current prescribed medications

_____

_____

_____

_____

Over-the-counter medications or supplements that you take on a regular basis

_____

_____

_____

_____

Your family history

Please use this section to provide information about any psychiatric or medical disorders that run in your biological family. Two categories of relatives are listed. First-degree relatives (parent/child or sibling) are the most important. "Other relatives" include anyone else who is your blood relative. Information about closer relatives is more useful than about those who are more distant kin. In many cases, you may not be sure whether a relative has had a specific disorder. Sometimes family members exhibit symptoms but we don't know whether they have ever been formally diagnosed or meet the full criteria for a condition. So, just provide the best information you can.

Check the boxes corresponding to any psychiatric disorders experienced by your biological relatives.

☐ Major depressive disorder
  o Parent/child or sibling with condition. Number with condition: _____
  o Other relative with condition. Number with condition _____

☐ Dysthymic disorder

  o Parent/child or sibling with condition. Number with condition _____

  o Other relative with condition. Number with condition _____

☐ Depressive disorder of unknown type

  o Parent/child or sibling with condition. Number with condition _____

  o Other relative with condition. Number with condition _____

☐ Bipolar type I disorder

  o Parent/child or sibling with condition. Number with condition _____

  o Other relative with condition. Number with condition _____

☐ Bipolar type II disorder

  o Parent/child or sibling with condition. Number with condition _____

  o Other relative with condition. Number with condition _____

☐ Cyclothymic disorder

  o Parent/child or sibling with condition. Number with condition _____

  o ther relative with condition. Number with condition _____

☐ Bipolar disorder of unknown type

  o Parent/child or sibling with condition. Number with condition _____

  o Other relative with condition. Number with condition _____

☐ Substance use disorder

  o Parent/child or sibling with condition. Number with condition _____

  o Other relative with condition. Number with condition _____

☐ Schizophrenia or other **psychotic disorder**

  o Parent/child or sibling with condition. Number with condition _____

  o Other relative with condition. Number with condition _____

□ Obsessive-compulsive disorder

   o Parent/child or sibling with condition. Number with condition _____

   o Other relative with condition. Number with condition _____

□ Generalized anxiety disorder

   o Parent/child or sibling with condition. Number with condition _____

   o Other relative with condition. Number with condition _____

□ Panic disorder

   o Parent/child or sibling with condition. Number with condition _____

   o Other relative with condition. Number with condition _____

□ Specific phobia

   o Parent/child or sibling with condition. Number with condition _____

   o Other relative with condition. Number with condition _____

□ Social phobia

   o Parent/child or sibling with condition. Number with condition _____

   o Other relative with condition. Number with condition _____

□ PTSD

   o Parent/child or sibling with condition. Number with condition _____

   o Other relative with condition. Number with condition _____

□ ADHD

   o Parent/child or sibling with condition. Number with condition _____

   o Other relative with condition. Number with condition _____

□ Eating disorder

   o Parent/child or sibling with condition. Number with condition _____

   o Other relative with condition. Number with condition _____

Questions to ask at the psychiatric evaluation

What is my primary psychiatric diagnosis?

What (if any) secondary diagnoses do I have?

What treatment(s) are you recommending?

Why are you recommending these specific treatment options?

Are there any alternative treatment strategies that I could consider?

What should I expect if I choose not to start treatment?

What are the possible risks and side effects associated with the recommended treatment?

What should I do if I start to experience side effects?

How soon should I expect to notice some improvement?

How frequently should I schedule follow-up appointments during treatment?

What should I do if I have a serious problem after hours or on the weekend?

How long will I likely have to continue treatment?

What is the long-term prognosis for my condition?

8

Medication and
Other Biological Treatments

THIS CHAPTER DESCRIBES MANY of the biological treatments used for
mood disorders. The aim of the chapter is to provide information about
the potential benefits as well as the risks associated with various options.
General recommendations for using these approaches are given in Chapter
11 for starting treatment, Chapter 13 for acute treatment, and Chapter 14
for maintenance treatment. Chapter 12 provides information about using
biological treatments when pregnant or breast-feeding.

As I've said before, this book cannot take the place of professional
advice. That is especially true of this chapter. The information I have provided can be used only to increase your knowledge so that you can work
more effectively with your treatment team and make well-informed decisions about your treatment. PLEASE DO NOT USE THIS CHAPTER
TO REPLACE THE ADVICE AND RECOMMENDATIONS OF
MEDICAL AND MENTAL HEALTH PROFESSIONALS. INFOR-
MATION IN THIS CHAPTER IS GENERAL AND MAY NOT AP-
PLY TO YOUR SPECIFIC SITUATION.

Finally, please do not be overly alarmed by the information about side effects. IN MANY CASES THE BENEFITS OF BIOLOGICAL TREATMENT FAR OUTWEIGH THE RISK OF SIDE EFFECTS.

General principles of biological interventions

In order for you to be able to make an informed decision about biological treatment options, it is important to first understand how researchers determine whether a given treatment is effective.

Effectiveness studies

In this section I will use studies of psychiatric medications to explain the process of studying treatment effectiveness. But, what I say also applies to other kinds of medications and to any other biological treatment for that matter. It also applies to nonbiological treatments, such as psychotherapy, but some of the specific research issues are different.

How are treatments developed and shown to be effective (or not)? The term *drug discovery* is used to describe the process by which drugs are discovered or designed. Historically, many drugs were discovered either by identifying the active ingredient from traditional remedies or by chance. More recently, scientists have attempted to develop medications using knowledge of the biological abnormality underlying disease or infection. Thus, medications are developed that are directly aimed at correcting the pathological process leading to the expression of symptoms. The pathological process is typically called a "target." For mood disorders, we are limited by the fact that we don't completely understand the biological causes (see Chapter 4). Nonetheless, we know these disorders involve problems with **neurotransmitters**, so an appropriate target might be a lack of neurotransmitter in **synapses** in the brain (again, see Chapter 4 for more on this). So, researchers might try to develop a medication that increases the level of a certain neurotransmitter—say, **serotonin**.

Once a target (e.g., lack of serotonin) has been identified, drug discovery involves a complicated process of identifying possible drugs followed by synthesis, characterization, and screening as well as studies of possible therapeutic efficacy. Candidate drugs that make it through this process can proceed to the clinical trials stage. In clinical trials, drugs are tested in humans for safety and effectiveness.

The clinical trial is the step of the drug discovery process that is most relevant for interpreting evidence of the effectiveness of medications used to treat mood disorders. Drugs progress through different levels of studies, known as "phases" in studies of both safety and effectiveness. For example, a potential drug going through a Phase III study would be at the stage of a large randomized study completed at several sites and involving many patients. The details of what each phase involves are not important; however, the following general points about drug studies may be useful for you to understand. In clinical trials, a drug's effectiveness is compared to the effectiveness of either a placebo or another medication that is known to be effective. A placebo is simulated intervention (e.g., an inert pill) that can produce an improvement, called the "placebo effect." This effect is not well understood. However, when we believe that a treatment will be helpful, this belief may produce either a subjective perception of improvement or an actual improvement. The goal of the drug comparison is to demonstrate whether the medication works better than a placebo. A difficulty with interpreting studies of antidepressant effectiveness is that the placebo response rate is high in **depression**.[239, 240] This fact has led to some controversy about the effectiveness of antidepressants (see the section on effectiveness below).

Now that you know something about how the effectiveness of biological treatment is determined, I want to discuss two very important points: (1) It is not possible to know everything about any given treatment, and (2) all potential treatments have risks. These two statements apply to all treatments, including psychotherapy strategies (Chapter 9) and complementary approaches (Chapter 10). These two ideas are particularly relevant to biological treatments that often have higher potential risks for adverse effects than psychotherapy and some complementary approaches. Let's talk about both of these issues.

We can't know everything about any given treatment

What do I mean by this? I mean that we will never know all of the potential benefits or risks of any biological intervention. Why? Part of the reason is the complexity of the human brain (see Chapter 4) and the human body in general. Another issue is the limitations of research that can be done. For reasons of both cost and feasibility, we cannot study every possibility. What does this mean for you and your prescriber? It means there will always be some uncertainty about any treatment approach you consider trying. This is not the ideal situation, but it is the reality. Please keep this in mind when you make treatment decisions. Let's discuss an example.

Studies of the effectiveness of medications generally evaluate either a specific dose or a dosage range. This makes sense. At the end of the study, we should know whether a specific dose or dosage range is effective. What we don't know is whether the dose is optimal for everyone. Because of individual variations in brain biology, some of us might need a higher (or lower) dose than that studied. Why aren't all the dosage possibilities studied? One reason is cost. Drug effectiveness studies are very expensive. Again, it is just not cost effective to study every possibility. So, that lack of information can sometimes result in a dilemma for prescribers and consumers. Suppose Joe is being treated with an antidepressant for an episode of depression. Let's further suppose he is taking the highest dose that is approved by the Food and Drug Administration (FDA) based on the studies that have been done. Finally, let's say Joe has improved but is not completely better after taking the medication for the recommended length of a clinical trial. The dilemma is whether to try a higher dose that isn't FDA approved or change to a different medication. The risk of trying a higher dose is that it hasn't been studied in terms of either benefits or side effects. The risk of changing medications is that a different medication might not be effective at all. Which option has the lower risk? That is something Joe and his prescriber would have to decide together. My point is that often these dilemmas result in what are known as off-label uses of medications. "Off label" means either using a nonapproved dose for an FDA-approved condition or using a medication for a nonapproved condition. In this case, Joe and his prescriber might decide that the best option is to try a higher dose. These decisions are neither right nor wrong. It is just a matter of choosing what seems like the best option when there isn't enough information available.

Another important consideration is that we often have variable levels of evidence in regard to the effectiveness of different interventions. Some treatments have been studied extensively with approaches that are very rigorous from a scientific standpoint. Other times the evidence isn't so strong, perhaps because of conflicting results from studies or because only less rigorous studies have been done.

Finally, all research is imperfect. Even studies that are very rigorous and well done have limitations. Sometimes these can be very minor. In other cases, these limitations can give an inadequate representation of the facts.

All biological treatments have risks

This point may seem obvious, but it is worth discussing. In an ideal world, science would allow us to develop risk-free interventions. We can't do that now and we may never be able to. Again, the problem is the complexity of the brain and body. Scientists can design a mood disorder medication to target one specific brain system—say, a neurotransmitter—but there are always other unwanted effects. Not everyone may experience these, but the possibility is there. Thus, it's always a matter of weighing the potential risks versus benefits of any treatment option. There are no perfect solutions. Even psychotherapy and self-help approaches have possible risks.

I want to make one very important point before we move on: The fact that a medication has some potential to cause side effects should not prevent you from considering it as a treatment option. In many cases, side effects either do not occur at all or are mild and go away quickly. Of course, some medications can cause more serious adverse effects, but one must always weigh the potential benefits and risks. Frequently, the benefit of biological treatments far outweighs any potential risks.

Medications used to treat mood disorders

In this section, I will discuss the specific medications used for the treatment of mood disorders. This section is intended to provide an overview of each medication. General recommendations for their use are presented in Chapters 11, 13, and 14 for starting, acute, and maintenance treatment, respectively.

Antidepressants

Antidepressants are used to treat **unipolar** and sometimes bipolar depression. These medications are categorized based on either their mechanism of action or their chemical structure. I will discuss each class separately.

Selective serotonin reuptake inhibitors (SSRIs)

The **selective serotonin reuptake inhibitors** have been extensively used because of their effectiveness and relatively benign side effect profile. The currently available SSRIs are fluoxetine, sertraline, paroxetine, fluvoxamine, citalopram, and escitalopram (see Table 8.1 on page 178 for trade names and dosing). SSRIs, as the name suggests, inhibit the reuptake of serotonin as their primary mechanism of action. The hypothesized role of the neurotransmitter serotonin in mood disorders is discussed in Chapter 4. By inhibiting the reuptake of serotonin, these agents cause more of the neurotransmitter to be available at the synapse. These medications are called "selective" because relative to other antidepressants, such as **tricyclic antidepressants** (TCAs) and **serotonin-norepinephrine reuptake inhibitors** (SNRIs), they primarily inhibit the uptake of only one neurotransmitter rather than several. However, reuptake inhibition may not completely explain how SSRIs and other antidepressants work. For more information on mechanisms of antidepressant action, see Chapter 4.

Some common "nuisance" side effects of SSRIs are stomach upset, diarrhea, restlessness, insomnia, sexual problems, headache, and weight gain (see Table 8.2 on page 182 for a summary). I use the word *nuisance* because many of these side effects may be very annoying but not dangerous. In contrast, some possible side effects have the potential to be much more harmful. For SSRIs, these side effects include **serotonin syndrome**, suicidal thinking, increased risk of falling, interactions with other medications, and discontinuation syndrome. These side effects will be defined and discussed in more detail in the later section on antidepressant side effects.

Selective serotonin reuptake inhibitors and 5-HT1A receptor partial agonists

Only one medication, vilazodone, is available in this class. Like the SSRIs, this medication inhibits the reuptake of serotonin as a primary mechanism of action. Additionally, it enhances the effectiveness of a specific kind of serotonin receptor (see Chapter 4 for more about receptors). This particular receptor is called the 5-HT1A receptor. There is some evidence that dysfunction of this receptor may contribute to the cause of depression in some cases. Therefore, improving the function of the receptor may add to this medication's effectiveness. Possible side effects are similar to those of SSRIs, with diarrhea and nausea being the most common.

Serotonin-norepinephrine reuptake inhibitors (SNRIs)

Like SSRIs, **serotonin-norepinephrine reuptake inhibitors** are a class of antidepressants with a name based on their presumptive mechanism of action. Thus, SNRIs inhibit the reuptake of two neurotransmitters, serotonin and **norepinephrine**, at the synapse. Currently available SNRIs are venlafaxine, desvenlafaxine, and duloxetine (see Table 8.1 for trade names and dosing). The common nuisance SNRI side effects are constipation, restlessness, rapid heartbeat, upset stomach, dry mouth, headache, and sexual problems. More serious possible side effects are **discontinuation syndrome**, elevated blood pressure, and serotonin syndrome. The later section on antidepressant side effects will provide more information on the adverse effects of SNRIs.

Dopamine-norepinephrine reuptake inhibitors

Bupropion is the only antidepressant currently available that inhibits the reuptake of **dopamine** and norepinephrine. However, its inhibition of dopamine reuptake is weak, and its mechanism of action is poorly understood.[241] Nuisance side effects include dry mouth, tremor, agitation, stomach upset, insomnia, and headache. More serious side effects include psychotic symptoms, elevated blood pressure, and seizures. Unlike most other antidepressants, bupropion does not cause sexual side effects or weight gain because it does not directly modulate serotonin function.[241] Bupropion is also effective for smoking cessation.

Serotonin modulators and norepinephrine-serotonin modulators

Nefazodone and trazodone are classified as serotonin modulators rather than reuptake inhibitors. Mirtazapine is a norepinephrine-serotonin modulator. The word *modulation* means that these drugs influence neurotransmitter function by a means other than reuptake inhibition.

Side effects with nefazodone include sedation, dry mouth, nausea, constipation, dizziness upon standing, and visual alterations.[241] Most important, nefazodone has been associated with rare but potentially fatal liver failure. Thus, its use has been limited in recent years. Although the risk of liver failure is low, I generally do not recommend this medication except in very limited circumstances. The one possibility for which it might be considered is someone who has had a good response to nefazodone and failed multiple other treatments. In that situation, the benefits might outweigh the risks. That said, a decision to take nefazodone would require careful thought and a detailed discussion between consumer and prescriber.

Trazodone is an antidepressant. It is rarely used as a primary treatment for depression, but it is often used as a sedative to treat insomnia associated with mood disorders. This is because its most common side effect is sedation and it is nonaddictive, unlike some other medications used for insomnia. Trazodone has a number of other potential side effects, including dizziness upon standing, irregular heartbeat, and erectile dysfunction in men.[241] Finally, a rare but dangerous side effect for males is priapism (persistent unwanted erection). In some cases, priapism might require surgical correction. If you are male, please discuss the pros and cons of using this medication with your prescriber.

Mirtazapine is also sedating and therefore can be a good choice for individuals who have insomnia as a symptom of depression. Common side effects are dry mouth, sedation, increased serum cholesterol levels, and weight gain.[241]

Tricyclic and tetracyclic antidepressants (TCAs)

Unlike the categories of antidepressants discussed above, tricyclic and tetracyclic antidepressants are named based on their chemical structure. Tricyclic antidepressants contain three rings of atoms in their chemical structure, while tetracyclics contain four rings. Medications in this class are amitriptyline, doxepin, imipramine, maprotiline, nortriptyline, and trimipramine.

In regard to mechanism of action, the primary action of most TCAs is the reuptake inhibition of serotonin and norepinephrine. Thus, these medications are also SNRIs, but this class was originally named based on chemical structure and that convention has continued. Further, most TCAs also affect other neurotransmitters and influence serotonergic neurotransmission in other ways in addition to reuptake inhibition. The TCAs also typically inhibit the function of two other neurotransmitters, histamine and acetylcholine. Thus, these medications have what are known as antihistamine and anticholinergic effects, which contribute to their side effect profile.

Compared to newer antidepressants, TCAs tend to cause more side effects and are very dangerous if taken in overdose. These problems have limited their use in recent years. However, they are very effective and may be used as second-line treatments if other medications are not effective. Side effects include irregular heartbeat, rapid heartbeat, dizziness upon standing, falls (because of dizziness), dry mouth, visual problems, constipation, difficult urination, problems with memory and concentration, sexual problems, sedation, and weight gain. Seizures are possible with overdose. These medications can have adverse interactions with a number of other drugs, so be sure to tell your prescriber about any other medications you are taking.

Monoamine oxidase inhibitors (MAOIs)

The final category of antidepressants we will discuss are the **monoamine oxidase inhibitors (MAOIs).** These medications are named for their mechanism of action. As the name implies, this mechanism is the inhibition of the enzyme monoamine oxidase. This enzyme breaks down the neurotransmitters serotonin, norepinephrine, and dopamine, so the inhibition makes more of these substances available at the synapse (see Chapter 4).

Isocarboxazid, phenelzine, and tranylcypromine are the MAOIs currently available to be taken by mouth. Selegiline is available as a transdermal patch. The use of oral MAOIs is limited by the fact that many foods have to be avoided when these medications are taken. Ingesting foods or medicines with tyramine or other amines can result in what is known as a "hypertensive crisis." A hypertensive crisis is a very dangerous elevation of blood pressure that can possibly lead to stroke or death. Symptoms of a hypertensive crisis include severe headache, nausea, stiff neck, sweating, and confusion, and emergency treatment is required. Foods that need to be avoided are aged cheeses and meats, fermented products, yeast extracts, fava and broad beans, red wine, draft beers, and overripe or spoiled foods. The lowest therapeutic dose of selegiline may not require this dietary

Table 8.1   Antidepressant medications and doses[241]

Generic name (trade name)	Class	Usual starting dose (mg/day)	Usual dose range (mg/day)
Amitriptyline (generic)	TCA	25–50	100–300
Amoxapine (generic)	TCA	25–50	200–300
Bupropion, immediate release (Wellbutrin)	Dopamine-norepinephrine reuptake inhibitor	150	100–300
Bupropion, sustained release (Wellbutrin SR, Zyban Sustained Release)	Dopamine-norepinephrine reuptake inhibitor	150	300–400
Bupropion, extended release (Aplenzin Extended-Release)	Dopamine-norepinephrine reuptake inhibitor	150	300–450
Citalopram (Celexa)	SSRI	20	20–60
Desvenlafaxine (Prestig Extended-Release)	SNRI	50	50
Doxepin (Silenor, Sinequan, Zonalon)	TCA	25–50	100–300
Duloxetine (Cymbalta Delayed-Release)	SNRI	60	60–120
Escitalopram (Lexapro)	SSRI	10	10–20
Fluoxetine (Prozac, Sarafem)	SSRI	20	20–60

restriction,[37] but discuss this with your prescriber if you are advised to take this medication. In addition to foods, a number of medications must be avoided because they can lead to a hypertensive crisis if taken with MAOIs. These include other antidepressants and St. John's wort as well as over-the-counter decongestants and cold medications. If you are prescribed any MAOI, please be sure to discuss the risks in detail with your provider and request a list of foods and medications that you must avoid.

Table 8.1   Antidepressants medication and doses[241] (*continued*)

Generic name (trade name)	Class	Usual starting dose (mg/day)	Usual dose range (mg/day)
Imipramine (Tofranil)	TCA	25–50	100–300
Isocarboxazid (Marplan)	MAOI	10–20	30–60
Maprotiline (generic)	TCA	75	100–225
Mirtazapine (Remeron)	Norepinephrine-serotonin modulators	15	15?45
Nefazodone (generic)	Serotonin modulators	150	150–600
Nortriptyline (generic)	TCA	25	50–200
Paroxetine (Paxil, Pexeva)	SSRI	20	20–60
Paroxetine, extended release (Paxil CR)	SSRI	12.5	25–75
Phenelzine (Nardil)	MAOI	15	45–90
Selegiline transdermal patch (Emsam)	MAOI	6	6–12
Sertraline (Zoloft)	SSRI	50	50–200
Tranylcypromine (Parnate)	MAOI	10	30–60
Trazodone (Desyrel)	Serotonin modulators	150	150–600
Trimipramine (Surmontil)	TCA	25–50	75–300
Venlafaxine, immediate release (Effexor)	SNRI	37.5	75–375

In addition to hypertensive crisis, MAOIs can cause a number of other side effects, including dizziness upon standing, weight gain, headache, insomnia, sedation, and sexual problems. Thus, while these medications are very effective, they are generally used only after a person has failed to respond to other treatments.

The currently available antidepressants and their doses are listed in Table 8.1.

How well do antidepressants work?

In order to make an informed decision about whether to take an antidepressant, you need to know the likelihood that it will be beneficial. Then it is critical to weigh the probability of success against the possibility of side effects. In this section, I will discuss what we know about antidepressant effectiveness.

Some studies seem to suggest that antidepressants have similar effectiveness to a placebo for mild (but not severe) episodes of unipolar illness.[242–244] These results have led to some questioning of whether these medications are effective. However, as discussed above, the placebo response in depression is large.[239, 240] This fact limits our ability to completely understand the results presented here. Here is my take: There is very strong evidence that antidepressants work better than a placebo for severe depression. In contrast, for mild and possibly moderate depression, antidepressants may not be significantly better than a placebo for acute treatment of a single depressive episode.

Deciding whether to use these medications is much more complicated than the information above might suggest because depression often is a **chronic illness** (see Chapter 4 for more information about this). Further, episodes that are incompletely treated are likely to recur, and with each recurrence the likelihood of more episodes increases. Thus, it is very important to achieve full remission for even mild episodes. So, even though the evidence of antidepressant effectiveness for mild depression is not strong, I recommend considering their use if other strategies fail or if it is not possible to implement other approaches (such as psychotherapy) for whatever reason.

All antidepressants are thought to be equally effective overall.[37] A few studies have suggested slight benefits for some agents over others—for example, there is some evidence that SNRIs might be more effective than other agents.[245] However, the facts are not conclusive, and experts consider the effectiveness of the various antidepressants to be generally equal.[37] Thus, decisions about which medication to choose are typically made based on previous response to antidepressant treatment, side effects, or factors such as cost (some of these are summarized in Table 8.3 on page 186). In regard to previous antidepressant response, if a medication has worked well before, then it is likely to work well again and in most cases should be the first choice. By the same token, if a particular drug has not worked well before, then it usually does not make sense to try it again.

Perhaps the most important point about antidepressants is this: Even though these treatments are equally effective overall, for reasons we do not understand some will work better than others for a given person. Currently, there isn't a way to predict this (other than prior response), so there is always the possibility that the first medication tried will not be effective and that another will need to be used. Studies suggest that the response rate to any antidepressant medication tried is in the 50%–75% range.[37] So, unfortunately some people will have to try more than one medication to find one that works well. This can be very frustrating, but it is the current state of the science. The same thing holds true for side effects. There isn't any way to know whether a person will experience one or more of the known side effects of a particular medication. Finally, different individuals require different doses. We know the dose ranges, but again we have to try a medication to determine the exact dose that is best for a given person.

Antidepressant side effects

In this section, I will say a little more about some common side effects associated with antidepressant treatment. In general, the risk of side effects varies between classes of antidepressants as well as between the individual medications in each class. Common side effects are listed in Table 8.2. This may look like a scary list with lots of potential problems that could result from taking these medications. Please keep in mind that many who take these agents either don't experience any side effects or experience only one or two. Further, side effects often improve significantly with time and in many cases go away completely. Sometimes there are interventions that can decrease adverse effects. Finally, even if some side effects persist, the suffering and functional impairment associated with untreated illness may greatly outweigh any discomfort associated with side effects. All of that said, you must decide for yourself based on having adequate information. That is the goal of this book—to provide the knowledge you need to make informed treatment decisions. Finally, some side effects can actually be beneficial. For example, antidepressants with a side effect of sedation can be

Table 8.2 Common antidepressant side effects by class or medication[241]

Side effect	May be caused by
Agitation/restlessness	Bupropion, SNRIs, SSRIs
Cholesterol level elevation	Mirtazapine
Constipation	SNRIs, TCAs, nefazodone
Discontinuation syndrome	SNRIs, SSRIs,
Dry mouth	Bupropion, SNRIs, TCAs, nefazodone, mirtazapine
Headache	Bupropion, SNRIs, SSRIs, MAOIs
High blood pressure	Bupropion, MAOIs, SNRIs
Insomnia	SNRIs, SSRIs, bupropion
Irregular heartbeat (arrhythmia)	TCAs, trazodone
Liver failure	Nefazodone
Low blood pressure (dizziness) on standing up	MAOIs, nefazodone, TCAs, trazodone
Rapid heartbeat	SNRIs, TCAs
Sedation	Nefazodone, trazodone, TCAs, MAOIs
Seizures	Amoxapine, bupropion, TCAs
Sexual problems (inhibited arousal)	SNRIs, SSRIs, TCAs, trazodone, MAOIs
Sexual problems (inhibited orgasm)	Desvenlafaxine, MAOIs, SSRIs, TCAs, venlafaxine
Sexual problems (priapism)	Trazodone
Stomach upset	Bupropion, SNRIs, SSRIs, nefazodone
Sweating	SNRIs
Urinary hesitancy	TCAs
Visual symptoms	TCAs
Weight gain	Mirtazapine, TCAs, MAOIs

useful for individuals who have insomnia if the medication is taken before bedtime. Some of these considerations are presented in Table 8.3.

Discontinuation syndrome

Both SSRIs and SNRIs can cause **discontinuation syndrome** if abruptly discontinued after extended therapy. Whenever possible, the dosage of these medications should be tapered off over several weeks to minimize or prevent discontinuation syndrome. Symptoms of discontinuation syndrome include insomnia, nausea, headache, lightheadedness, chills, body aches, and "electric shock–like" sensations. Usually these symptoms go away without treatment in one or two weeks.

Mania and rapid cycling in bipolar disorder

The use of antidepressants for treating bipolar depression is controversial.[246] In general, antidepressants are thought to be effective for bipolar depression,[247, 248] although there is contradictory evidence.[249–251] Further, some, but not all, investigations suggest that the use of antidepressants may contribute to the development of **mania** and **rapid cycling** among those with bipolar spectrum illness.[1, 18, 247] This problem may be especially likely with TCAs.[248] Also, some research indicates that antidepressants can be safely used if combined with a mood stabilizer.[252] Thus, many unanswered questions remain about antidepressant use in bipolar disorder. My assessment is that antidepressant monotherapy for bipolar depression should always be avoided—that is, taking any antidepressant as the only medication treatment. While this issue is incompletely resolved, I think there is enough evidence that it is not worth the risk. Antidepressant use along with a mood stabilizer may be considered, but some research suggests limited effectiveness. Based on what we know at present, my thinking is that, in general, it is safer to avoid antidepressants altogether in bipolar disorder if possible. But this may not be possible in many cases, and any risk associated with antidepressant use in bipolar disorder may be outweighed by the potential benefit of treating depressive symptoms. Please discuss this issue with your provider and decide together what is the best approach for your specific situation.

Serotonin syndrome

Serotonin syndrome is caused by too much serotonergic activity in the body. Symptoms include abdominal pain, diarrhea, flushing, sweating, elevated body temperature, tiredness, confusion, and tremor.[37] In some cases serotonin syndrome can lead to kidney failure, rhabdomyolysis (the rapid breakdown of muscle tissue), renal failure, cardiovascular shock, and even death.

One cause of serotonin syndrome is taking an MAOI at the same time as other serotonergic agents, such as antidepressants or the antianxiety agent buspirone. Serotonin syndrome may result when medications, other than MAOIs, that increase serotonin are combined. Thus, always be sure that all your prescribers know about all the medications you take.

Sexual side effects

The exact incidence of sexual side effects associated with SSRIs is difficult to determine and precise numbers are unknown; however, a range of 30%–50% has been suggested.[253] As Table 8.2 indicates, most antidepressants, other than bupropion, can also cause sexual dysfunction. Some people find it uncomfortable to discuss this problem with their prescriber. However, I want to strongly encourage you to do so if you experience sexual side effects. Many times solutions can be found to sexual and other side effects, so please bring any side effect problems up with your provider.

Suicide

An FDA advisory warned that antidepressants might be associated with an increased risk of suicidal thoughts and behaviors in adolescents. As a result, all antidepressants contain a so-called "black box" warning about suicide risk. In part, this warning states: "Antidepressants increased the risk of suicidal thinking and behavior (suicidality) in short-term studies in children, adolescents, and young adults with major depressive disorder. . . ." As stated in the Introduction, this book does not cover the treatment of mood disorders in children and adolescents. Nonetheless, this warning certainly brings up the question of whether antidepressants contribute to the risk of suicide in adults.

The relationship between suicide risk and antidepressant treatment is incompletely understood. One study concluded that antidepressant treatment did not increase suicide risk in adults but might in younger individuals.[254] There is also some evidence that TCAs might be associated with suicide risk but that newer antidepressants, such as SSRIs, dopamine-norepinephrine reuptake inhibitors, norepinephrine-serotonin modulators, and SNRIs, are not.[255] However, the authors of that study point out that the relationship may not be one of TCAs causing suicide because other factors may have contributed. Finally, numerous studies suggest that antidepressants generally decrease the risk of suicide.[256–260]

The conclusion is that it is almost impossible to absolutely prove whether or not antidepressants ever cause increased suicide risk. One of the major difficulties is that mood disorders by themselves are major risk factors for suicide. My take on this issue is that it is possible that antidepressant treatment might very rarely increase the risk of suicide in specific adults, but for most people antidepressant treatment will decrease the risk. In my opinion, the potential benefits outweigh the risks, especially for those with severe or chronic depression.

Since suicidal thinking and behavior are always a risk for those with mood disorders, the most important thing is for you to monitor yourself for thoughts of death or suicide. If such thoughts develop, please seek help immediately. One option is to call the National Suicide Prevention Lifeline 1-800-273-TALK (8255). Additional options are listed in Chapter 1.

Table 8.3 lists factors that may guide antidepressant selection, including depressive symptoms and other medical and psychiatric conditions as well as individual concerns and preferences. The table does not take into consideration other important factors such as previous response to medications or severity of illness. Thus, other information must also be considered in the medication selection process. Also, please keep in mind that these are POSSIBLE side effects. Not everyone who takes the medication will experience side effects. For those who do, the side effects may be mild and go away after a short time. The MAOIs are not included in this discussion because their use is typically limited to situations of failure to respond to other medications.

Table 8.3   Factors to consider in selecting an antidepressant

Symptoms, coexisting conditions, and concerns	May be helpful	Use with caution or avoid (if possible)
Chronic pain	Duloxetine	
Desire to stop smoking	Bupropion	
Dizziness		Nefazodone, TCAs, trazodone
Insomnia	Mirtazapine, TCAs	SSRIs, SNRIs, bupropion
Irregular heartbeat		TCAs
Sedation		Mirtazapine, TCAs
Seizure disorder		Bupropion, TCAs
Sexual side effects	Bupropion	SSRIs, SNRIs, TCAs
Unsteady gait		Nefazodone, TCAs, trazodone
Urinary hesitancy		TCAs
Weight gain	Bupropion	Mirtazapine, TCAs
Weight loss	Mirtazapine	Bupropion

Mood stabilizers

Mood stabilizers are used to treat bipolar spectrum disorders. Some also have a role in the treatment of unipolar illness. In regard to bipolar spectrum illness, some mood stabilizers are effective for mania and **hypomania**, mixed episodes, bipolar depression, maintenance treatment, or all of these. All mood stabilizers have the potential to cause significant, and in some cases potentially dangerous, side effects, at least compared with the newer antidepressants. Unfortunately, medications are needed to control **mood** symptoms for those with bipolar spectrum disorders (with the possible exception of mild **cyclothymic disorder** or **bipolar disorder NOS**). So, while problematic side effects are frequently associated with the use of mood stabilizers, no alternatives are currently available.

Table 8.4 Anticonvulsants indicated for the treatment of mood disorders[262, 263]

Generic name (trade name)	Evidence for use in major depression	Evidence for use in bipolar disorder		
		Mania	Depression	Maintenance
Carbamazepine (Carbatrol)	x	xxx	x	xx
Gabapentin (Neurontin)				x
Lamotrigine (Lamictal)	x		x	xxx
Levetiracetam (Keppra)			x	
Oxcarbazepine (Trileptal)		x	x	x
Tiagabine (Gabitril)	x			
Topiramate (Topamax)	x			x
Valproate/Divalproex (Depakote)		xxx	x	xx
Zonisamide (Zonegram)				x

x = minimal evidence, xx = moderate evidence, xxx = strong evidence

Let's start by discussing the anticonvulsant mood stabilizers.

Anticonvulsants

Anticonvulsants are medications developed to treat epilepsy or seizure disorders. Some are also effective as mood stabilizers for bipolar disorders. There is weak evidence of beneficial effects of carbamazepine, lamotrigine, and valproate for patients with recurring unipolar depression who experience prominent irritability or agitation.[261] Two anticonvulsants, carbamazepine and valproate, are approved by the FDA for treating acute manic or mixed episodes associated with **bipolar I disorder** in adults, and lamotrigine is FDA approved for maintenance treatment of bipolar I disorder in adults. There is also evidence that lamotrigine and valproate have some effectiveness for bipolar depression.[262, 263] Table 8.4 lists the generic and trade names of anticonvulsants as well as my interpretation of the evidence supporting their use in treating mood disorders.

As with all medications, a number of potential side effects are associated with anticonvulsant use. I will limit our discussion to those agents that are most commonly used to treat mood disorders. Let's start with two of the most concerning, skin rash and birth defects.

Skin rashes have been reported as side effects with all anticonvulsants, but the highest risk is associated with carbamazepine and particularly lamotrigine.[264] Several factors increase the risk of rash secondary to lamotrigine, including high initial dose, rapid dose increase, and a previous history of anticonvulsant-induced rash. Any anticonvulsant-induced skin rash has the possibility of progressing to a fatal reaction, such as toxic epidermal necrolysis or Stevens-Johnson syndrome. Carbamazepine and lamotrigine are most likely to cause these severe reactions.[264] If a rash develops, the drug must be immediately stopped. If you get a rash, stop taking the medication and call your prescriber right away. Once the rash has gone away, a thorough risk-benefit analysis must be conducted before considering trying the medication again.

Taking carbamazepine, lamotrigine, and valproate should be avoided during pregnancy, as all three can cause birth defects.[265] Carbamazepine and valproate are thought to be safe for women who are breast-feeding (also see Chapter 12).[266] There is not enough information available to assess the safety of using gabapentin, levetiracetam, oxcarbazepine, tiagabine, topiramate, and zonisamide during pregnancy and lactation.[265, 266]

A number of other potentially serious side effects are associated with these medications. Carbamazepine may cause heart conduction problems and therefore must be used with caution in those with some kinds of heart problems.[266] Anticonvulsant treatment can also affect the number of blood cells in circulation. Thus, baseline (before treatment) and ongoing monitoring of blood cell counts is required when receiving treatment with these medications. Carbamazepine can cause leukopenia (decrease in the number of white blood cells) and has a black-box warning for risks of agranulocytosis (decreased concentration of the granulocyte class of white blood cells, which includes neutrophils, basophils, and eosinophils) and aplastic anemia (bone marrow does not produce enough new blood cells). Further, thrombocytopenia (decreased levels of platelets in the blood) can occur during treatment with carbamazepine, lamotrigine, and valproate.[266] Both low levels of sodium in the circulation (hyponatremia) and a condition known as syndrome of inappropriate antidiuretic hormone secretion (SIADH) have been reported with carbamazepine and oxcarbazepine.[266] Topiramate and zonisamide increase the risk of developing an abnormality of the acid-base balance in the bloodstream. Thus, serum bicarbonate levels should be monitored at baseline and during treatment.[264] Carbamazepine, valproate, and zonisamide can have short-term effects on tests that monitor liver functions, commonly known as liver function tests (LFTs). Baseline and ongoing LFT monitoring is required with these medications. Valproate has the greatest risk of liver damage, known as hepatotoxicity.[266] Valproate-induced pancreatitis is a rare, life-threatening adverse effect.[266] Valproate also is linked to polycystic ovaries in females, but this side effect seems to be more likely to occur in women with seizures rather than in those with mood disorders.[267] Topiramate and zonisamide elevate the risk of developing kidney stones with long-term use.[264] Finally, a rare but potentially fatal angioedema (swelling of the dermis layer of the skin and underlying tissue) has been reported with oxcarbazepine.[264]

In addition to more serious side effects, anticonvulsants can produce a number of less serious but potentially bothersome adverse reactions. Some anticonvulsants can affect appetite and weight. Weight gain frequently results from treatment with valproate and may also occur with carbamazepine and gabapentin.[266] Weight gain does not appear to be related to the dose; that is, higher doses do not cause greater weight gain. In contrast, weight and appetite loss and **anorexia nervosa** have been reported with both topiramate and zonisamide.[266] Finally, lamotrigine and levetiracetam do not appear to affect weight. Carbamazepine and valproate can cause problems with attention, learning, memory, and psychomotor speed in some individuals. Topiramate is associated with the highest rate of cognitive dysfunction, and persons being treated with this medication can experience problems with concentration, attention, word-finding, and memory.[266, 268] Other side effects include sedation, dizziness, and unsteady gait.[266] Gabapentin and zonisamide are the most sedating.[266] Ironically, although they are used to treat psychiatric disorders, anticonvulsants can also cause psychiatric symptoms. Carbamazepine, gabapentin, lamotrigine, oxcarbazepine, and valproate may have a lower risk of adverse psychiatric effects than other anticonvulsants.[264] Most important, an FDA analysis suggested that persons who take anticonvulsants have an elevated risk of suicidal ideation or behaviors, regardless of the reason the medication is prescribed. The evidence for increased suicidality is stronger for those taking these medications for epilepsy than for those with a psychiatric diagnosis. In bipolar disorder, these agents may not be associated with increased risk of suicidality and are most likely protective.[269] Nonetheless, anyone taking anticonvulsants must be alert for worsening depression, suicidal thoughts, and other emotional changes.

Therapeutic serum drug concentration monitoring is used to help assess whether an adequate dose is being taken as well as to help prevent side effects from occurring due to a dose that is too high for a given person. Therapeutic monitoring is required for valproate and carbamazepine. The concentration range recommended for valproate is 50–125 μg/mL and 4–12 μg/mL for carbamazepine. Serum concentrations of gabapentin, lamotrigine, levetiracetam, oxcarbazepine, tiagabine, topiramate, and zonisamide do not correlate with treatment response. Therefore monitoring of serum concentrations is not necessary for these anticonvulsants.

Antipsychotics

The psychiatric medications known as antipsychotics were developed to treat disorders that have symptoms of **psychosis**, such as **schizophrenia**. There are two general subcategories of these medications. The older class is known as first-generation, "typical antipsychotics" or neuroleptics. Medications that have been developed more recently are known as "atypical" or second-generation antipsychotics. I use the term **second-generation antipsychotics (SGAs)** in this book. The first-generation agents are rarely used for mood disorders, so I will not discuss them. SGAs are used as mood stabilizers for bipolar spectrum disorders and as adjunctive agents for the treatment of unipolar illness. The uses of these medications are listed in Table 8.5.

The second-generation antipsychotics have a number of potentially serious side effects. There is evidence that elderly patients with dementia-related psychosis treated with antipsychotic drugs are at an increased risk of death. These agents should be avoided in that group of individuals, if possible.

Table 8.5 Second-generation antipsychotics used to treat mood disorders

Generic name (Trade name)	FDA approved MDD adjunctive	FDA approved BD	Approximate dose range (mg/day)	Common side effects
Aripiprazole (Abilify)	Yes	Mania & mixed	10–30 (BD) 2–15 (MDD)	Tremor, anxiety, insomnia, sedation, constipation, dizziness, weight gain, nausea
Olanzapine (Zyprexa)	Yes	Mania, mixed depression & maintenance	5-18 (MDD) 10-20 (BD)	Low blood pressure, constipation, dry mouth, weight gain, sedation, dizziness, upset stomach, tremor, increased appetite, abdominal pain, headache, insomnia
Paliperidone (Invega)	Not approved	Not approved	NA	Rapid heartbeat, sedation, upset stomach, weight gain, dizziness, headache, nausea, constipation, tremors
Quetiapine (Seroquel)	Not approved	Mania, depression & maintenance	400–800 (BD)	Headache, sedation, dizziness, dry mouth, constipation, rapid heartbeat, weight gain, nausea
Risperidone (Risperdal)	Not approved	mania & mixed	1–6 (BD)	Sedation, increased appetite, fatigue, nausea, cough, constipation, anxiety, dizziness, tremor, insomnia
Ziprasidone	Not approved	Mania, mixed & maintenance	80–160 (BD)	Irregular heartbeat, sedation, dizziness, dizziness and (Geodon) upset stomach, dry mouth, dizziness, nausea, drop in blood pressure

Dosages are general ranges. Dosage adjustments may be required when taken with certain other medications and/or with some medical conditions. BD = bipolar disorder. MDD = major depressive disorder.

One of the most significant concerns with the SGAs is the association with weight gain, hyperglycemia, and diabetes. These conditions are generally referred to as metabolic effects, and all of the SGAs carry a warning about them. Weight gain and other metabolic side effects are common adverse effects of the SGAs used to treat mood disorders, particularly olanzapine, risperidone, and quetiapine.[241] Thus, regular monitoring of weight, body mass index, serum lipid levels, and fasting glucose levels is recommended. If weight gain does occur, then a risk-benefit analysis of continuing the medication must be considered. Individuals with an established diagnosis of diabetes mellitus who are started on SGAs must be monitored regularly for worsening of glucose control. Finally, persons who have risk factors for diabetes, such as obesity or a family history of diabetes, should be monitored very carefully during treatment for any evidence of the onset of diabetes. If you take an SGA, let your prescriber know if you develop symptoms that could indicate elevated blood glucose levels, which include increased thirst, increased urination, increased appetite, and weakness.

Another category of adverse reactions is a group of neurological effects generally referred to as extrapyramidal side effects (EPS). These are much more common with first-generation antipsychotics, but there is some limited risk with SGAs as well.[241] EPS can broadly be divided into those that are related to early treatment and those that are related to long-term or chronic treatment. Early-treatment EPS occur in the first days and weeks of taking the medication, are dose dependent, and are reversible when the medication dose is reduced or discontinued. There are three types of early treatment EPS: parkinsonism, dystonia, and akathisia. Antipsychotic-induced parkinsonism is characterized by the same symptoms as Parkinson's disease—muscle rigidity, tremor, and slowing of movements. Dystonia is the spastic contraction of discrete muscle groups. Akathisia is a sense of restlessness or need to keep moving. In contrast, chronic EPS occur after months and years of antipsychotic treatment, are not clearly dose dependent, and may persist after medication is discontinued.[241] The chronic EPS include tardive dyskinesia and dystonia. Tardive dyskinesia is a disorder of abnormal involuntary movements. Abnormal movements can occur in any muscle group but are most commonly seen in the oral-facial region. This condition is potentially irreversible and there is no proven treatment. That said, the syndrome might go away either partially or completely if the medication is stopped. Finally, a potentially fatal symptom complex known as neuroleptic malignant syndrome has been reported in association with antipsychotic drugs. Symptoms of this condition include fever, muscle rigidity, confusion, irregular pulse or blood pressure, and rapid and irregular heartbeat.

Other side effects seen to various degrees with the SGAs are dry mouth, constipation, blurred vision, sexual dysfunction, sedation, rapid heartbeat, dizziness upon standing, and irregular heartbeat. In regard to irregular heartbeat, one condition is known as "QTc prolongation." The time required for the heart ventricles to repolarize is measured by what is known as the QT interval on electrocardiograms. The QT interval varies with heart rate and is therefore corrected for heart rate and then called "QTc." Significant prolongation of the QTc is associated with increased risk for dangerous irregularities of heart rate that can result in fainting or even sudden death.[241] Of the SGAs, ziprasidone is associated with QTc prolongation, but the clinical significance of this is unclear[241, 270] and a recent study found no increased mortality from ziprasidone as compared to olanzapine.[271] Thus, the risk of dangerous irregular heartbeat with ziprasidone appears to be low. Nonetheless, it is recommended that those treated with ziprasidone be monitored for other risk factors, including congenital prolonged QT syndrome as well as liver or kidney failure. Also, the use of ziprasidone with other drugs known to significantly prolong the QTc interval should be avoided. Finally, elevated levels of the hormone prolactin (hyperprolactinemia) are associated with risperidone.[241] Hyperprolactinemia can cause impaired sexual function, breast tenderness and enlargement, lactation, and decreased production of estrogen and testosterone. In women, this condition may disrupt menstrual cycles.

Lithium

Lithium has been used for the treatment of bipolar disorder for more than fifty years. It is effective for mania, depression, and maintenance treatment. It is also sometimes used as an adjunctive treatment for major depression. Like the other mood stabilizers, lithium has a number of side effects, including increased urination, increased thirst, weight gain, problems with memory and concentration, tremor, sedation, impaired coordination, nausea, vomiting, diarrhea, hair loss, and acne.

More serious side effects include hypothyroidism, irregular heartbeat, impaired kidney concentrating capacity, psoriasis, and chronic kidney changes. Lithium is very toxic if the serum level gets too high. Most people experience some symptoms of toxicity with serum levels higher than 1.5 meq/L, and levels higher than 2.0 meq/L can cause life-threatening side effects. Mild toxicity causes symptoms that include tremor, nausea, diarrhea, blurred vision, vertigo, and confusion. Higher serum levels can result in seizures, coma, irregular heartbeat, and death. Anything beyond mild toxicity is a medical emergency that requires hospital treatment and frequently dialysis to remove excess lithium from the body. A number of other medications, including some over-the-counter preparations, can have an impact on lithium levels, so it is critical to let your prescriber know about any other medications you are taking and obtain a list of medications to avoid. Finally, lithium can cause birth defects if taken during pregnancy.

Because of lithium's side effects, a number of baseline and ongoing tests are recommended for those receiving treatment with this medication. Most experts recommend tests of kidney function (BUN and creatinine), pregnancy test, thyroid function test, complete blood count, ECG, and pregnancy test for females before starting lithium. These tests should be repeated at regular intervals while taking lithium along with monitoring of the serum lithium levels. Therapeutic serum lithium levels are between 0.5 meq/L and 1.2 meq/L. Lithium treatment is usually started in low, divided doses to minimize side effects—for example, 300 mg three times per day or less. The dose is then increased until a therapeutic serum level is reached.

Additional biological treatments

In addition to medication, there are other biological treatments for mood disorders: transcranial magnetic stimulation, electroconvulsive therapy, vagus nerve stimulation, and light therapy.

Transcranial magnetic stimulation (TMS)

In October 2008 the FDA approved TMS for the treatment of major depression. TMS is approved for those who have not achieved satisfactory improvement from a trial of at least one antidepressant at or above the minimum dose and duration. A number of studies indicate that TMS is effective for major depression.[272, 273] However, the need for daily treatments may result in its use being challenging for some.

TMS works based on the fact that a magnetic field induces an electric current that runs perpendicular to the motion of the field. In TMS, a magnetic field is applied directly to the scalp and the cortical region directly below is stimulated electrically. Most individuals receive daily treatments for four to six weeks, with each treatment lasting about an hour. No sedation is required and treatment does not affect cognition. Side effects are minimal, with the most common being scalp pain or discomfort. There is a very slight risk of seizure and therefore TMS should be used with caution, if at all, for persons with epilepsy. TMS must be used with caution in persons who have implantable devices, such as pacemakers, and must not be used if there is ferromagnetic material (metal that can become magnetic or is attracted to magnets) in the body within 1 foot of where the coil will be placed.

Electroconvulsive therapy (ECT)

ECT is a very effective treatment that has the highest rates of response (70%–90%) and remission of any form of antidepressant treatment.[37] Therefore, the American Psychiatric Association[37] recommends that ECT be considered for severe major depression that does not respond to other treatments. Further, the use of ECT as a first-line treatment is recommended for those with high suicide risk as well as those who are so depressed that they are unable to eat. ECT may also be effective for mania but is rarely used for this condition.

Electroconvulsive therapy has a bad reputation, which is, to a great extent, undeserved. Still, it is a treatment that certainly has a number of potential adverse effects. The fact that electrical stimulation is applied to the brain to induce a seizure may make ECT seem like a very extreme intervention. However, viewed objectively, it is difficult to make an argument that ECT is more "extreme" than other medical interventions, such as open-heart surgery. Nonetheless, the general public has a negative perception of ECT, perhaps because of inaccurate portrayals of the procedure in the popular media. The classic example is the movie *One Flew Over the Cuckoo's Nest*, in which ECT was wrongly depicted as a tool of terror. Further, the belief persists that ECT is administered without anesthesia or muscle relaxants. In fact, ECT is administered under general anesthesia, and muscle relaxants are used to prevent a generalized convulsion or seizure. Thus, individuals are not consciously aware of the seizure, and the experience of the procedure is similar to that of minor surgeries that require anesthesia.

In regard to side effects, ECT can cause a short-term increase in heart rate and blood pressure as well as irregular heartbeat. It also causes a period of confusion after treatment that usually lasts for 30–60 minutes, and some people experience more significant memory loss.[37] As mentioned, ECT requires general anesthesia and so all the risks normally associated with anesthesia apply to ECT.

A decision to undergo ECT must be made with a complete understanding of all the potential risks and benefits. If at all possible, input from significant others should be sought to assist in the decision-making process. A decision to receive ECT treatment should not be made lightly. Nonetheless, given the disability and suffering associated with severe depression, my recommendation is that ECT at least be considered as a possible option for severe depression that is unresponsive to other treatments.

ECT is usually administered two or three times per week for a total of six to twelve treatments.[37] Treatment should be continued until depressive symptoms have resolved completely or until there is no further improvement.

Vagus nerve stimulation (VNS)

The vagus nerve is also known as the tenth cranial nerve. It arises from the medulla region of the brain and connects to a region known as the nucleus of the solitary tract, which in turn projects into other locations in the central nervous system. VNS involves electrical stimulation of this nerve. The mechanism of action is incompletely understood.

VNS is approved for use in individuals with depression whose symptoms have not responded to at least four adequate trials of antidepressant medications and/or ECT.[37] There is evidence of effectiveness, but the benefit for depression has not been completely established.[37]

VNS requires the surgical implantation of a stimulator device. Possible side effects are postsurgical infection, hoarseness or voice alteration, coughing, shortness of breath, and neck discomfort. VNS is recommended for consideration for persons with depression who have not responded to other treatments.[37]

As with ECT, decisions about VNS treatment must be made with a complete understanding of both the potential benefits and risks. I strongly recommend that, if at all possible, you seek input from significant others to assist in the decision-making process.

Light therapy

There is evidence that bright light therapy provides some benefit for both seasonal and nonseasonal depression.[37] Light therapy may also enhance response to antidepressants. The only side effect is possible induced hypomania. Given the low risk of adverse events, this strategy warrants consideration as monotherapy for mild seasonal depression as well as use in conjunction with other biological or psychological approaches.

Summary of biological treatments

Biological treatments play an important role in the treatment of mood disorders. However, most of these approaches have a much greater risk of side effects than either psychological or complementary approaches. Currently, biological strategies are strongly recommended for severe depression and bipolar spectrum disorders (along with psychotherapy and complementary approaches). As with all treatments, the important thing to remember is that each person must weigh the potential benefits against the potential risks. Given the disability and suffering as well as the suicide risk associated with severe depression and bipolar disorder, biological treatment is likely to be the best choice for most people. For unipolar illness, recent studies suggest the effectiveness of psychotherapy approaches to prevent **relapse** (see Chapter 9). One approach may be to use medication to achieve full remission and then consider psychotherapy to prevent relapse. This strategy has not been adequately studied, however, and it is unclear whether staying on medication along with psychotherapy may prevent relapse better than psychotherapy alone. Finally, for a first episode of mild to moderate unipolar depression, initial treatment with psychotherapy and/or complementary approaches may be appropriate for some people (see Chapters 9, 10, and 11). If this strategy does not result in symptom improvement and ultimately full remission, then biological approaches should be considered. For those who have had more than one episode of depression and thus have a **recurrent illness**, more aggressive treatment may be warranted at the first sign of return of illness.

Perhaps one of the most important points about biological treatments is that in order to be effective, these methods must be used as directed. This can be of particular concern for psychiatric medications because it can be easy to forget to take one or more doses. Ann, who (you will remember) has depression, says, "Some days, it can be hard to remember whether I have taken my antidepressant. I think this is because there isn't an immediate effect from missing a dose."

If many doses are missed, medications will most likely either be less effective or perhaps not work at all. Several strategies can be used to help people remember to take their medication. Perhaps the most effective is a "pill box" with separate boxes for specific doses on particular days—for example, "Monday morning." These boxes can be bought at most pharmacies and are inexpensive. There is also a row on the daily mood chart to help you keep track of whether you have taken all your psychiatric prescriptions as prescribed on any given day.

As I have emphasized throughout this book, the best treatment approach is the one that is best for your specific situation. Please discuss options with your treatment team. Using as many appropriate strategies as possible will give you the best chance of achieving full remission and staying well for life. I hope this book will help you develop a comprehensive recovery plan. Finally, the purpose of this chapter is to provide information to help you work effectively with your treatment team and assist you to make informed decisions about treatment. It cannot replace the advice of medical and mental health professionals. Please do not make decisions based only on the information in this chapter.

9

Psychotherapy

PSYCHOTHERAPY SHOULD BE ONE COMPONENT of treatment for most people who have a **mood disorder**. I say "most" because there may be situations where engaging in psychotherapy just isn't feasible. If at all possible, however, I strongly encourage you to include this treatment approach in your recovery plan. For those with **unipolar** depression of mild to moderate severity, psychotherapy may be the only treatment necessary. Before we move on, a word about terminology: Psychotherapy is often known simply as "therapy." I use the terms *psychotherapy* and *therapy* interchangeably in this book.

Why psychotherapy?

Several types of therapy have been shown to be very effective for **depression**,[37] including severe depression,[274] and bipolar disorder (along with biological treatments).[275-279] For example, there is evidence that adding psychotherapy to medication can decrease the **relapse** rate by about 40% for bipolar disorder.[280] This is a huge difference in outcome for a disorder that can be difficult to treat. Furthermore, psychotherapy has a number of advantages over treatment with medication alone, including helping individuals develop an understanding of the sources of depression and enhancing interpersonal relationships.[37] Psychotherapies also frequently address the complicated relationships between our sense of self and depression (also see Chapter 4).

Ann, whom you met in earlier chapters, has received both medication and psychotherapy for depression. She says, "Therapy helped me develop insight about thinking errors that contributed to my depression. Changing my thinking really helped to improve my mood. Therapy was also helpful in terms of increasing my self-esteem."

I strongly recommend psychotherapy either as monotherapy for mild or moderate unipolar depression or in combination with biological treatments for more severe illness and for bipolar disorder. However, if you start treatment with psychotherapy alone and do not get better, then other approaches, such as medication, should be considered. Please see Chapters 11 and 13 for more information. Combining psychotherapy with complementary approaches (see Chapter 10) should also be considered. Finally, if you have had previous episodes of depression that required medication treatment, it may not make sense to try psychotherapy without medication. As I've said in other chapters, this book provides only general information to help you make informed treatment decisions and work effectively with your treatment team. Please discuss options with your medical or mental health treatment team before making any treatment decisions.

What is psychotherapy?

Psychotherapy is a general term for a variety of techniques aimed at increasing awareness, self-observation, and insight. The ultimate goal of therapy is to change behaviors and patterns of thinking as well as decrease emotional distress. Psychotherapy is sometimes called "talk therapy" and can occur in an individual, couple, family, or group setting. In the next section, we'll take a look at how some common psychotherapy methods work.

Developing self-awareness

The purpose of therapy is to help you feel better. Therapy can help you by directly decreasing your mood disorder symptoms or by increasing your general level of happiness and satisfaction. It can also help you more indirectly by bringing about behavior changes that lead to decreased depression. In most cases, its effect is a bit of both.

Regardless of the therapy used, a major component involves developing self-awareness. Fundamentally, psychotherapy is a process of getting to know yourself better. Most of us probably tend to think that we know ourselves very well. But, in fact, we all have many blind spots. Blind spots can be dangerous—think about driving on the freeway. Finding ways to see through the blind spots can decrease mood symptoms and help us lead more productive and satisfying lives.

Why do we have blind spots about ourselves? One reason is that our brains tend to automatically try to keep us from feeling bad by pushing information that is uncomfortable or painful out of our conscious awareness. The technical term for this is *denial*. A classic example is when someone experiencing chest pain refuses to believe he is having a heart attack and delays seeking treatment. In that case, the denial is a result of fear.

Here's another example: Many individuals with substance use disorders are unable to see that their substance use is causing a problem in their life. Their denial may be the result of thinking that having a substance use problem makes the individual a bad person. Denial can also prevent a person from recognizing that she has a mood disorder. As with addictions, having a mood disorder may carry a stigma. One aim of this book is to get rid of that stigma by making it clear that mood disorders are not the fault of the person with the illness. Furthermore, having a mood disorder does not mean anything negative about you or about someone you love.

Before we move on, an important take-home point is that we don't recognize denial when it is happening. That is why we have to make a special effort to look for it. All of that said, our thoughts and behaviors frequently cause or worsen mood symptoms. They can also prevent us from leading happy and satisfying lives. Changing thinking and behavior patterns can therefore be very helpful, but first we have to recognize them for what they are.

Another reason we may not notice our thoughts and actions is that they occur automatically and we are frequently paying attention to something else. A simple example is brushing your teeth. You can brush away without giving it any thought and your mind can be anywhere or thinking about anything. Did you ever complete a simple task and then not remember whether you had actually done it because your mind was somewhere else? It happens to me all the time. Once we start to pay attention to the here and now, it's amazing how much of our lives happen on autopilot with our brains focused on the past or future—rather than on the present moment.

Similarly, thought processes usually occur automatically. A good example is worry. Most of the time we don't make a conscious decision to worry about some stressful event; it just happens. It may seem surprising but we often don't even identify our thinking as worry. We are aware of our thoughts at some level and recognize that we are feeling bad emotionally. What we don't often do is think, "Oh, I'm worrying now." In other words, we don't look objectively at our subjective experience.

This is an important concept because our thoughts often drive both our emotional state and our behaviors. Learning to recognize thinking patterns is very important for your recovery. Once you become aware, you can decide to change how you think or diminish the power thoughts have over your mood and life. This transformation allows you to evaluate behaviors objectively. We become aware of the mental processes that are driving our behavior. Then we have the opportunity to look objectively at those thoughts or feelings and decide whether we want to respond in our habitual way or try something new.

These processes form the basis for most psychotherapy approaches and particularly for those methods discussed in the next section. However, in order to develop self-awareness, it is critical to first cultivate an attitude of compassion and kindness toward yourself. Otherwise, there may be a tendency to avoid recognizing personality traits that you want to change. This tendency is the "denial" discussed above. The other possibility is that you might want to beat yourself up over your imperfections. This is not only unhelpful but also illogical. As I discussed in Chapter 4, our personalities, habits, and traits develop from complex interactions between our inherited characteristics and life experiences. We didn't sign up for them and it makes no sense to criticize ourselves for who we are. However, it does make sense to recognize what we can change and then make an effort to do so. Psychotherapy can help you accomplish this important step in your recovery plan. Some of the complementary strategies discussed in Chapter 10 can be helpful too.

There are a number of specific psychotherapy approaches in use today. In this section, I will provide a brief overview of several of these approaches. It is important to point out that in practice it is common and appropriate to combine more than one approach over a course of treatment. Your therapy might include a combination of several of these methods. Also, this section is not all-inclusive. Other treatment approaches not listed in this chapter may be appropriate for your situation. The purpose of this section is to provide information about some of the more common approaches. Psychotherapy needs to be tailored to your life situation and goals, so please discuss the best option for you with your therapist.

Cognitive and mindfulness-based therapies

I focus on **cognitive therapies** (CT) and mindfulness-based approaches in this book for several reasons. Most important, there is considerable evidence that supports their effectiveness. Also, cognitive therapy is widely available, and both CT and **mindfulness** practices can be implemented by using self-help approaches (see Chapter 10). Furthermore, the theories underlying these approaches provide a straightforward way to understand some key components of the **psychology** of depression. Finally, these methods not only are useful for symptom reduction but also have the potential to help you lead a happier and more satisfying life.

Before moving on, I want to make a very important point: These methods may not be the best for you. Please discuss appropriate therapy options with your therapist. There are too many variables for me to make a specific recommendation. However, regardless of the recommended psychotherapy, these methods may be added as a complementary approach (see Chapter 10) in most cases.

In Chapter 4, I discussed how certain thinking patterns, particularly irrational cognitions about the self, are associated with depressive symptoms. Let's discuss cognitive therapy, which is targeted at changing those thinking patterns.

Cognitive therapy (CT)

CT arose as a blending of cognitive and behavioral approaches (also see Chapter 4) and is often referred to as cognitive behavioral therapy or CBT. Cognitive strategies involve changing one's thought patterns. Broadly speaking, behavioral therapy includes techniques designed to reinforce desired and eliminate undesired behaviors. CT is generally a short-term "here and now" therapy. A number of techniques are employed in CT to help individuals change thinking patterns and behaviors that may be related to the experience of depression. Perhaps the most important is the questioning and testing of thoughts, assumptions, and beliefs to determine whether they are realistic. The aim is to identify inaccurate thoughts that may result in depression and subsequently counter these thinking patterns with objective evidence.

There is considerable evidence of the effectiveness of CT for treating unipolar depression[1, 37, 281] as well as bipolar spectrum illness.[277, 278] Some, but not all, studies suggest this treatment approach may be similar in effectiveness to antidepressant medication, especially for less severe unipolar depression.[37] Cognitive therapy also has the advantage of preventing relapse after the completion of treatment, which is not the case for medications (in other words, medications need to be continued to prevent relapse).[37]

CT typically focuses on current problems in one's life, rather than issues from the past. The therapist works in a collaborative relationship with the depressed individual. Together, they form a "team" investigating thinking patterns and schemas to determine their validity.[1] Schemas are beliefs or patterns of thinking, particularly about the self. Similarly, recurrent behaviors are reviewed with the aim of determining whether they help or hinder. Based on the results of these explorations, solutions are devised. One solution involves the recognition and modification of negatively distorted and illogical automatic thoughts and schemas.[1] Recognition of distorted thinking patterns occurs by way of a process of examining relevant evidence. Specific thoughts and schemas are conceptualized as hypotheses, and the patient and therapist team sort through evidence supporting or refuting the hypothesis (thought/schema).[1] Thus, change occurs as a result of a very logical approach to determining whether thinking patterns are valid or not. Finally, behavioral techniques are used to assist the process as well as change any recurrent behaviors that are not helpful.[1]

It may be useful to provide an example of how CT can be used. Remember Ann, whom you met in earlier chapters. She has experienced emotional pain because of problems with family relationships. Of course, it is normal to feel sad or hurt when relationships with those we love aren't going well. However, sometimes we also experience negative emotions because of how we think about the situation. In other words, our belief system and thinking patterns may make us feel even worse. For example, Ann has a tendency to experience low self-esteem. For people with low self-esteem, family stress can bring up negative thoughts about the self, such as: "There must be something wrong with me or these things wouldn't happen." So it is common for them to feel bad not only because of the actual situation but also because of negative thinking.

One aim of CT is to help us become aware of these negative thinking patterns. The next step is to recognize that these patterns may be irrational or disorted by negative past experiences. At that point, it is possible to examine the evidence in support of and against the belief or idea. Most of us do, in fact, have irrational negative beliefs about ourselves, but when we examine the evidence, we can see that the beliefs are mostly, or entirely, irrational and illogical. That recognition results in the belief losing the power to make us feel bad.

As the example illustrates, CT is a powerful method that can help us change our thinking patterns and feel better emotionally. I strongly recommend that you consider incorporating CT into your comprehensive recovery plan.

Mindfulness-based psychotherapies

What is mindfulness? The original concept of mindfulness was associated with meditation and developed primarily from Eastern religious and philosophical thought, particularly Buddhism. That said, there is nothing inherently religious about mindfulness. People with many different religious beliefs, as well as those who aren't religious at all, practice mindfulness. There are a number of definitions of mindfulness; most include focusing attention on the present moment—that is, being aware of the sensations (including thoughts and emotions) that we are experiencing right now. As a familiar example, when driving, some of us tend to go on autopilot. This seems to be especially likely when we are on a familiar route. We may be thinking about the grocery list or anything other than driving. Our minds are capable of completing routine tasks without using all of our attention capabilities, so we can do one thing and think about something else. This allows us to multitask. In the case of driving, however, it may also contribute to accidents.

The opposite of being on autopilot is paying attention to all incoming sensory information. When we are driving, new visual and auditory data is coming in all the time as we progress along our route. Besides the changing scene through the windshield and the variations in traffic noise, there is incoming data from inside our vehicle. If we pay attention, we can notice the sensation of our bodies on the seat and our hands on the steering wheel. Maybe there are odors too—perhaps exhaust fumes from a passing truck or the smell of leather from the jacket we are wearing. My point is that there is a wealth of sensory information that we frequently block out.

Is blocking out sensory information a bad thing? What about multitasking? The answer is no and yes. In a general sense, it is wonderful that our brain can suppress incoming sensory information that may not be relevant. This process allows us to focus brain resources on what is most important for the immediate situation. For example, when we are driving on the freeway, it is very useful for us to focus on what the other cars are doing, rather than paying attention to every detail of the surrounding landscape. By the same token, our ability to multitask is often beneficial. That said, both of these processes can prevent us from paying attention to what is going on in the moment.

What are the advantages of focusing our attention on the here-and-now experiences of each moment? One potential benefit is that by spending more time living in the moment we can actually experience all the richness of our lives. We all have a short time on this planet. As we get older, we invariably realize that time really does fly. By not living in the moment, we risk realizing one day that we have missed most of our lives by spending so much of our time on autopilot. The old saying "Stop and smell the roses" applies. The point is that we can't stop and enjoy the fragrance if we don't even notice that there are roses nearby.

Another reason to be mindful is to become aware of our thoughts and emotions in an accepting and nonjudgmental way. This is critically important for the development of self-awareness that I discussed earlier in this chapter. But, you may be thinking, "I'm aware of my thoughts all the time." I invite you to consider that this is likely to be only partially true. Most of us are aware of the constant stream of thoughts that go through our heads, but we don't often actually pay much attention to their content. One facet of mindfulness is becoming aware of our *thoughts* along with the many other sensations that occur on a moment-to-moment basis. Further, mindfulness specifically includes developing a nonjudgmental view of each thought, feeling, or sensation that we experience. In other words, developing a mindfulness practice means cultivating an attitude of curiosity, openness, and acceptance about our experiences and thoughts.

As discussed in Chapter 4, both the amount of time spent thinking about self and the patterns of thinking about self (specifically, analytic as opposed to experiential self-focus) are likely major contributors to the development of depressive symptoms. Practicing mindfulness has the potential to prevent thinking patterns related to self from leading to depression. First, by paying more attention to the immediate experience, one is able to decrease the overall level of self-focus. Further, shifting more of one's time from analytic self-focus to direct experience of the moment has the potential to decrease depression.

Another advantage to direct experience of the moment involves developing awareness that our thoughts are passing mental events without any real substance. At first, this notion may seem counterintuitive. After all, we tend to trust our brains, right? Well, I would argue that we can trust our brains, but only sometimes. Our minds deal pretty well with concrete facts, such as the name of the current president or the shortest route to the grocery store. I invite you to consider that our stream of thoughts is not very reliable when it comes to how we see our selves or how we perceive our selves in relation to others. As described above in the section on cognitive therapy, most of us develop irrational negative thoughts and beliefs about "self." Further, we attach great significance to these thoughts. We do this to the point that they can control our emotions. Developing mindfulness allows us to be aware of these thoughts about self when they occur and recognize them as simply transient mental phenomena. As we develop this view, we recognize that these mental events are ephemeral, like passing clouds in the sky. This practice allows us to realize that most of our thoughts do not represent accurate reflections of reality either about life in general or specifically about aspects of self. As a result, our thoughts become less powerful and less likely to bring on negative emotion. Furthermore, by practicing mindfulness we develop the skill to let thoughts go and move on. Both of these processes can greatly decrease the negative thinking associated with depression (see Chapter 4 for a detailed discussion).

Finally, at a deeper level, the practice of mindfulness has the potential to fundamentally change our thinking about the entire concept of self. As we come to develop an understanding that our ceaseless stream of thoughts is frequently not reality based, we also see that the idea of self is not nearly as important as we once thought. Like all of our thoughts, the idea of self is just a concept in our minds. It is a useful concept, but it is an ever-changing idea about who we are and what it means to be "me." As we have new experiences and lay down new memories, our notion of who we are evolves. As we come to appreciate that self is not a static or permanent thing but rather a collection of thoughts and memories at any given moment, we may recognize that the idea of self lacks substance.

Letting go of self is incredibly freeing. Less focus on self frees us to be what we truly are without being constrained by ideas or beliefs about who or what we are, or should be. Less self-focus also makes room in our brain for more "other-focus." This enhances our relationships by allowing us to fully invest in others without needing to think about the impact on self. For example, if we meet someone, we can stay focused on that person rather than self. We all know what goes through our minds when we meet someone new. We think, "Will he like me?" Or maybe, "She won't be interested in anything I have to say." Just think how good it would feel not to be chained to constantly evaluating life in terms of self-focused thinking. This is one potential benefit of learning to let go of self. Less self-focus also allows us to put more of our mental energy into giving love and being compassionate. Our world can certainly use more of both. Finally, less general investment in self helps us see that those negative cognitions and schemas are really not so powerful after all. At that point, we frequently can just observe them floating on our thought stream. Like a twig on a stream, they move along and don't cause a disruption in our emotional state.

I hope you find the idea of mindfulness intriguing and will consider giving this practice a try. One way to do this is through meditation; I discuss this in Chapter 10. Another approach is to use the secular evidence-based psychological treatments discussed below.

Mindfulness-based stress reduction (MBSR)

MBSR was developed by Dr. Jon Kabat-Zinn at the University of Massachusetts Medical Center.[282] MBSR is a group therapy that includes education about stress, coping strategies, and assertiveness in addition to mindfulness. The mindfulness component includes sitting meditation, a body scan (focusing on bodily sensations), and hatha yoga. Furthermore, MBSR involves the cultivation of a number of attitudes, including becoming an impartial witness to one's own experience and accepting things as they actually are in the present moment.[282] More information is available on the University of Massachusetts Medical School Center for Mindfulness website (http://www.umassmed.edu/cfm/home).

Considerable evidence supports the effectiveness of MBSR on several psychological outcomes, including studies of social anxiety disorder,[283] generalized anxiety disorder,[284] and insomnia.[285] MBSR has been shown to improve psychological functioning among individuals with a large variety of medical disorders,[286-290] including fibromyalgia,[291, 292] cancer,[286, 290, 293-296] HIV,[297] and pain[287, 291, 298-301] as well as healthy individuals.[302] There is extensive evidence that MBSR can be effective for coping with the general stresses of life as well as those stresses associated with illness.[283, 286–290, 298, 301, 303–310] However, one analysis of several studies suggested that some benefits could be relatively modest.[311]

Mindfulness-based cognitive therapy (MBCT)

MBCT is a group therapy that was developed by Zindel Segal, Mark Williams, and John Teasdale.[312] MBCT is based on MBSR and combines the principles of cognitive therapy with those of mindfulness to prevent relapse of depression.[312] It uses the principles of mindfulness as described above as well as the "differential activation" hypothesis developed by Teasdale.[313] This theory suggests that individuals who have had prior depressive episodes are vulnerable to relapse because depressive thinking patterns can easily be reactivated and thus precipitate a new episode. The aim of MBCT is to teach individuals how to disengage from these thought patterns linked to relapse by practicing mindfulness. MBCT, like MBSR, utilizes secular mindfulness techniques, including seated meditation. The program specifically teaches people to recognize deteriorating mood with the aim of disengaging from patterns of ruminative, negative thought that contribute to relapse.[312]

As with MBSR, many investigations have evaluated the effectiveness of MBCT. Evidence indicates that MBCT is beneficial for unipolar depression relapse prevention,[314–319] generalized anxiety disorder,[284] panic disorder,[320] hypochondriasis,[321] and social phobia.[322] The strongest evidence is for relapse prevention in major depression. A recent analysis of several studies[323] concluded that MBCT was significantly better than usual care for reducing relapses in those with three or more prior depressive episodes. The authors also concluded that MBCT's effectiveness for relapse prevention was similar to that of antidepressants and that adding MBCT to other treatments could be useful for reducing symptoms. A subsequent study[319] provided strong evidence that MBCT offers protection against relapse equal to that of maintenance antidepressant treatment. While MBCT has mostly been used for relapse prevention in depression, there is also evidence of its effectiveness for those still experiencing symptoms.[324] Finally, there is preliminary evidence that MBCT may change sleep in ways similar to treatment with antidepressants.[325]

Summary of mindfulness therapies

As you can see, there is a lot of evidence supporting the effectiveness of mindfulness treatment approaches. A recent review and analysis of several studies[326] concluded that mindfulness-based therapy improves symptoms of anxiety and depression across a wide range of severity. Furthermore, preliminary evidence suggests that MBCT is feasible for use in bipolar disorder and may decrease symptoms of anxiety and depression in this condition.[327–329] Finally, evidence is accumulating in support of the use of mindfulness interventions for suicide prevention;[330–333] additional research is being conducted in this area.[334]

Despite the evidence described above, a number of unanswered questions remain about mindfulness-based treatments. First, many studies have had methodological limitations, which means that the results suggest but do not prove effectiveness. Another question is whether these approaches work equally well for everyone. It is very likely that mindfulness-based treatments will work better for some people than others. Right now we don't know what characteristics are associated with the best response. So, mindfulness might not work well for you. Also, you will notice that I have often used the expression *mindfulness practice*. For mindfulness to be most helpful, you should have an ongoing daily practice. This typically means some form of daily meditation. Thus, mindfulness approaches are not likely to be a good choice for those who cannot develop a consistent ongoing practice.

Even though we don't know everything about them yet, I strongly recommend mindfulness-based approaches as a component of your recovery program. If MBSR or MBCT is not available in your area, you can begin a mindfulness practice as a complementary strategy. I will discuss this in Chapter 10.

Other psychotherapy methods

The rest of this chapter will discuss some additional psychotherapy methods that you may encounter. Some of these have been included because there is evidence for their effectiveness; however, please be aware that they are not all widely available. Please don't be discouraged if some of the following options are not available in your area. The important thing is to start treatment with a licensed therapist and decide together with her or him on the best approach for your specific situation.

Family-focused therapy (FFT)

FFT consists of psychoeducation, communication training, and problem-solving skills training for individuals with bipolar spectrum disorders and their families. FFT is typically administered in twenty-one sessions over a nine-month period.[335] Educational components focus on helping families learn about the nature and treatment of bipolar disorder as well as the concept that **mood episodes** come about as an interaction among genetic, biological, familial, and social-environmental factors.[335] FFT also focuses on relapse prevention, which involves identifying both relapse triggers and early warning signs of mood recurrence as well as developing a plan of action to implement if symptoms increase. FFT includes training in family communication and problem solving. Multiple studies suggest that FFT, when provided along with medication, is effective for controlling symptoms and assists patients with adhering to their medication regimen in bipolar disorder.[336–338]

Group therapy

Group therapy is not a specific therapy but a general category that can include a variety of therapeutic approaches. In group therapy, one (or sometimes more) therapist leads a therapy session involving several individuals. These group sessions may have a variety of themes. Some are focused on a specific disorder and others might be aimed at a symptom, such as anger. Psychoeducation (see below) is often provided in a group setting. Group approaches offer the advantage of learning from the experiences of other attendees; however, this benefit may be offset by a lack of individual attention. Also, some people are uncomfortable discussing personal information and feelings with others. So, group therapy isn't for everyone. One approach is to start with individual therapy and then eventually make the transition to a group setting. Also, individual and group approaches can be used simultaneously.

Interpersonal therapy (IPT)

As described in Chapter 4, IPT focuses on problems in interpersonal relationships that may contribute to depression as well as those problems that may be caused by the depression. Multiple studies have confirmed the effectiveness of IPT for the acute and maintenance treatment of depression.[205]

IPT is a time-limited, here-and-now therapy that focuses on developing an understanding of the interpersonal problems in one's life and then developing concrete solutions.[205] The early stages of treatment focus on learning about depression and identifying the major interpersonal problem area. After that, the focus is on the development and implementation of specific strategies to solve the problem. Most of the time, therapy involves working on interpersonal issues. It is not necessary to have a therapist who practices IPT to do this work. Almost any therapy approach can facilitate the exploration of relationship issues.

Interpersonal and social rhythm therapy (IPSRT)

IPSRT is psychotherapy designed specifically for the treatment for bipolar disorder.[339, 340] As the name suggests, IPSRT is based on the interpersonal psychotherapy model of depression as discussed above and in Chapter 4. The other component of this approach is based on a model of bipolar disorder suggesting that individuals with this condition have a genetic predisposition to circadian rhythm and sleep-wake cycle abnormalities.[339] Further, positive and negative life events are thought to cause disruptions in social and circadian rhythms that can lead to the development of symptoms.[339] IPSRT aims to prevent these disruptions by combining IPT and behavior techniques to help individuals regularize their daily routines, diminish interpersonal problems, adhere to medication regimens, and mitigate circadian and sleep-wake cycle vulnerabilities.[339] Studies suggest that this approach is effective, along with medication, for preventing relapse[341] and increasing occupational functioning[342] in bipolar disorder.

Marital and family therapy (MFT)

As the name suggests, these therapies focus specifically on relationships with domestic partners or the entire family unit. Mood disorders can disrupt family relationships, and family discord can contribute to the onset of mood episodes. Thus, addressing these issues can be an important component of recovery.

Problem-solving therapy (PST)

PST is a brief therapy that typically involves six to twelve sessions.[37] It combines elements of IPT and CT,[37] which are described in this chapter. There is some evidence for the effectiveness of this approach for those with mild depressive symptoms.[37]

Psychodynamic psychotherapy

Broadly speaking, psychodynamic therapies originated from psychoanalytic theories and treatment strategies developed by Freud and others. Psychodynamic treatments typically focus on psychological factors that may contribute to the expression of depressive symptoms.[37] These factors include personality development, internal conflicts related to guilt or shame, the management of anxiety, and repressed or unacceptable impulses. Developmental psychological causes, such as a poor relationship between the child and emotional caretakers that may result in problems with self-esteem or emotional regulation, may also be addressed.

Psychodynamic treatment is usually a longer-term approach, with aims extending beyond immediate symptom relief.[37] These aims may include the modification of underlying psychological conflicts that may contribute to the development of mood symptoms.

Psychoeducation

Psychoeducation is not really psychotherapy in the traditional sense. It is a process of providing education and information about psychiatric disorders. Typically mental health clinicians provide this instruction to individuals who are suffering from psychiatric disorders. Many times family members are also included. Information may be provided in written or lecture formats. This book is psychoeducation. Research indicates that psychoeducation is an effective intervention.[343]

Summary of psychological approaches

As this chapter illustrates, there is compelling evidence that psychotherapeutic approaches are effective for both unipolar and bipolar spectrum disorders (along with medication). For mild to moderate unipolar spectrum illness, psychotherapy alone may be adequate treatment, especially if combined with some of the complementary approaches discussed in Chapter 10. However, the benefits of combining psychotherapy and complementary approaches have not been studied, so it is just my opinion that there is likely to be an additive effect. For bipolar spectrum illness, the evidence supports using psychotherapy along with medication. Whether or not psychotherapy alone could control mild bipolar spectrum symptoms (cyclothymia and bipolar disorder NOS) is currently unknown.

In my view, there is particularly strong evidence for the benefits of CT and MBCT for mood disorders and MBSR for general stress and coping with illness. However, the choice of a therapy approach needs to be based on individual needs. For example, if you are experiencing significant interpersonal stress or relationship problems, then IPT or MFT would most likely be the treatment of choice. Furthermore, more than one approach may often be combined in practice. My opinion is that psychoeducation is always helpful. That's why I wrote this book.

I have emphasized mindfulness-based theories and approaches to some extent in this book (also see Chapters 4 and 10). I made this choice because of the extensive literature that supports these strategies for treating mood disorders as well as coping with the stresses of life. There is new evidence that mindfulness practices appear to affect brain function as demonstrated by both electroencephalographic and functional imaging studies[344, 345] as well as specifically change the brain's response to sadness.[346] A recent investigation also suggests a positive impact on immune function.[306] Finally, a study indicated that mindfulness training is associated with changes in gray matter concentration in brain regions involved in learning and memory processes, emotion regulation, self-referential processing, and perspective taking.[347] Despite all the positive evidence, many studies have a number of limitations[323, 344, 348] and more research is needed. Nonetheless, my take on these studies is that while all of the various effects of mindfulness have not yet been absolutely proven, there is convincing evidence that many people benefit from this approach. Further, I am not aware of any evidence of potential adverse effects. Thus, I recommend that you consider adding a mindfulness practice to your recovery plan.

Whatever psychotherapy approach you may pursue, it is important to keep in mind that these strategies require your active participation. I like the analogy of working with a coach to develop athletic ability. No matter how good the coach is, no improvement in skills will occur without lots of practice. Sitting in a therapist's office once a week is likely to have limited benefit unless it is accompanied by effort on a daily basis to implement changes. I hope you will consider psychotherapy either as monotherapy or in combination with biological treatments. I think that we all have psychological imperfections and that recognizing these and implementing change is the best formula for staying symptom free as well as achieving lasting happiness.

10

Complementary Approaches to Recovery

This chapter describes a number of recovery strategies that may be helpful in addition to, or in some cases instead of, treatments provided by mental health or medical professionals. I strongly encourage you to consider some of these approaches to maximize your chances of getting well and staying in recovery.

What's in this chapter? I include some approaches that might be broadly considered complementary or alternative medicine. Some are strategies that you can implement on your own, or at least without the assistance of a medical or mental health professional. So, some of what you'll find here could be considered "self-help." Maybe the best description is a selection of tools for your recovery toolbox. The tools I have included are those for which there is enough evidence of benefit that I recommend that you consider using them. I also discuss some options for which there is considerably less evidence for benefit. They are included because you may hear about them from other sources and perhaps my review will be helpful.

Most of what is in this chapter may be most useful to consider as an add-on or "adjunctive" treatment. By that I mean strategies that you might consider in addition to medication or traditional psychotherapy. However, some approaches may be sufficient as monotherapy for those with very mild depressive spectrum disorders. In this book, I use the term *complementary* for all of these strategies. Finally, as I have said elsewhere in this book, please develop a comprehensive recovery plan. A comprehensive plan includes as many strategies as are appropriate for your situation. Adding some of the approaches in this chapter to more conventional treatments is one way to make your plan comprehensive.

Acupuncture

Acupuncture is a traditional Chinese medicine approach. Some studies have found that acupuncture is effective in treating **depression**. These studies are difficult to evaluate, though, because some are published in Asian languages and there is significant variation in the acupuncture techniques used.[241] A number of studies, [349–352] but not all,[353] suggest possible benefit; however, recent reviews of the evidence have concluded that the benefit is uncertain[354–357] and that there is insufficient evidence to recommend this treatment approach for depression.[241, 358] Nonetheless, it is possible that future rigorous studies may demonstrate a benefit.

Aerobic exercise

Some studies have shown that higher levels of physical activity are generally associated with lower levels of depression.[359] Further, a fairly large body of literature suggests that aerobic exercise may be associated with reduced depressive symptoms.[359] There is also some evidence for the benefits of nonaerobic exercise.[359] Reviews of the evidence published in scientific journals generally conclude that exercise is beneficial for depression.[359–363] However, further research is needed to establish the degree of effectiveness.[362, 363] Nonetheless, there is some indication that aerobic exercise may be similar in effectiveness to treatments with either antidepressants or psychotherapy.[359, 364] It has been proposed that exercise might be beneficial for bipolar disorder,[365, 366] but studies are lacking.

There are a number of unanswered questions in regard to the extent of the therapeutic benefit of exercise for depression; however, there is fairly convincing evidence of some benefit and exercise certainly has general health benefits. Therefore, implementing an exercise program is definitely worth trying for depression. It may be reasonable to try exercise alone for very mild depression, and exercise should be considered as an adjunctive treatment for more severe episodes of depression. Although exercise has not been studied as a treatment for bipolar disorder, given the general health benefits it seems worth trying.

As discussed in Chapter 4, the endorphin hypothesis suggests that exercise releases endorphin **neurotransmitters**, which results in the decrease of depressive symptoms. This hypothesis has been based on the idea that the runner's high occurs as a result of endorphin release.

Like all interventions, exercise is not without risk. Please check with your primary health care provider before starting an exercise program. In regard to how much aerobic exercise is needed for treating depression, one recommendation is for three 30-minute sessions per week of aerobic exercise at 60%–80% of maximum heart rate for at least eight weeks.[367] For some individuals, it may be necessary to start at a lower level and increase to that intensity. I said above that it might be reasonable to try exercise alone for treating mild depression. However, if you do start to improve quickly, then other approaches such as psychotherapy or medication must be considered. Also, if you previously had depression that required medication or psychotherapy, then trying exercise alone may not be a good strategy. I strongly recommend that you seek a professional evaluation even if you want to try exercise alone. That way you can discuss whether exercise alone is a good option for your specific situation. Also, if you find that other treatments are needed, then you will already have a relationship established with a provider.

Dietary supplements

In this section, I will discuss a group of treatment approaches that fall into the general category of dietary, food, or nutritional supplements; another definition might be "natural health products." Some countries may define several of these supplements as drugs. For ease of discussion, I use the term *supplement* to encompass all of these labels. Supplements are generally substances intended to provide nutrients that may be missing or may not be consumed in sufficient quantities in an individual's regular diet.

Folate

Folate is a B vitamin found in some vegetables and fruits. Folate is necessary for the brain to synthesize the neurotransmitters **norepinephrine**, **serotonin**, and **dopamine**,[368] which are involved in **mood disorders** (see Chapter 4). There is evidence that folate deficiency may be associated with the occurrence of depression, poor response to antidepressants, and **relapse** of illness.[369] The three commercially available folate formulations that can be taken as a supplement are folic acid, 5-methyltetrahydrofolate (5-MTHF; also known as methylfolate and L-methylfolate), and folinic acid.[369]

Folate supplementation has been studied as an adjunctive and monotherapy treatment for **unipolar** depression. These studies have a number of limitations but suggest possible benefit, particularly for those with low folate levels.[369] Therefore, folate has been recommended for consideration as an adjunctive treatment for unipolar depression.[241, 368, 369] There may be some side effects of folate supplementation, however, including increasing the cancer risk, masking vitamin B12 deficiency, and worsening depressive symptoms.[368, 369] Thus, a decision to take folate supplements should be made only in consultation with a health care provider.

Omega-3 fatty acids

Omega-3 fatty acids are a family of unsaturated fatty acids that are essential for normal growth and health. These substances are not manufactured by the body and must be taken in as part of a person's diet. The two omega-3 fatty acids that have been most studied are eicosapentaenoic acid (EPA) and docosahexaenoic acid (DHA).[370] Most of the health benefits that have been demonstrated with omega-3 fatty acids are specifically associated with these two acids. The most efficient natural dietary source of EPA and DHA is fish and shellfish. Another omega-3 fatty acid, linolenic acid, is available from plant sources but requires more enzymatic steps to be used by the body than EPA.[370]

Studies have shown that omega-3 fatty acids have a number of medical benefits, many involving the health of the heart and circulatory system.[371] American Heart Association (AHA) experts have concluded that omega-3 fatty acids may positively influence cardiovascular health in several ways, including decreasing the risk for irregular heartbeat, decreasing triglyceride levels, lowering blood pressure, and reducing inflammation.[371] Thus, the AHA recommends consumption of these substances.

There is evidence that omega-3 fatty acids may have benefits for the prevention of mood disorders as well as the reduction of symptoms.[370] In regard to prevention, studies have found that higher fish and seafood consumption is associated with lower rates of major depression, postpartum depression, and bipolar disorder.[370] A number of studies have evaluated the possibility that omega-3 fatty acids might have treatment benefits for depressive and bipolar spectrum disorders. Most of these investigations have assessed whether these substances might contribute to symptom reduction when used as an adjunctive treatment.[241] The results are difficult to interpret because of different methods used and different omega-3 fatty acids studied.[241, 370] Nonetheless, there is some evidence that omega-3 fatty acids may help treat unipolar and bipolar depression, but not all studies have demonstrated benefit.[241, 368, 370, 372, 373] For example, one major study[373] found no benefit for depression among patients with coronary artery disease when omega-3 fatty acids were added to treatment with the antidepressant sertraline. Perinatal depression is depression in the mother during pregnancy or after childbirth. Omega-3 treatment has also been evaluated for this condition by a number of studies, but the results are inconclusive.[374]

In summary, there is some evidence that omega-3 fatty acid supplementation may be beneficial for unipolar depression, but the jury is still out. Further, we do not currently know which dosage levels and which specific omega-3 acids should be used.[370] Despite the lack of conclusive evidence for benefit, a current recommendation[241, 368, 370] is to *consider* omega-3 fatty acids as an adjunctive treatment for major depression. Specifically, adding EPA or the combination of EPA and DHA to other treatments is suggested.[241] One reason for the recommendation is the evidence for health benefits, aside from the possibility of improving mood.[375, 376] Further, levels of omega-3 fatty acids tend to be low in the typical American diet.[370] Finally, the risk of adverse effects appears low; however, at very high doses, omega-3 fatty acids may have an anticoagulant effect[370] that might put one at risk of bleeding. Thus, a decision to add omega-3 fatty acids to your treatment should be discussed with your health care provider.

SAM-e

S-adenosyl methionine (SAM-e) is a naturally occurring molecule present in all living human cells that plays a key role in the synthesis of the neurotransmitters norepinephrine, serotonin, and dopamine.[368] There is some evidence that SAM-e may have benefits for unipolar depression.[241] However, the strongest evidence is for intravenous or intramuscular administration,[377] which limits the usefulness of this agent. There is less evidence supporting the use of oral SAM-e.[377] SAM-e may cause such side effects as gastrointestinal symptoms, headache, anxiety, fatigue, insomnia, tachycardia, and restlessness.[368]

Based on the current evidence, I cannot recommend SAM-e as a treatment for depression. However, this recommendation may change if additional studies suggesting benefit are completed. See your health care provider for the latest information.

St. John's wort

St. John's wort (*Hypericum perforatum*) is a plant that has been used to treat depression. St. John's wort contains a number of substances. Two of these substances in particular, hypericin and hyperforin, are thought to have actions similar to antidepressant medications.[378] Multiple studies have examined the effectiveness of St. John's wort for mild or more severe depression. Some of these, but not all, have suggested benefit.[241] Expert reviews[241, 378] of these investigations conclude that there is a possibility of effectiveness for mild depression but that St. John's wort is likely not effective for more severe cases.

In addition to limited evidence of effectiveness, there is a significant risk of interactions with a number of prescribed medications.[241, 378, 379] Specifically, St. John's wort can reduce the efficacy of medications such as antiretroviral medications, immunosuppressants, anticancer agents, anticoagulants, oral contraceptives, and hormone replacement therapy.[241] Further, there are concerns about adverse effects of combining St. John's wort with the SSRI class of prescribed antidepressants.[379, 380]

In summary, the evidence provides little support for the use of St. John's wort, at least when compared with other approaches discussed in this and other chapters. IF YOU DO TAKE ST. JOHN'S WORT, BE SURE TO DISCUSS POSSIBLE DRUG INTERACTIONS WITH YOUR MEDICAL AND MENTAL HEALTH PRESCRIBERS.

Mindfulness meditation

Mindfulness approaches are discussed extensively in Chapters 4 and 9. In this section, I will talk specifically about mindfulness meditation because it is an approach that you can implement without the assistance of a health care professional.

The word *meditation* generally means a practice by which one trains her or his mind to enter a specific mode of consciousness or internal state. There are a variety of different meditation practices. As the name suggests, mindfulness meditation involves focusing awareness on the present experience on a moment-to-moment basis. Mindfulness involves developing the ability to focus attention on the here and now and observing each moment with curiosity, openness, and acceptance. It is particularly important to develop a nonjudgmental awareness of one's thinking patterns. The concept of mindfulness meditation was developed from Eastern religious and philosophical thought, particularly Buddhism. That said, there is nothing inherently religious about meditation in general or mindfulness in particular. Today, persons with many different religious beliefs, as well as those who aren't religious at all, practice mindfulness meditation. The evidence for the effectiveness of mindfulness is discussed in Chapter 9.

Should you try a mindfulness meditation practice? I think there is enough evidence in support of this general approach that it should be considered as another tool in your comprehensive recovery toolbox. How do you go about starting a mindfulness practice?

One specific nonreligious program is mindfulness-based stress reduction (MBSR), discussed in Chapter 9. MBSR has been extensively studied, and its effectiveness has been demonstrated for the reduction of both medical and psychological symptoms. Information is available on the University of Massachusetts Medical School Center for Mindfulness website (http://www.umassmed.edu/cfm/home). In addition, many mindfulness training programs now exist, and a variety of books and other media products are available. The quality of some of these is difficult to evaluate. Further, it is impossible to know whether minor differences in programs result in differences in effectiveness. Nonetheless, implementing some type of mindfulness practice is a recovery strategy worth your consideration. Please see the self-help book section later in this chapter for specific recommendations that may help you initiate a mindfulness practice.

Religion and spirituality

The aim of this section is not to advocate for any particular religious point of view or belief system. Religious belief and affiliation, or lack thereof, are obviously individual choices, and I am not arguing for or against religion and spirituality. However, a handful of scientific studies have looked for possible relationships between depression and religious involvement. Since the goal of this book is to provide evidence-based information to support your recovery, I will briefly discuss the possible role of religion.

Some of the research that has been done suggests that religious involvement may be inversely associated with depression.[381–384] In other words, more religious involvement may be related to less depression. However, religious involvement can be difficult to study for a number of reasons. As one example, it could be the social support from belonging to a religious group that has an impact on depression rather than the actual religious practice. That said, a recent study[385] found that frequency of prayer or meditation, not church attendance, predicted lower hopelessness and depression severity scores in older adults treated for depression. This investigation argues against the social support idea, but it is only one study. The conclusion is that we do not have enough research to understand the relationship between religious involvement and depression. Still, the few studies that have been done suggest that a religious or spiritual practice could be a recovery tool for those who are so inclined.

Social support

Social support refers to your network of relationships with other people. A number of psychosocial stressors have been shown to be related to depression.[386, 387] One of the most important factors may be level of social support. Inadequate social support is associated with depression,[386, 388–391] and higher levels of social support have been associated with better outcomes.[392] Deficits in social support have also been associated with relapse and delayed recovery in bipolar depression.[393–395] These studies suggest that one of the most important steps you can take to foster your recovery is to make sure that you have adequate social support in your life.

So, where do you start? My recommendation is to first evaluate your current level of support. One way to go about this is to take a look at both the quantity and quality of your current relationships. Quantity, of course, refers to the number of relationships; however, perhaps more important is the quality. Quality is more difficult to define because there are many facets to each of our relationships. For our purposes, let's define quality as the amount of support that you feel you get from each relationship. Of course, this probably varies over time, but just try to think of an average level of support over the last few months. I think it can be helpful to use a numerical scale when doing ratings. I invite you to use that approach in this process. In the following exercise, please rate each of your important relationships on a scale from −5 to +5. A score of +5 means that you feel you are getting the maximum social support possible from a relationship. In contrast, a −5 means that the relationship feels like it is draining your emotional resources rather than adding to them. One important point: This scale is not intended to say anything at all about how much you care for others or how much they care about you. It is simply a rating of the level of support. For example, you may have a best friend whom you love very much; however, he may be going through a difficult time and you are providing support for him. Right now, your providing support may feel like an emotional drain, even though he is one of your dearest friends. Sometimes

I find the analogy of a battery useful. Is the relationship charging or discharging your battery? One final point: Please do not limit your list of relationships to individuals. You may belong to groups or organizations that are either supporting or draining—for example, clubs, groups, or classes that you attend. Now please complete the following exercise.

Evaluation of your level of social support

List the ten relationships that you currently feel are most important in your life. These can be individuals or groups. Then rate the average amount of emotional and social support you feel you have received from that relationship during the past six months. Negative numbers mean that you are giving more support than you are receiving. Positive numbers reflect support you are getting. Zero means neutral—the relationship is neither charging nor discharging your emotional battery. The social support evaluation is included in this book as Form 10.1 and is also available as a PDF file that can be freely downloaded from our website (http://www.bullpub.com).

Form 10.1   Social support evaluation form

Relationship
(name of individual or group)   Level of support you receive

Relationship											
_____	−5	−4	−3	−2	−1	0	1	2	3	4	5
_____	−5	−4	−3	−2	−1	0	1	2	3	4	5
_____	−5	−4	−3	−2	−1	0	1	2	3	4	5
_____	−5	−4	−3	−2	−1	0	1	2	3	4	5
_____	−5	−4	−3	−2	−1	0	1	2	3	4	5
_____	−5	−4	−3	−2	−1	0	1	2	3	4	5
_____	−5	−4	−3	−2	−1	0	1	2	3	4	5
_____	−5	−4	−3	−2	−1	0	1	2	3	4	5
_____	−5	−4	−3	−2	−1	0	1	2	3	4	5
_____	−5	−4	−3	−2	−1	0	1	2	3	4	5

Total score (add all
of the numbers)

Now that you have completed your evaluation, let's talk about the results. What is your total score? If it's highly positive, with lots of +4s and +5s, then you are probably receiving adequate social and emotional support. That said, it still might be beneficial for you to increase your support further. You don't have to worry about damaging your emotional batteries by overcharging them. If your scores are mainly +2 or lower, there may be opportunity for improvement.

What about negative numbers? If you have one or more relationships that seem to be discharging your emotional battery, you may be wondering what to do about those. Often there aren't easy answers. Relationships are complex. However, just being aware is a good starting point. If you are working with a therapist, then perhaps you will want to explore in therapy why a certain relationship feels draining. If not, introspection may help you sort out what is going on. Maybe there are ways that you can continue to be supportive to the other person that do not feel so draining. Often, helping others can be very therapeutic for us if we are able to change our perspective so that it feels positive rather than draining. Mindfulness meditation (discussed above) may help in this regard.

Besides looking at any negative numbers, the other approach is to increase the score for relationships you already have or add new relationships with positive numbers. Let's talk about increasing the positive score for existing relationships first.

Sometimes we don't receive as much support as possible from our relationships simply because we don't ask. Many of us think that we have to "be strong" or shouldn't "burden" others with our problems. If that applies to you, then I invite you to reconsider. We all need emotional support and it is unrealistic to always be the "strong one." Further, asking for help can make our relationships stronger. When we ask for support, we are being authentic and honest. This is much more intimate than keeping our feelings bottled up and not letting the other person know what is really going on with us. I invite you to consider assessing how well you are doing with asking for the support you need.

Another way to increase support might be to devote more time to the relationship. Some of us tend to isolate ourselves when we feel bad emotionally, and this is usually not helpful for recovery. Perhaps you could

Table 10.1   Options to increase social and emotional support

- Take an adult enrichment class on a topic that interests you from your local school district or college.
- Join a religious or spiritual group or organization.
- Join a health club or sports team.
- Get to know your neighbors.
- Volunteer with an organization.
- Join a support group.
- Get a companion animal.
- Become a "regular" at a local coffee shop.

spend more time with individuals on your list. Or, for groups, maybe you could increase your participation or involvement.

Finally, consider adding some new relationships that could be supportive. Table 10.1 lists some ideas for you to consider. One option is to join a support group. It may be especially beneficial to become a member of a support group for individuals with mood disorders. An Internet search is a good way to find out what is available in your area. Also see the resources listed at the end of this book and in Chapter 5.

Companion animals

The preceding section focused on emotional support from humans. Companion animals also provide caring and comfort to many. In some ways, animals are more reliable than humans. Think about the dogs you have known. They love us no matter what. They don't care if we have a bad hair day or aren't in the best mood; our canine companions will always be there for us. Of course, other animals can also be great companions, but I think the love that dogs have for humans is a great example of what we can get from our furry friends. Still, it's a two-way street: We give our companion animals a lot too. This can be especially true if we take in an animal from a shelter or rescue organization. This is just my opinion, but I think that adopting an animal that needs a home is an act of compassion that may help you recover. That said, adopting an animal and taking on the responsibility of caring for a pet are very personal decisions and are not feasible for everyone. Please think carefully about whether it is a good option for you. Talk with your loved ones and maybe your treatment team before making a decision.

There isn't enough research, but there is some evidence that interacting with animals is beneficial for humans. Benefits may include enhanced socialization; reduced levels of stress, anxiety, and loneliness; improved mood; and development of recreation skills.[396-399] Although this section mostly represents my opinion, there is some preliminary evidence that having an animal friend may support your recovery.

Self-help books and websites

Many excellent resources are available that complement this book, including other books and online sources of information. However, there is unfortunately a lot of information out there that may not be helpful and, even worse, may be inaccurate. I have listed recommended websites and books in Appendixes B and C, respectively. My lists are not meant to be exhaustive; there are many good resources available that I did not include. However, please use appropriate caution when considering sources of information other than those I have listed. One way to do this is evaluate the credentials of the author or owner of the site. Is she or he a trained professional and/ or affiliated with an organization, such as a university or hospital? For a website, is it an official site of a professional organization or government entity? Another good approach is to ask a member of your treatment team about books or sites you find.

Along these lines, an important question is whether self-help books are effective. Of course, what "effectiveness" means may vary from one book to another. For books that provide information (like this one), effectiveness might be measured by how much one's knowledge is increased after reading it. However, some books are directly aimed at decreasing mood symptoms.

Is there any evidence that this approach, known as "bibliotherapy," actually works? The answer is that, in fact, there is some evidence for its effectiveness for depressive symptoms.[400–403] Still, there are many unanswered questions. For example, we don't know whether bibliotherapy works equally well for everyone. Further, many of the available books have not been studied. I think the conclusion is that some books may be helpful for some people in terms of symptom reduction. As I've said throughout this book, I recommend doing everything possible to get well. Thus, I encourage you to consider adding some of the books listed in Appendix C to your recovery toolbox. Even if reading them does not directly contribute to symptom reduction, I believe the knowledge you gain can help guide your recovery. Some also have the potential to help you beyond recovery by providing a pathway to a more satisfying and happier life. Before ending this chapter, I want to specifically mention some books in that category along with others that I think may be particularly worth reading (see Appendix C for complete citations).

The first recommendation is *An Unquiet Mind: A Memoir of Moods and Madness* by Kay Redfield Jamison. Dr. Jamison is Professor of Psychiatry at the Johns Hopkins University School of Medicine, and she also has bipolar disorder. Her book provides a compelling and intimate account of living with this illness from the unique perspective of a mental health professional. While this book is not aimed at helping you lead a happier life or reduce your symptoms, I think it can be particularly helpful in a couple of ways. It can help those with bipolar disorder avoid feeling like they are the only ones with this condition. It can seem that way if you don't personally know anyone else with the illness. More important, Jamison's story is a story of courage. I find it inspiring and hope that you will too.

Another recommendation is the classic *Feeling Good: The New Mood Therapy* by David Burns. This book was originally published in 1980 and has been a best seller. It is one book that has been studied, and there is evidence that reading it and completing the included exercises can help reduce depressive symptoms. There is a companion text, also by Dr. Burns, *The Feeling Good Handbook*. Both books explain cognitive behavior therapy (see Chapter 9 for more information) in a simple and easy-to-read fashion. Most important, both books provide a model of cognitive behavior therapy that it is easy to understand and incorporate into your life. These books contain many useful exercises to help you include cognitive therapy methods in your overall recovery plan. Either or both of these books can definitely provide information to help guide your recovery and may directly contribute to a reduction in depressive symptoms.

I highly recommend several books about mindfulness. Mindfulness refers to a practice that usually involves meditation and is aimed at developing the capacity to live in the present moment. Practicing mindfulness also facilitates the development of compassion for self and others. Finally, mindfulness practice can enable us to detach from many negative thoughts and emotions associated with mood disorders. I discuss mindfulness in much more detail in Chapters 4, 9, and 10. As I said in those chapters, there is compelling evidence that a mindfulness practice can help decrease symptoms of depression and anxiety as well as increase general feelings of psychological well-being, happiness, and life satisfaction. Therefore, I encourage you to consider adding a mindfulness practice to your recovery plan. The following recommendations can help to guide you in that process and may be beneficial for both reducing symptoms and increasing life satisfaction and happiness.

The first title is *Full Catastrophe Living: Using the Wisdom of Your Body and Mind to Face Stress, Pain, and Illness* by Jon Kabat-Zinn. Dr. Kabat-Zinn is Professor of Medicine Emeritus and founding director of the Stress Reduction Clinic and the Center for Mindfulness in Medicine, Health Care, and Society at the University of Massachusetts Medical School. As described in Chapter 9, he developed the psychotherapy approach known as mindfulness-based stress reduction (MBSR). His book provides a description of the main components of MBSR, such as yoga and mindfulness meditation, along with instructions on how to do these techniques on your own. The book also provides statistical information on how well this program works and case studies. Two other books by Kabat-Zinn are *Coming to Our Senses: Healing Ourselves and the World through Mindfulness* and *Wherever You Go, There You Are: Mindfulness Meditation in Everyday Life*. Both are worth reading to enhance your understanding of the relationship

Table 10.2   Summary of complementary strategies

Strategy	Recommendation	Conditions
Acupuncture	Not recommended	N/A
Aerobic exercise*	Monotherapy	Mild unipolar depression/medical and emotional health
	Adjunctive	All mood disorders/medical and emotional health (effectiveness evidence for unipolar illness only)
Folate*	Possibly as adjunctive	Unipolar depression (consider risk of adverse effects)
Mindfulness meditation	Adjunctive	All mood disorders/general emotional health (most effectiveness evidence for unipolar illness)
Omega-3 fatty acids*	Adjunctive	All mood disorders/medical health (most effectiveness evidence for unipolar illness)
Religion	Adjunctive	All mood disorders/general spiritual health (very limited effectiveness evidence for unipolar illness) and spirituality
SAM-e	Not recommended	N/A
Self-help books	Adjunctive	All mood disorders/general emotional health
Social support	Adjunctive	All mood disorders/general emotional health
St. John's wort	Not recommended	N/A

*Discuss with your health care provider before starting.

between mindfulness and emotional and spiritual well-being as well as the practice of meditation for its own sake. Finally, please consider reading *The Mindful Way through Depression: Freeing Yourself from Chronic Unhappiness*. Drs. Mark Williams, John Teasdale, and Zindel Segal along with Dr. Kabat-Zinn wrote this book. It is aimed specifically at implementing a mindfulness practice to reduce depressive symptoms.

Summary of alternative and adjunctive recovery strategies

This chapter has covered a lot of territory. Table 10.2 provides a summary of my recommendations. Please keep in mind that new research results are reported every day. Thus, new information might change my opinion of some of these recovery approaches. Please ask your mental health providers for the latest data. Finally, please consider implementing some of these recommended strategies as part of your comprehensive recovery plan.

11

Starting Treatment

THE GOAL OF THIS SECTION IS TO PROVIDE information you will need if
you are starting treatment for the first time. Information for those already
in treatment is given in Chapters 13 and 14. If you are already receiving
treatment, reading this section will likely still be useful because it provides
a good starting point in thinking about treatment in general. Finally, the
information in Chapter 13 is particularly important for those starting treatment, so please be sure to read that chapter too. Please also start a **mood**
chart to track your progress (see Chapter 13).

The limitations of the information provided in this section are
similar to those we have discussed earlier in the book. THIS CHAPTER
CANNOT REPLACE ADVICE AND TREATMENT FROM A
QUALIFIED PROFESSIONAL. I PRESENT GENERAL TREAT-
MENT GUIDELINES THAT MAY OR MAY NOT BE APPROPRI-
ATE FOR YOUR SITUATION. ONLY A MEDICAL OR MENTAL
HEALTH PROFESSIONAL CAN MAKE A SPECIFIC RECOM-
MENDATION. There are just too many variables to take into account.
That said, the goal of this section is to provide the information you will

need to work with a professional to determine the best option in your particular situation.

Which initial treatment approach?

Please note that this chapter is written primarily for those who are starting treatment for the *first time*. This is an important point because if you have had treatment before but stopped for whatever reason, your response to prior treatment must be taken into consideration. The best predictor of treatment response is an individual's previous response to any particular intervention. This is true for both benefits and adverse effects. For example, if you have taken a particular medication before and it either was not effective or caused significant side effects, then in most cases it would not make sense to try that medication again. As another example, consider someone who had a prior depressive episode and tried psychotherapy alone. Then, after several months, psychotherapy resulted in only partial remission and antidepressant medication was ultimately required for the person to get completely better. In that situation, it would make the most sense to start treatment for a new episode with both psychotherapy and medication. This is why it is so critical to keep a record of any prior treatment. Be sure you complete the exercise in Chapter 7, which is designed to help you organize information about prior treatment in a way that will facilitate discussion with your treatment team.

Before we move on, there is one more critical point I want to make: THE FINAL DECISION ABOUT TREATMENT MUST BE YOURS. Professionals and this book can provide the information you need to make a good decision, but only you can evaluate the risks versus the benefits of any approach and decide what is best for you.

Potential risks versus benefits

In all fields of medicine, a risk-benefit analysis is used to evaluate potential treatment approaches. Why? ALL TREATMENTS HAVE POTENTIAL RISKS—even those that seem to be the safest. For example, the self-help strategy of exercise seems to be pretty risk free, but you could injure yourself, perhaps even seriously. Another example not related to mental health is the over-the-counter medicine aspirin. We think of this medication as being safe, but in fact it can increase the risk of bleeding. What about "no treatment"? Well, that can be risky too. By choosing not to start treatment, some may take on the risk of not getting better.

Looking at this analysis from the other side, we should ask: Do all treatments have the potential of providing benefit? The answer is unequivocally no. For a treatment to have the potential to be effective, two conditions must generally be met:

- ◆ THERE IS RESEARCH DEMONSTRATING THE TREATMENT'S BENEFIT FOR THE CONDITION YOU HAVE.

- ◆ YOU ARE USING THE TREATMENT CORRECTLY.

What do I mean by "research demonstrating benefit"? Simply that the treatment has been studied using appropriate scientific methods and the results were positive and published in a peer-reviewed medical or mental health journal. In regard to the second item above, I mean that you are using the treatment in the way that it has been shown to be effective. For example, perhaps a study of **depression** found a particular antidepressant to be effective at doses between 20 and 60 milligrams (mg) per day. If you are taking the wrong dose (e.g., 10 mg per day) or frequently forget to take the medication, it may not be effective.

But, you may ask, can't treatments be effective even without evidence that they work? Yes, of course. The fact that a treatment hasn't been studied generally just means that we don't know. But, the issue is that it MAY NOT WORK. So, there is the possibility of wasting time and money with no chance of benefit whatsoever. There may also be unknown risks. Should you ever consider trying an untested treatment? The answer is maybe. But, if you do, it should be with the knowledge that the treatment might not work and might also be associated with unrecognized risk.

Three general treatment strategies

In this book, I have divided treatment methods into three general categories: biological treatments (Chapter 8), psychotherapy (Chapter 9), and complementary approaches (Chapter 10). Before we move on, you must be aware of two critical points about treatment:

- ◆ MAXIMIZE YOUR CHANCES OF RECOVERY BY USING ALL APPROPRIATE OPTIONS.

- ◆ USE THE BEST TREATMENT OR COMBINATION OF TREATMENTS FOR YOUR SPECIFIC SITUATION.

Let me clarify what I mean. **Mood disorders** are often difficult to treat and are frequently **chronic illnesses**. Please give yourself the best chance of achieving full recovery by using all the methods of treatment that are appropriate for you. For example, a combination of psychotherapy and exercise or perhaps the combination of medication, psychotherapy, and increasing social support is best for you. The point is to do everything you can to get well. By finding the best combination for you, I mean working with your medical and mental health professionals to put together a comprehensive plan that is logical and makes sense for you. For example, if you have already failed a trial of a certain medication, it usually will not make sense to try it again. The treatment plan must be individualized to your specific situation. The information and exercises in this book can help you work with your providers to develop a comprehensive recovery plan that is tailored to your specific situation.

Starting treatment for a depressive disorder

The most important step in starting treatment for a depressive disorder is to be sure that it is a **unipolar** depressive disorder and not bipolar depression. As discussed in Chapter 4, bipolar depression can be mistaken for unipolar illness. Please complete the diagnostic exercise in Chapter 3, if you have not already done so, to be absolutely sure that you do not have a bipolar spectrum disorder. If that exercise suggests the possibility that you might have bipolar spectrum disorder, discuss this with your treatment team *before* starting any medication.

Table 11.1 lists five possible options for those who begin treatment for depression. In general, the decision of which strategy or strategies to use is based on the specific disorder, the severity of the disorder, your specific

---

Table 11.1 Options for initial treatment for a depressive disorder

---

- Complementary monotherapy (very mild depression only and if recommended by a medical or mental health professional)
- Psychotherapy monotherapy (mild to moderate depression only)
- Pharmacotherapy or other biological monotherapy
- Combination psychotherapy and biological treatment
- Complementary approaches in combination with psychotherapy and/or biological treatment

---

situation and preferences, and whether you have more than one condition. The word *monotherapy* is typically used to mean one approach used alone, while *combination treatment* refers to using more than one strategy at a time.

In general, for less severe or complicated (e.g., only one disorder) conditions, initially trying a complementary treatment or psychotherapy alone may be reasonable. In contrast, for those with more severe or complicated illness, biological treatment in combination with psychotherapy is usually recommended as an initial approach. However, it is important to point out that treatment using complementary approaches (see Chapter 10) alone has not been adequately studied. There is a risk of not getting better, even for those with very mild depression. Therefore, I do not recommend making a decision to try complementary monotherapy on your own. I recommend that you have a professional evaluation and then decide together with your provider whether trying complementary monotherapy may be appropriate. Another reason for this approach is that you can have a backup plan in place. For example, you and your provider might decide that trying exercise and meditation is reasonable. However, you can decide how long to try these approaches and schedule a follow-up appointment at the end of that time period. At that appointment, the two of you can assess your response and decide whether additional interventions are warranted. Based on the current evidence, I think this is the only safe way to try complementary monotherapy. That said, I strongly recommend using complementary approaches along with other treatments. Complementary approaches can always be combined with either psychotherapy or biological treatment as monotherapy or with the two in combination.

In addition to the above, please keep the following two points about depression treatment in mind:

- ◆ WHATEVER TREATMENT YOU TRY FIRST, IF YOU AREN'T GETTING BETTER IN A REASONABLE TIME, THEN THE STRATEGY NEEDS TO BE REEVALUATED.

- ◆ A COMBINATION OF TREATMENT WITH BIOLOGI- CAL, PSYCHOTHERAPEUTIC, AND COMPLEMENTARY METHODS MAY GIVE THOSE WITH MAJOR DEPRES- SION THE BEST CHANCE FOR A RAPID AND FULL RECOVERY.

The first point above means that if you aren't getting better, then your treatment must be reassessed. Strategies to respond to inadequate response are discussed in Chapter 13. In general, you should expect to see some improvement in response to biological treatments within a few weeks and in response to psychotherapy treatments within a few months.[241] Some individuals may choose biological or combination treatment because of the possibility of a more rapid response. There isn't good evidence about how soon improvements should be expected from complementary approaches; however, a trial of several weeks might be reasonable.

Whatever the initial approach, if there is inadequate or no improve- ment within the time frames given above, then changes should be consid- ered. Of course, if you are getting worse, then changes will almost certainly be required. These changes might include a dosage change for medication or a frequency change for psychotherapy. After an adequate trial of any treatment (or treatments) without response, an entirely new approach may be necessary (see Chapter 13).

The second point above is similar to one of the critical points about treatment. For those with more severe depression, the best chance of a rapid and complete recovery comes from a combination of treatments.[241]

Table 11.2 lists the options to consider for starting treatment for the depressive disorders. Though not specifically listed in the combination treatment column, complementary approaches are recommended for consideration in combination with biological and psychotherapy approaches for all depressive disorders. Details about the various approaches are given in Chapters 8 (biological) and 9 (psychotherapy).

Major depressive disorder

In the following sections, I will review current recommendations for starting treatment for **major depressive disorder**. I will start with major depression that is not complicated with either **comorbidity** or symptoms that may require a specific approach. Once again, I want to emphasize that these are only general recommendations. Please work with a professional to determine the best option for your specific situation. If you have had prior treatment, then it is critical to consider your response to those interventions when planning your current treatment.

Uncomplicated major depression

As presented in Table 11.2, one key element in the treatment decision-making process involves the severity of symptoms. In general, current recommendations suggest biological approaches combined with psychotherapy for severe episodes. For mild or moderate symptoms, either psychotherapy or antidepressant treatment is a reasonable starting point. If recommended by a medical or mental health provider, a short trial of complementary approaches alone may be considered for very mild depression. But, if there isn't any improvement within a few weeks or if there is any worsening of symptoms, then more conventional treatments should definitely be considered.

Major depression with psychotic symptoms

An episode of depression with **hallucinations** or **delusions** is categorized as very severe depression and requires aggressive treatment. Most research suggests that treatment should start with either a combination of an antidepressant and an antipsychotic or electroconvulsive therapy (see Chapter 8 for more information about ECT).[37] Psychotherapy should be considered as well but may not be practical until the psychotic symptoms have resolved.

Table 11.2 Initial treatment approaches for depressive disorders[241, 405, 406, 409, 410, 416–422]

	Initial treatment for depressive disorders				
Disorder	**Complementary monotherapy**	**Psychotherapy monotherapy***	**Biological monotherapy***	**Combined biological and psychotherapy***
Major depression, mild to moderate (without psychiatric comorbidity)	Limited evidence but may be reasonable for very mild depression if recommended by a medical or mental health professional	CT, IPT, PST, or psychodynamic	SSRI, SNRI, mirtazapine, or bupropion Light therapy if clearly seasonal**	Strongly recommended if interpersonal or psychosocial problems or stress May be the best option in most situations when biological treatment is indicated
Major depression, severe (without psychiatric comorbidity)	Not recommended	Not recommended	SSRI, SNRI, mirtazapine, or bupropion	Strongly recommended
Major depression, with psychosis (without psychiatric comorbidity)	Not recommended	Not recommended	Antidepressant and antipsychotic or ECT	Add psychotherapy as soon as practical (may need to wait until resolution of psychotic symptoms)
Major depression (any severity with one or more comorbid conditions)	Utilize evidence-based treatment for coexisting disorder(s) AND recommendations for major depression alone. See text for additional information.			

Condition				
Dysthymic disorder (without psychiatric comorbidity)	Not recommended	Some evidence for CT or IPT	Some evidence for SSRI, SNRI, mirtazapine, or bupropion	Strongly recommended
Dysthymic disorder (with one or more comorbid conditions)	Utilize evidence-based treatment for coexisting disorder(s) AND recommendations for dysthymic disorder alone. See text for additional information.			
Depressive disorder not otherwise specified	No evidence. Utilize recommendations for mild major depression or dysthymic disorder depending on duration of illness.			
Adjustment disorder with depressed mood	Might consider but no evidence	Recommended	Limited evidence for effectiveness	No evidence available
Depressed mood due to a medical condition	Treat underlying medical condition. If symptoms persist, use appropriate row above.			

This table provides general information only and cannot take the place of advice from a medical or mental health professional. Also, this table assumes no prior treatment. For those who have had previous treatment for major depression, response to previous treatment should be considered.

*Complementary approaches are recommended for consideration in combination with biological and psychotherapy approaches for all depressive disorders.

**Light therapy can be used as monotherapy for seasonal illness or in combination with any other treatment for both seasonal and nonseasonal depression.

CBT = cognitive behavior therapy, IPT = interpersonal therapy, PST = problem-solving therapy, SSRI = selective serotonin reuptake inhibitor, SNRI = serotonin-norepinephrine reuptake inhibitor, ECT = electroconvulsive therapy

Major depression with catatonic symptoms

The word *catatonia* refers to symptoms of immobility, severe agitation, or other unusual motor or verbal behaviors. This condition is a rare but very severe form of depression that requires emergent aggressive treatment. Hospitalization is typically required along with nutritional support, such as intravenous fluids. Immediate treatment may require intravenous benzodiazepines or ECT.[37] Antidepressants are normally also required.

Major depression with a seasonal pattern

Major depression with a seasonal pattern is characterized by a regular and recurring relationship between seasons and the onset and remission of symptoms. Depression is not considered seasonal if the relationship is the result of season-specific psychosocial stressors, such as the winter holidays. Seasonal depression usually comes on in the fall in the Northern Hemisphere. Typically onset is between early October and late November and remission occurs in mid-February to mid-April.[37] All the standard treatments for major depression are thought to be effective for **seasonal affective disorder**;[37] however, light therapy may be considered as a monotherapy for mild to moderate episodes.[37] If there is no response to light therapy alone within a few weeks, then another approach should be tried. For more severe episodes, light therapy can be started as adjunctive treatment along with medication and/or psychotherapy.

Major depression with a comorbid anxiety disorder

Anxiety disorders frequently co-occur with major depression. There is evidence that 40%–60% of persons with major depression will also meet the diagnostic criteria for an anxiety disorder.[37] It is critical to develop a treatment plan that addresses both disorders. The good news is that often the same one treatment will be effective for both conditions. Psychotherapy can be effective for symptoms of both depression and anxiety, as can some of the complementary approaches. Antidepressant medications are generally effective for both depressive and anxiety symptoms too. However, both SSRIs and TCAs (see Chapter 8 for more information about these medications) can sometimes worsen anxiety symptoms at the start of treatment. Moderate to severe anxiety may warrant short-term adjunctive treatment with one of the antianxiety medications known as benzodiazepines,[37] as these agents reduce symptoms immediately. These medications do have some risk of abuse and dependence (addiction), however, and can cause excess sedation. The risk of dependence is relatively low with short-term use among those who do not have a substance use disorder. The sedative effects can be very impairing for some people. For example, those individuals who are particularly sensitive to benzodiazepine sedation may not be able to drive or engage in other activities that require alertness and motor skills. Thus, the risks and benefits of these medications must be carefully considered.

Major depression with a comorbid substance use disorder

As with anxiety disorders, substance use disorders frequently co-exist with major depression. Both disorders must be addressed in the development of a treatment plan. Some individuals may need detoxification prior to starting treatment for depression. Since substance use can induce depressive symptoms, it is possible that these symptoms will resolve with abstinence without additional treatment. Currently it is not possible to predict which individuals will require additional treatment for depression. The advantage to waiting for a time to see if depressive symptoms resolve is that specific treatment for depression may not be required if symptoms go away after the substance use is stopped. However, ongoing depression may complicate the process of substance abuse recovery. Some factors that may suggest starting specific treatment for depression early include a family history of mood disorders and previous major depressive episodes that occurred either before the onset of substance use or during periods of abstinence.[37] My opinion is that, in general, starting specific treatment for depression sooner rather than later makes the most sense, especially if symptoms are in the moderate to severe range.

Major depression with a comorbid eating disorder

Both antidepressants and some psychotherapy strategies have been shown to be effective for eating disorders. In many cases a treatment approach may be chosen for depression that will also be helpful for the eating disorder.

Cognitive therapy (CT) and SSRIs have the most evidence of effectiveness, but there has also been success with interpersonal therapy (IPT).[37]

Major depression with comorbid dementia

Individuals with dementia frequently develop depression. Antidepressants are effective for treating depression in this population, but they do not improve cognition.[37] The main treatment issue to be aware of is that those with dementia may be especially vulnerable to some medication side effects, particularly those involving the cholinergic system. Thus, medications with lower anticholinergic effects should be considered, such as bupropion, fluoxetine, or sertraline.[37] ECT is also effective and may be considered if antidepressants are not effective.[37] Whether or not psychotherapy or alternative strategies should be considered will obviously depend on the extent of cognitive impairment.

Dysthymic disorder

Psychotherapy treatments for **dysthymic disorder** have not been adequately studied, but there is some evidence of effectiveness.[404] One short-term study found CT and an SSRI to be equally effective.[405] However, another found an SSRI in combination with IPT or an SSRI alone to both be more effective than IPT alone.[406] Despite a lack of adequate studies and some conflicting results, combined psychotherapy and antidepressant treatment is thought to provide the best response.[37] Psychotherapy alone could be considered, but if the response is incomplete, then the addition of an antidepressant should be considered. There is not a lot of evidence to guide treatment of dysthymic disorder that is comorbid with other psychiatric conditions. Nonetheless, I recommend following the same recommendations as are given for episodes of major depression.

Adjustment disorder with depressed mood

Though often thought of as a less severe depressive disorder, **adjustment disorder with depressed mood** should be taken very seriously. For example, a recent Danish study found that persons with the diagnosis of adjustment disorder had twelve times the rate of suicide as those without this diagnosis.[407]

This condition is fairly common and the prevalence is thought to be in the 11%–18% range among individuals studied seeking routine primary care.[408] There is very little research on the treatment of this disorder;[408] however, there is limited evidence for the effectiveness of antidepressants[409] and some recommend psychotherapy as the treatment of choice.[410] Alternative approaches should also be considered as part of the treatment plan.

Starting treatment for bipolar disorder

In this section, I will discuss starting treatment for bipolar depression and then for **mania** and **hypomania**. Our current understanding is that biological treatments are always required for bipolar spectrum disorders. Thus, in this section, I present medications as the primary treatment approach. However, I strongly recommend psychotherapy in addition to medication. We know very little about using complementary treatments for bipolar disorders, so I will not discuss these approaches in the following section. However, as I've said throughout this book, combining as many recovery strategies as possible may give you the best chance of getting completely better and staying well. The same important points apply to bipolar disorder as were stated for unipolar depression:

* WHATEVER TREATMENT YOU TRY FIRST, IF YOU AREN'T GETTING BETTER IN A REASONABLE TIME, THEN THE STRATEGY NEEDS TO BE REEVALUATED.

* A COMBINATION OF TREATMENT WITH BIOLOGI-CAL, PSYCHOTHERAPEUTIC, AND COMPLEMENTARY METHODS MAY PROVIDE THE BEST CHANCE OF A GETTING BETTER AS QUICKLY AS POSSIBLE AND ACHIEVING A FULL RECOVERY.

Bipolar depression

The first step in treating bipolar depression is recognizing that it is bipolar and not unipolar depression. There is considerable evidence that bipolar depression is often misdiagnosed as unipolar illness. Once the depressive episode is correctly diagnosed, it is critical to start the proper treatment.

One of the difficulties confronting us is that the treatment of bipolar depression has not been adequately studied.[411] Another problem is that, because of a lack of solid research, experts do not always agree on the best treatment approaches. For example, A. M. Nivoli and colleagues[246] completed a review of a number of recently published guidelines for the treatment of bipolar depression. They found some areas of consensus among the guidelines, but there were also differences of opinion. In the following section, I will try to summarize the various recommendations in way that will be helpful to you.

Biological treatments for bipolar depression

The most important recommendation is that antidepressants should not be used as monotherapy for bipolar depression. As discussed in Chapter 8, many[1, 18, 247] but not all[248] studies suggest that there is a risk of inducing mania and cycle acceleration (more frequent shifts between mania and depression). Although this finding is controversial, my opinion is that there is enough evidence that this can happen that it is not worth the risk to ever use antidepressant monotherapy for bipolar disorder.

The use of antidepressants for bipolar depression in general is also controversial.[246] Some research suggests that antidepressants can be safely used if combined with a mood stabilizer.[252] However, the effectiveness of antidepressants for bipolar depression in general has been questioned. There is support for effectiveness[247, 248] as well as contradictory evidence.[249–251] Thus, many unanswered questions remain about antidepressant use in bipolar depression. My assessment is that antidepressant monotherapy for bipolar depression should be absolutely avoided. I think antidepressants along with mood stabilizers should be considered, but probably not as first-line therapy in most cases. In other words, it may be best to try a mood stabilizer first (see Chapter 8) and then consider adding an antidepressant if necessary. If antidepressants are used, then consideration should be given to discontinuation (of the antidepressant only, the mood stabilizer is continued) when the depressive episode is in remission.[412, 413] Of course, these are only general

Table 11.3   Initial treatment for bipolar depression

	Not currently on medication	**Already taking a mood stabilizer**
Bipolar I depression	Quetiapine monotherapy[411, 413, 414, 423] Olanzapine monotherapy[411] Olanzapine and fluoxetine[411] Lamotrigine monotherapy[411, 413, 414, 423] Valproate monotherapy[411, 413, 423] Lithium monotherapy[413, 414, 423]	If on lithium, add lamotrigine[411] Add quetiapine[412]
Bipolar II depression	Quetiapine monotherapy[411, 423] Valproate monotherapy[411]	Optimize mood stabilizer dose

This table provides general information only and cannot take the place of advice from a medical or mental health professional. Also, this table assumes no prior treatment. For those who have had previous treatment for bipolar depression, response to previous treatment should be considered.

recommendations that cannot take the variables of your specific situation into consideration. Please discuss the pros and cons in detail with your prescriber if antidepressants are being considered for bipolar depression.

Table 11.3 lists some of the recent expert consensus recommendations for the initial treatment of bipolar I and II depressive episodes. As you can see, the most consistent recommendation for both **bipolar I and II disorders** is quetiapine monotherapy. Lamotrigine and valproate are both strongly recommended for bipolar I depression. Based on the evidence that is currently available, if all other factors are equal, then I recommend considering quetiapine as a possible first choice for both bipolar I and II disorders for those not already receiving treatment. However, other factors (such as side effects and prior treatment history) may lead to a different choice in your specific situation. For those already receiving pharmacotherapy, optimizing the current treatment is likely to be the best first option. Depending on the severity of the depression and other factors, additional interventions may be warranted. Again, these are only general recommendations and do not take the variables of your specific situation into consideration. So please work with your prescriber to determine the best option for you.

Psychotherapy for bipolar depression

Although the treatment recommendations for bipolar disorder all include biological treatments, psychological approaches also play an important role.[275–279] For example, adding psychotherapy to medication can decrease the **relapse** rate by about 40% for some people with bipolar disorder.[280] Several psychotherapies have been recommended as adjunctive treatments for bipolar depression, including IPSRT,[411] CT,[411, 413, 414] IPT,[413, 414] and FFT.[411, 413, 414] Though not really psychotherapy, providing education and information (psychoeducation) has also been shown to be effective.[343] Thus, I strongly recommend adding psychotherapy to your comprehensive recovery plan (see Chapter 9 for more information). Some of the psychotherapies listed above may not be available in your area; I listed them for your information. The most important thing is to start therapy even if none of the listed approaches are available.

Manic, hypomanic, and mixed episodes

In this section, I will review the treatment of manic and mixed episodes. For manic episodes, I will differentiate between milder and more severe episodes. As you may recall from Chapters 2 and 3, milder manic episodes are known as hypomania. For the purposes of this chapter, let's think of mania as occurring along a continuum of severity, from mild to moderate to severe. The severity rating depends on the degree of impairment. Thinking about it this way is more useful than a strict definition of mania or hypomania. For treatment purposes, the issue is the level of impairment. Obviously, a person with severe impairment will need more aggressive treatment to quickly restore functioning than someone who is only minimally impaired.

Severe manic and mixed episodes frequently result in significant impairment and require immediate treatment. The short-term aim of treatment is to control symptoms as quickly as possible. In most cases, hospitalization is required to ensure safety as well as to closely monitor treatment.[413] In contrast, milder episodes can often be treated on an outpatient basis.

Biological treatments

Three categories of medications are effective antimanic agents: (1) anti-psychotics, (2) **lithium**, and (3) **anticonvulsants** (see Chapter 8 for more information).[413] Additionally, a class of antianxiety medications known as benzodiazepines are sometimes indicated for short-term rapid control of mania-induced agitation.[413] Finally, ECT is an option for very severe mania or manic episodes that do not respond to medication.[413] In regard to anti-psychotics, both first- and second-generation agents are effective, but only **second-generation antipsychotics (SGAs)** are discussed in detail in this book due to the infrequent use of first-generation medications in the United States. Two anticonvulsants have antimanic effectiveness: valproate and carbamazepine.[413] Finally, since antidepressants are thought to contribute to mania in some cases, it is frequently recommended that these medications be discontinued at the time of onset of a manic or mixed episode.

For individuals who are not taking any antimanic agents and have more severe manic or mixed symptoms, treatment might include starting either valproate or an SGA as monotherapy.[413] If psychotic symptoms are present, then the use of an antipsychotic should be considered. There is some evidence that combining SGAs with mood stabilizers is the most effective treatment for mania.[78] Therefore, combination treatment may be an option in some cases of more severe symptomatology. However, using two agents has the potential disadvantage of increasing the risk of side effects. Short-term use of a benzodiazepine may be warranted[413] if agitation or insomnia is a significant problem. For those with milder mania, SGA, lithium, val-proate, or carbamazepine monotherapy is a reasonable starting option.[413] Finally, for individuals who develop mania while on an antimanic agent, the recommendation is to optimize the current medication.[413] We have very little information about the treatment of hypomania or mood elevations associated with **cyclothymic disorder** or **bipolar disorder NOS**. There is very limited evidence suggesting that low-dose quetiapine might be effective.[415]

Psychotherapy

There is currently no evidence to suggest that any psychotherapy treatment is effective for mania.[413] Further, many or perhaps most people experiencing mania are unable to participate in psychotherapy. Thus, until there is some symptom improvement, even attempting psychotherapy may not be fruitful. However, as discussed above, psychotherapy is strongly recommended for persons with bipolar disorder and can be implemented during depressed or euthymic episodes.

Treatment setting

Most mood disorder treatment occurs in an outpatient setting. Outpatient means that you go to your doctor's or mental health professional's office to receive treatment. Other treatment settings sometimes used are inpatient, residential, and intensive outpatient. Inpatient treatment means that you are admitted to a hospital. Nowadays, inpatient psychiatric treatment is typically short term, often lasting just a few days. In most cases, individuals are discharged to outpatient treatment as soon as they are clinically stable. The term *residential treatment* is used in a variety of different situations but often describes a treatment program that, as the name implies, is "residential," meaning that individuals live at the treatment facility during treatment. Residential programs are often less intense than inpatient treatment but last longer. These approaches are often used for substance abuse treatment. *Intensive outpatient* can refer to a variety of programs but often means that persons come to the program in an outpatient setting frequently, perhaps daily or several times per week. These programs sometimes serve as a bridge between inpatient and regular outpatient treatment.

Which treatment setting is right for you?

As discussed above, outpatient treatment is usually the method of choice for persons with mood disorders. However, inpatient treatment should be considered if an individual is having thoughts of harming self or others or is so ill that she or he cannot take care of him/herself.[241] Hospitalization or admission to an intensive outpatient program may also be the treatment of choice for those who are severely ill and who lack adequate social support, have complicating psychiatric or medical comorbidity, or have not improved with outpatient treatment.

What about involuntary treatment?

The issue of involuntary treatment is complex and has the potential to be very stressful for individuals with mood disorders as well as for involved clinicians. Various jurisdictions specify the criteria for which persons can be admitted to hospitals against their will. The criteria all involve situations in which an individual may be a danger to self or others if not admitted. Involuntary admission to a hospital is a last resort but is sometimes necessary to ensure safety. This usually happens when an individual with a mood disorder is unable to think clearly because of the illness—for example, is experiencing psychotic symptoms. IF HOSPITALIZATION IS RECOMMENDED FOR YOU, PLEASE CONSIDER CAREFULLY BEFORE REFUSING. THE ADAGE "BETTER SAFE THAN SORRY" APPLIES HERE. THERE IS LITTLE TO LOSE FROM A FEW DAYS IN A HOSPITAL BUT OFTEN A LOT TO LOSE BY NOT BEING ADMITTED IF YOU ARE UNSAFE ON YOUR OWN. MANY TIMES A TRUSTED FRIEND OR FAMILY MEMBER CAN PROVIDE HELPFUL PERSPECTIVE IF HOSPITALIZATION IS RECOMMENDED BUT YOU FEEL IT IS UNNECESSARY.

12

Special Considerations for Women

Mood disorders are common among women of childbearing age.[424] For example, in one study of young women seen in gynecologic settings, about 22% had major **depression**.[425] Thus, many mothers must make decisions about mood disorder treatment while pregnant or breast-feeding. Further, some women must make decisions about when to become pregnant or whether to become pregnant at all. Such decisions can be very difficult because all options may involve trade-offs. Treatment choices are much more complicated during pregnancy and breast-feeding because, in addition to the risk-benefit analysis for the mother, the risks to the child of both getting and not getting treatment must be considered. The first part of this chapter will provide information that may be helpful if you are pregnant or thinking about having a baby. In the final section, I will discuss another topic relevant for women, premenstrual dysphoric disorder.

As I've said in other chapters, this book can only provide general information. The goal is to help you work effectively with your treatment team and make informed decisions. Please discuss all treatment decisions with your treatment team. Now let's start with major depression.

Major depression

Depressive episodes are common in women both during pregnancy and after delivery. One study[426] found that 9% of pregnant women suffer from depression, and even higher rates have been reported.[427] The onset of depression within four weeks after delivery,[38, 428] known as postpartum depression, also occurs frequently. Studies suggest that 6%–12% of women will experience a depressive episode after giving birth.[429, 430] Furthermore, women with a prior history of depression have a twofold increased risk of developing depressive symptoms during or after pregnancy.[431] For women who have had one episode of postpartum-onset depression, the risk of recurrence is also high. A study[432] of women with a prior episode of postpartum-onset depression found that 26% experienced recurrence of major depression in the first twenty weeks after delivery and 40% experienced recurrence within one year.

Decisions about pregnancy for those who have, or who are at risk for, major depression must be informed by a complete understanding of two issues: (1) the potential consequences of depression for both mother and child and (2) the possibility that some treatments for depression could cause adverse effects for the child. These concerns must be considered in addition to the general risk-benefit analysis that I recommend everyone complete before starting treatment (see Chapter 11).

Diagnosis of depression during pregnancy and after delivery

There are two considerations to be aware of in determining whether you are suffering from depression if you are currently pregnant or recently gave birth (see Chapters 2 and 3 for more information about the diagnoses of depression).

First, normal symptoms experienced in pregnancy, such as decreased energy, appetite changes, and sleep disturbance, can mimic depressive symptoms. So, if you are being evaluated for depression, be sure to tell your health care provider if you are currently pregnant.

The other consideration is the "baby blues." Many women experience transient depressive symptoms after delivery that typically last for seven to ten days and do not require treatment.[37, 433] However, if symptoms do not go away within ten days, then they could indicate major depression and a professional evaluation is warranted (see Chapter 3 for more information on the diagnosis of depression and Chapter 5 for advice on seeking treatment).

Some women may experience symptoms of postpartum depression that require emergency treatment. If at any time you have thoughts of harming yourself, this is an emergency even if you have been depressed for only a few days. Please seek help immediately (see Chapter 1 for more information). Symptoms of **obsessions** or **compulsions** can occur with postpartum depression (see Chapter 3 for more information on these symptoms). Obsessions are recurrent, intrusive thoughts that are experienced as unpleasant and that are not consistent with an individual's personality. In the postpartum period, obsessions can include thoughts of harming the baby.[37] This too represents an emergency and professional help must be obtained immediately. However, if a mother has thoughts of harming her baby, it is critical for the mother to avoid castigating herself for such thoughts. While obviously very disturbing, these obsessions are a result of the depression and do not mean anything about the mother's character or love for her child. These thoughts are a symptom and nothing more. Finally, postpartum **psychosis** is a rare condition in which a woman may experience **delusions** and possibly **hallucinations** (see Chapter 3 for more information on these symptoms). Again, professional assistance is required on an emergency basis.

Depression and your child

In addition to the impact of depressive symptoms on the mother, there is some evidence that depressive symptoms may affect the child both before and after birth. During pregnancy, a mother's depression appears to be associated with a variety of complications, including preterm deliveries, fetal distress, caesarean sections, and admission of the child to a neonatal intensive care unit.[434-439] There is also evidence that depression after birth may, in some cases, adversely affect infants and children. Investigators have shown an association between postpartum maternal depression and childhood attachment problems, symptoms of depression and anxiety, behavior problems, and delays in cognitive and language development.[440-444]

Furthermore, one study[445] reported that more than 75% of mothers with major depression reported that their symptoms made it difficult for them to care for their children.

It is important to note that in the preceding paragraph I used the words *associated with* rather than *cause*. Studies suggest that relationships exist between maternal depression and the concerns stated above, but these investigations do not prove that there is a direct cause-and-effect interaction. There may be other factors involved in some cases that the investigators were not aware of. Most important, these studies certainly do *not* indicate that such complications *will* occur. The research indicates only that there is most likely some increase in risk. However, I think the evidence of risk is strong enough to be taken into consideration when making decisions about pregnancy and mood disorder treatment. I want to be very clear about one thing: These findings do not mean that you cannot have children if you suffer from major depression. However, my recommendation is that you do everything possible to avoid potential problems. I will suggest some strategies after we discuss treatment.

Depression treatment during pregnancy and breast-feeding

This section will review the risks and benefits of treatments for depression during pregnancy. I will first discuss treatment with antidepressants.

Antidepressant treatment during pregnancy

Research indicates that women frequently take antidepressants during pregnancy,[446] so it is very important for you to completely understand their pros and cons before making a decision. All antidepressants are believed to cross the placenta.[447, 448] This means that when a pregnant woman takes antidepressant medication, the unborn child is exposed to the medication as well. Many medications and substances that cross the placenta have some potential to harm the developing child. The first trimester of pregnancy is the period of fetal organ development. It is during these three months that the fetus is at greatest risk of the adverse effects of medications taken by the mother. Three general types of adverse effects can occur when a child is exposed to harmful substances before birth. The first is known as embryo-toxicity. This means that exposure of the child to medication or harmful substances during pregnancy may cause some type of problem that occurs after birth but does not result in physical birth defects.[448] Examples of this type of effect include the development of childhood behavioral problems and the child experiencing withdrawal symptoms after birth. A second possible adverse effect is known as teratogenicity. This means that there is a malformation of fetal organs or skeletal structures—in other words, a birth defect.[449] Finally, the third adverse effect is the risk of miscarriage and problems at the time of birth, such as premature birth or caesarean section. Just to be clear, these are just general examples. I will talk about specific risks thought to be associated with antidepressants a little later in this section—but first a bit more background information.

In order to classify the risk of various medications to an unborn child, the U.S. Food and Drug Administration (FDA) uses five categories to indicate the potential of a drug that crosses the placenta to cause birth defects (Table 12.1). The rating given to a particular medication must be interpreted with care, however,[450] because the level of evidence used to categorize individual medications varies from medication to medication as does the level of risk actually imposed by a particular drug.[450] Thus, medications in the same category may have very different levels of risk and/or different levels of evidence supporting their categorization.[450] The FDA has proposed major revisions in prescription drug labeling to give health care providers and consumers better information about the use of medications by women who are pregnant or breast-feeding. Thus, the categories listed in Table 12.1 may change in the future; consult the FDA website (http://www.fda.gov) for the latest information. Finally, the FDA uses "black box" warnings on the labels of some medications when the FDA determines that a potential side effect is serious enough to warrant drawing the clinician's attention to it right away.[450]

Unfortunately, the potential risks and benefits of antidepressant treatment during pregnancy and breast-feeding are difficult to determine with certainty. First of all, for ethical reasons, there are no controlled trials of antidepressant use in pregnant women.[447] What does this mean? To

Table 12.1 FDA pregnancy categories

Category A

Adequate and well-controlled studies have failed to demonstrate a risk to the fetus in the first trimester of pregnancy (and there is no evidence of risk in later trimesters).

Category B

Animal studies have revealed no evidence of harm to the fetus; however, there are no adequate and well-controlled studies in pregnant women.

or

Animal studies have shown an adverse effect, but adequate and well-controlled studies in pregnant women have failed to demonstrate a risk to the fetus.

Category C

Animal studies have shown an adverse effect, and there are no adequate and well-controlled studies in pregnant women.

or

No animal studies have been conducted, and there are no adequate and well-controlled studies in pregnant women.

Category D

Studies—adequate, well-controlled, or observational—in pregnant women have demonstrated a risk to the fetus; however, the benefits of therapy may outweigh the potential risk.

Category X

Studies—adequate, well-controlled, or observational—in animals or pregnant women have demonstrated positive evidence of fetal abnormalities. The use of the product is contraindicated in women who are or may become pregnant.

absolutely establish cause-and-effect relationships, studies would have to be conducted in which depressed women were randomly assigned to either take an antidepressant or not take an antidepressant and then become pregnant. Then the investigators would determine whether there was a higher risk of adverse effects among the children of those women who took the medication. In contrast, the information we have is from studies that do not clearly indicate cause and effect,[447] often called "association studies." An example of this is to compare a group of women who took antidepressants during pregnancy to a group who did not and see whether either group has a statistically significant difference in some particular outcome. If the children of the antidepressant group were found to have a higher incidence of a particular birth defect, then one could say that treatment with antidepressants is "associated" with that birth defect. The most these studies can tell us is that there might be a higher risk of certain outcomes if a medication is taken during pregnancy or breast-feeding. Many studies have other limitations as well,[451] frequently involving what we call "confounding variables." A confounding variable is a condition that may cause a study result to be incorrect. For example, a study might report that among the children of women taking a certain antidepressant while pregnant there were more cases of an adverse outcome than among the children of women who were not taking the medication. The adverse outcome might be a result of taking the medication; however, it might also be the result of a confounding variable. In this case, perhaps the effect of the depression itself on the child could be the actual cause.[451]

Researchers try to control for these confounding variables, but it is often impossible to completely sort out the effects of one variable from another. Of course, the more studies that report a relationship between a specific medication and a certain adverse outcome, the more likely it is to be a "real" interaction, but in some cases it may be impossible to ever be absolutely certain. We just do not know enough about the risks of taking some medications during pregnancy or breast-feeding. In the following section, I will review some of the evidence that is currently available. As I have said elsewhere in this book, this information is presented to help you evaluate treatment options; it cannot replace a detailed discussion with your health care providers. Furthermore, new information will become available after this book is published. So, my aim is to help you think through possibilities but not to provide specific recommendations for your unique situation.

I will first discuss the issue of the effectiveness of antidepressant medication during pregnancy. As mentioned above, ethical considerations prohibit the studies that would absolutely answer this question. Nonetheless, at least one study suggests that antidepressant treatment during pregnancy can control depressive symptoms.[452] Also, there is some evidence that stopping antidepressant treatment during pregnancy may result in **relapse** of depression.[453-456] In contrast, a recent large study[457] found evidence that taking antidepressants during pregnancy may not reduce the risk of developing a new episode of depression among women with a history of this illness. Given the limited and somewhat conflicting information available, it is difficult to know for sure whether antidepressants have the same effectiveness during pregnancy as when taken by individuals who are not currently pregnant.[37]

There are also many unanswered questions about the safety of antidepressant use during pregnancy. Unfortunately, the available studies have many limitations and some have produced conflicting results.[450, 451, 458, 459]

Some studies suggest that antidepressant use during pregnancy might be relatively safe. One such study[460] found that antidepressant use in the first trimester of pregnancy is not associated with an increased risk for major birth defects. Further, in a recent review[458] the authors evaluated the safety of different classes of antidepressants and concluded that there was no convincing evidence of an increased risk for any adverse outcomes. In contrast to these reports, a fairly large body of literature suggests that at least some risk to the unborn child may be associated with taking antidepressants during pregnancy. For example, there have been reported associations between the use of these medications and increased rates of induced delivery and caesarean section,[461] poor pregnancy outcome and neonatal withdrawal reactions,[462] preterm births,[463] and spontaneous abortion.[464]

Among the classes of antidepressants, some experts[447] have recommended the **selective serotonin reuptake inhibitors (SSRIs)** as the first choice if antidepressants are used for the treatment of depression during pregnancy. This is both because of the general favorable tolerability profile of this class of drugs and because a reasonable amount of reproductive safety data is available. Therefore, this chapter will focus on the use of SSRIs in pregnancy (see Chapter 8 for more information on SSRIs). In regard to FDA pregnancy category risks, all SSRIs are category C except paroxetine, which is category D (see Table 12.1 for a list of the categories).

A recent study[465] found that prenatal exposure to SSRIs, especially during the first trimester, may modestly increase the risk of the development of autism spectrum disorders. Another study reported that infants exposed to SSRIs continuously during gestation were more likely to be born preterm than infants with partial or no exposure.[434] However, the same study found no increased risk for minor physical anomalies or reduced maternal weight gain.[434] One relatively large study[466] of the risk of birth defects when SSRIs are used during the first trimester was published in 2007. That study of 9849 pregnancies found no increased risk of birth defects in women who took fluoxetine, citalopram, escitalopram, or fluvoxamine during the first trimester. However, all the studies discovered a small but statistically significant increased risk of certain birth defects in women taking sertraline or paroxetine during the first trimester. The authors pointed out that birth defects associated with SSRIs are rare and the absolute risks are small. Another large study of fluoxetine, sertraline, paroxetine, and citalopram[467] found a small increase in the rate of certain birth defects in women taking SSRIs during the first trimester. Finally, there is some evidence[468, 469] suggesting a higher risk of newborns having a condition known as persistent pulmonary hypertension, which is a serious and life-threatening lung condition, when SSRIs were used during the final twenty weeks of gestation. As a result, the FDA issued a black box warning regarding the use of SSRIs and their possible association with an increased risk for pulmonary hypertension. The FDA also issued a Public Health Advisory entitled "Treatment Challenges of Depression in Pregnancy and the Possibility of Persistent Pulmonary Hypertension in Newborns," which is available on its website (http://www.fda.gov/Drugs/DrugSafety/PostmarketDrugSafetyInformationforPatientsandProviders/DrugSafetyInformationforHeathcareProfessionals/PublicHealthAdvisories/ucm124348.htm). However, it is important to note that a more recent study[470] did not find an association between SSRI use during pregnancy and pulmonary hypertension.

In regard to specific SSRIs, considerable data is available on the use of fluoxetine during pregnancy. Many studies[471–481] have found no increase in the risk of birth defects. However, studies have reported an increase in spontaneous abortions,[472] low birth weight,[473, 476] preterm delivery, and withdrawal-like symptoms.[473] Finally, two studies[482, 483] have found no evidence of long-term developmental delays with fluoxetine. One other specific SSRI, paroxetine, warrants mention. There is evidence that the use of this medication during pregnancy may be associated with an increase in the risk of cardiovascular birth defects.[459, 461, 466] For this reason the FDA recommended that the manufacturer of paroxetine change the drug to pregnancy category D in 2005. In contrast, a number of studies have found no adverse outcomes associated with paroxetine.[471, 478, 484, 485]

In summary, we do not have enough information to completely understand the risks of antidepressant use during pregnancy. SSRIs are most commonly used and have the most information available. The data we have suggests that taking antidepressants during pregnancy appears to be associated with some risk to the developing child. But, untreated depression can also be associated with risks for both mother and child. Later in this chapter I will discuss alternative approaches, such as psychotherapy. However, in some cases the benefits of antidepressant treatment during pregnancy may outweigh the possible risks,[37, 450] particularly for severe depression or when symptoms include thoughts of suicide or are causing significant disability. Please do not make a decision based only on reading this chapter. My goal is to provide general information that may be helpful, but a book cannot consider all of the factors that may apply to your individual situation. Please discuss the options with your health care providers and your loved ones.

Antidepressant treatment while breast-feeding

Human milk is the ideal source of nutrients, immunological defenses, and growth-promoting factors for the newborn child; it provides the mother and child with both short- and long-term health benefits.[486] As with pregnancy, information about the safety of antidepressant use when breast-feeding is limited.[486] As in the preceding section, I will discuss only SSRIs in this chapter. In regard to SSRI effectiveness for postpartum depression, there is evidence of benefit.[487-490] However, all antidepressants are excreted into breast milk and thus there is at least a potential risk of adverse effects in breast-fed infants of mothers who take these medications. Still, any potential risk must be weighed against the possible adverse consequences of not getting treatment. That said, there have been very few reports in the literature suggesting that infant exposure to SSRIs may be associated with adverse effects for the child.[486]

In regard to specific medications, a number of studies have demonstrated that the concentration of sertraline in breast milk is generally low and is not detectable in the serum of breast-fed infants of mothers taking the drug.[491–493] Furthermore, no adverse effects were observed in any of the infants who participated in these studies.[491–493] When compared with sertraline, some other SSRIs result in higher concentrations in breast milk.[494–497] While it makes sense to think that lower concentrations are better, in fact we do not know that undetectable levels of drugs have no short- or long- term effects, nor do we know that measurable drug levels in infant serum are associated with adverse events.[486] A recent review[486] concluded that either sertraline or paroxetine could be considered as the first choice among SSRIs for use during breast-feeding. However, other factors would need to be considered. For example, if one of these agents has been tried before and found to be ineffective for a given person, it would not make sense to try it again.

Psychotherapy treatment while pregnant or breast-feeding

Because of the lack of risk to the child, psychotherapy should always be considered as a treatment option for women who are pregnant and breast-feeding (see Chapter 9 for more about psychotherapies).[37] As I have said elsewhere in this book, even if medications are used, I recommend that psychotherapy also be a part of the treatment plan in most cases. There have been a few studies of psychotherapy use during pregnancy.[498–502] In particular, a controlled trial of interpersonal psychotherapy demonstrated this it was an effective antidepressant treatment during pregnancy.[502] In regard to postpartum depression, several well-designed studies have shown various psychotherapy modalities to be effective, including cognitive therapy,[489, 490] psychodynamic psychotherapy,[503] and interpersonal psychotherapy.[504]

Recommendations

As you can see from the information provided earlier in this chapter, decisions about depression treatment during pregnancy and breast-feeding are

---

Table 12.2   Key points about depression treatment during
pregnancy and breast-feeding

◆   Episodes of depression during or after pregnancy are relatively
    common.

◆   The risk is much greater for women who have had prior episodes of
    depression.

◆   Untreated maternal depression may be associated with some risk for
    the child.

◆   Treatment decisions must consider the risks and benefits of both
    using and not using a particular treatment for both mother and child.

◆   Taking antidepressants during pregnancy appears to be associated
    with some potential risk to the child, but the risk is likely relatively low.

◆   Psychotherapy treatment appears to be effective during pregnancy
    and nursing but may not be adequate by itself for more severe
    depression.

---

complicated. This is due to the fact that potential risks and benefits for both
mother and child must be carefully considered. Further, the consequences
of both using and not using any potential treatment must be evaluated. Finally, we do not have enough information about the potential benefits and
risks of antidepressant treatment during pregnancy and breast-feeding.[37] A
summary of key information is presented in Table 12.2.

As I said earlier, the goal of this chapter is to provide information
that may be helpful. All treatment decisions must be made as a result of
discussions with your treatment team and loved ones. Some general strategies are listed in Table 12.3.

My main recommendation is that, whenever possible, pregnancies
should be planned well in advance. Plans should include depression treatment during both the pregnancy and when breast-feeding, if you plan to
nurse your child. One recommendation[450] that I like is to try to achieve
a period of at least three months of stable remission before becoming

---

Table 12.3   Strategies for the management of depression during pregnancy and breast-feeding

---

♦ Be sure you are not pregnant before starting any medication.

♦ Avoid unplanned pregnancy.

♦ If you become pregnant, do not stop taking any medication without first talking with your health care providers about possible risks and benefits.

♦ Tell your health care providers if you are planning to get pregnant or think you may be pregnant now.

♦ Begin the treatment planning process well before becoming pregnant.[450]

♦ Consider breast-feeding when planning pregnancy.[450]

♦ If possible, become pregnant after at least three months of being stabilized in a period of remission.[450]

♦ If you take an antidepressant during pregnancy or breast-feeding, if possible select one for which we know more about the potential risks.[450]

♦ Make any medication changes before becoming pregnant.[4]

---

pregnant. Though evidence is lacking, I think this approach could have three benefits. First, it may minimize the chances of a relapse during pregnancy. Second, it may prevent the need to change medications while you are pregnant or nursing. Finally, it may provide an opportunity for you to use the safest maintenance treatment possible when you become pregnant (see Chapter 14 for more about maintenance treatment). By that, I simply mean the treatment with the least risk for the child that is effective for you. For some, that may be psychotherapy alone. For others, it might mean using one of the antidepressants that we know the most about during pregnancy and breast-feeding. You may already know which maintenance treatment or treatment combination works best for you. If not, advance planning for pregnancy can provide the opportunity to determine that before getting pregnant. This could take a year or more because the longer you stay in remission as a result of a particular treatment, the more confident you can be that it works well for you. Also, you may need to try more than one approach to find what works best for you.

Even with advance planning, relapse is possible, so I recommend deciding before you get pregnant what steps you will take if relapse occurs. Having a plan in place can greatly decrease stress if your depression returns. For example, if you are receiving weekly psychotherapy, the first step might be to increase the frequency to twice a week. The second step, if necessary, might be to start an antidepressant. Of course, these are just examples. The point is that these decisions can be difficult and stressful, so try to make contingency plans in advance if you can.

Planning is good, but we all know life doesn't always work out the way we plan. What if you are pregnant or breast-feeding now? The most important step is to talk to your treatment team and decide together what the safest approach is for your specific situation. There are many factors to consider when making treatment decisions (see Chapter 11); however, treatment with psychotherapy alone may be the safest option if you are experiencing mild depression. For more severe depression or mild depression that does not respond to psychotherapy, the risks versus benefits of medication treatment should be considered.

Bipolar disorder

Bipolar disorder presents many challenges for women who want to have children. This is because of the severity of the illness as well as the fact that many medications used to treat this disorder are known to cause birth defects (also see Chapter 8).[505] As with major depression, women with bipolar disorder have a high risk of relapse during pregnancy[506] and after delivery.[507, 508] But, these rates are similar to those among nonpregnant women, which suggests that pregnancy itself may neither increase nor decrease the risk of relapse.[505] Unfortunately, the baseline risk of relapse after stopping medication is very high for bipolar disorders. Further, while treatment with psychotherapy alone may be effective in preventing relapse for some women with major depression, there is currently no evidence that this strategy is effective for bipolar disorder.[509] The conclusion is that there may be no available option that is completely free of risk. On the one hand, stopping medication is associated with a risk of relapse of illness; on the other, taking medications may expose the child to some risk of adverse effects. So, advance planning is essential for those who have bipolar disorder and want to become pregnant. It may not be possible to eliminate risk completely, but you can develop a plan that minimizes risks for both you and your child.

Medication treatment for bipolar disorder during pregnancy and breast-feeding

Antidepressants are sometimes used for the treatment of bipolar depression (see Chapters 8 and 11 for more information). Please see the preceding section for information about using these medications when pregnant or nursing. Everything I said about using antidepressants for major depression applies to bipolar disorder. Current evidence indicates that individuals with bipolar disorder require ongoing treatment with a mood stabilizer to avoid relapse (see Chapter 11 for more information). Unfortunately, many medications that provide mood stabilization also are known to cause birth defects when taken by pregnant women.

Lithium is one of the most effective treatments for bipolar disorders (see Chapter 8 for more detailed information about lithium). The risk of birth defects has been thought to be very high with lithium, although some recent evidence suggests that the risk may be less than originally thought.[510] Nonetheless, first-trimester exposure to lithium is associated with a greater relative incidence of cardiovascular malformations compared with that in the general population.[505, 510] Several anticonvulsants are also effective as mood stabilizers (see Chapter 8 for more information). Among these, valproate and carbamazepine are known to increase the risk of birth defects during pregnancy, and there is some evidence that lamotrigine may as well.[505] Finally, **second-generation antipsychotics** are also used for bipolar disorder. There is very limited evidence in regard to the potential risks associated with the use of these medications during pregnancy.[505, 511]

Table 12.4   General recommendations concerning pregnancy and breast-feeding for those with bipolar disorder

---

◆ Be absolutely sure you are not pregnant before starting any medication.

◆ Avoid unplanned pregnancy.

◆ If you become pregnant, let your health care providers know immediately.

◆ Tell your health care providers if you are planning to get pregnant or think you may be pregnant now.

◆ Advance planning for pregnancy and breast-feeding is critical to minimize risk.

In regard to treatment during breast-feeding, lithium, valproate, carbamazepine, and lamotrigine are secreted in breast milk.[509] Please discuss with your treatment team the risks and benefits of breast-feeding while taking these medications.

Recommendations

As I said earlier in this section, bipolar disorder presents many challenges for women who want to have children. Decisions about pregnancy and treatment are very complicated and must be made on an individual basis. Thus, I can make only very general recommendations that may be helpful. These are listed in Table 12.4.

In order to minimize risk, advance planning is critical. If you have bipolar disorder, please take precautions to avoid unplanned pregnancy. My strongest recommendation is to take your time and gather as much information as possible when considering pregnancy. Also, please do not make a decision based only on reading this book. Each woman's situation is unique and the various options can be complicated. Talk to your treatment team, including your obstetrician, about your desire to have a child. Once you have gathered information and all of your questions have been answered, you can make a thoughtful and well-informed decision about pregnancy.

Premenstrual dysphoric disorder

Premenstrual dysphoric disorder (PMDD) is a mood disorder related to a woman's menstrual cycle.[512] The DSM-IV-TR (see Chapter 2 for more information about this manual) lists PMDD in an appendix as a disorder that requires further study.[38] PMDD was placed in the appendix because the experts felt there was not enough evidence available to include it as an "official" disorder. The diagnostic criteria may be revised over time based on further research. Currently, PMDD is defined as a condition causing symptoms such as depressed **mood**, anxiety, loss of interest in activities, and rapid changes in emotional state (labile mood).[38] These symptoms typically come on during the week prior to menses and disappear after the onset of menstruation. As currently defined, the diagnosis requires at least five of the symptoms listed in Table 12.5.[38] These symptoms must be present most of the time during the week prior to menses, and at least one of the symptoms must be one of the first four on the list. Also, the symptoms must have occurred most months for at least twelve consecutive months. Finally, the symptoms must cause impairment in functioning. The DSM-IV-TR differentiates PMDD from more common minor premenstrual symptoms, commonly known as premenstrual syndrome or PMS, which may affect as many as 70% of women.[512]

A number of disorders can result in symptoms similar to those of PMDD associated with menstruation and should be ruled out. These include autoimmune disorders, diabetes mellitus, anemia, hypothyroidism, dysmenorrhea, and endometriosis.[512] Symptoms of both depression and bipolar disorder worsen prior to menses, so it is important to determine whether the condition is actually PMDD or another mood disorder.

The biological cause or causes of PMDD are currently unknown. The primary hypothesis at this time is that dysfunction in female sex hormonal changes related to the menstrual cycle underlie this condition.[512] Abnormal function of the **neurotransmitter serotonin** has also been implicated.[512] There is some evidence for an inherited increase in risk for developing PMDD.[512] Finally, in regard to psychological factors, stress is associated with this illness.

Table 12.5 DSM-IV-TR symptoms of premenstrual dysphoric disorder (PMDD)[38]

PMDD diagnosis requires at that least five symptoms (and at least one of the first four) must have occurred most months for at least twelve consecutive months. Additional symptoms may include muscle pain or suicidal thoughts.

1. Feeling sad, hopeless, or self-deprecating

2. Feeling tense, anxious, or on edge

3. Marked lability of mood interspersed with frequent tearfulness

4. Persistent irritability, anger, and increased interpersonal conflicts

5. Deceased interest in usual activities, which may be associated with withdrawal from social relationships

6. Difficulty concentrating

7. Feeling fatigued, lethargic, or lacking in energy

8. Marked changes in appetite, which may be associated with binge eating or craving certain foods

9. Hypersomnia or insomnia

10. A subjective feeling of being overwhelmed or out of control

11. Physical symptoms such as breast tenderness or swelling, headaches or sensations of bloating, or weight gain with tightness of fit of clothing, shoes, or ring

Several treatment approaches may be beneficial for PMDD. Adopting a more healthy lifestyle may be helpful for some.[512] Additionally, relaxation therapy and psychotherapy can lead to a reduction of symptoms.[512, 513] If medication is required, the SSRI antidepressants are frequently effective (see Chapter 8 for more about these medications).[512, 514, 515] Finally, suppressing ovulation by controlling the usual hormonal fluctuations associated with the menstrual cycle can be effective.[512] Oral contraceptives and other medications have been used for this purpose.

13

Getting Well:
The Acute Phase of Treatment

THIS CHAPTER IS ABOUT GETTING WELL. The acute phase begins when you start treatment and continues until you are in full remission. Once you are completely well, it is likely that you will enter a maintenance phase of treatment (see Chapter 14). The aim of acute treatment is for you to get completely well as quickly as possible. The purpose of this chapter is to help you achieve that goal. ONCE AGAIN, I WANT TO EMPHASIZE THAT THIS BOOK PROVIDES ONLY GENERAL GUIDELINES AND CANNOT REPLACE ADVICE AND TREATMENT FROM A QUALIFIED PROFESSIONAL.

Most of the time the decisions that will be critical to your recovery occur during a follow-up appointment with your medical or mental health providers. Let's talk about what happens during these visits.

Follow-up appointments

Follow-up visits are typically very different depending on whether your appointment is with your therapist or with your prescriber. While many of the same principles apply, this chapter will focus on what are commonly known as medication follow-up appointments or "med checks." Med checks generally occur every few weeks during acute treatment, but the frequency can vary considerably from one provider to another.

The duration of these appointments is also variable but often is in the range of fifteen to thirty minutes (see Chapter 5 for more about this). Thus, it is critical to use the time effectively. Most of this chapter is about helping you prepare so that you can do just that (also see Chapter 6).

The goal of medication follow-up appointments is to find out how you are responding to treatment and determine whether any changes need to be made. This means determining whether you are getting better as well as whether you are having any medication side effects. Given the short time typically available for the appointment, it is usually best to stay focused on this specific issue. Med check visits are usually not about psychotherapy; however, some prescribers may provide very brief psychotherapy during follow-up visits. I recommend asking your provider directly about this issue so that you both have the same expectations of the visit. Unless your prescriber provides psychotherapy, she or he will likely want to keep the session focused on your medication treatment. It is to your advantage to follow this strategy and maximize your medication treatment. I also strongly recommend therapy for most people (see Chapters 9 and 11), but in most cases that will be with a different provider. Of course, it is useful to let your prescriber know about any major stressors that may influence your treatment response. However, this information should be provided in a short summary rather than excessive detail. Save the detail for your therapy session. That said, if you are in crisis or have thoughts about harming yourself or others and need immediate help, then your prescriber needs to know that. In that case, tell your prescriber at the beginning of the session so that she or he will know that issue needs to be the primary focus of the session. In those situations, issues related to your medication treatment may have to be deferred to another day and the session devoted to helping you manage the immediate concerns.

I want to mention two more very important points about medication management. The first is that some medications require monitoring of blood levels to determine whether the level of medication is within a certain therapeutic range. "Therapeutic range" means that a certain amount of medication is required to be in the bloodstream either for a treatment response or to prevent side effects. Many psychiatric medications do not have a therapeutic range, so monitoring is not necessary (this information is provided in Chapter 8). For those medications that do require monitoring of therapeutic levels, it is very important to have your blood drawn as recommended by your prescriber. For example, **lithium** is a medication that requires a certain level in the bloodstream to be effective; also, if the level of lithium gets too high, side effects can develop. Some medications require blood work to monitor for possible side effects. Again, lithium is an example of this. Some medications, like lithium, require monitoring for both therapeutic levels and side effects, while some require only one or the other (see Chapter 8 for information about specific medications). The important point here is that in many cases the results from your blood work may be necessary to make treatment decisions at follow-up appointments. In most cases, your prescriber will give you a prescription or lab order to get the required blood work done before you next appointment. For some medications and side effects, the lab work must be done at a specific time of day and/or at a specific time in relation to when you take your medication. In some cases, blood tests need to be done after you have been on the medication for a specific length of time. Be sure you understand exactly when and what time of day to get your blood work done. In most cases, your prescriber will want to see the results of your blood work at the time of your next appointment to facilitate the decision-making process. If so, please be sure you have your lab work done in time for the results to be available on the day of your appointment. It can take hours to days for results to be available, depending on the specific test and the laboratory doing the analysis. So, ask your provider exactly when you need to get your blood drawn in order for her or him to have the results when you come in for your office visit.

The second point about medication management is that medications need to be taken as prescribed in order to be effective. However, we all can forget to take one or more doses. In Chapter 11, I suggested using a medication box to help keep track of your doses. This can be especially useful if you take several different medications. The daily **mood** chart (described later in this chapter) provides a row with boxes to check on days when you have taken all your medications as prescribed. I mention this issue here because it is critical to let your prescriber know if you have missed more than a few doses of medication. Admitting that you have missed doses might seem embarrassing, but your prescriber will understand. We all have a hard time remembering to take medications. The important thing is to work together to come up with a strategy that will help you remember. Equally important is to avoid making an incorrect treatment decision. For example, if you have been taking a prescription for several weeks but are not getting better, it is critical to consider whether you may have skipped many doses. If not, then the appropriate decision might be to change the dose or medication because it isn't working. But, if you have missed more than a few doses, then any lack of response may be a result of missed doses rather than the medication being ineffective. In that situation, the appropriate strategy would most likely be to focus on taking the medication correctly rather than changing it.

Before we talk more about getting ready for follow-up appointments, let's discuss the issue of individual treatment response.

Individual variations in treatment response

One important point to keep in mind is that response to psychiatric treatments varies considerably from one person to another. This applies to both benefits and side effects. Thus, psychiatric treatment depends much more on any given person's individual response than do other branches of medicine. For example, we know that a number of classes of antidepressants are effective in general, but unfortunately we don't know which one will work for any given individual. The same holds true for side effects. We know what side effects any given medication can cause; we just don't have a way to know in advance whether any specific person will experience any or all of these side effects. This leaves us with a less than ideal situation. We just have to try a treatment approach to see whether it works. We cannot know until we try a treatment whether it will be effective or cause side effects. Therefore, your individual response to treatment must be monitored carefully.

Based on the discussion above, we can identify two key components to achieving a full recovery and getting well as quickly as possible: (1) monitoring progress and side effects and (2) maximizing treatment and other interventions. We'll discuss monitoring first.

Are you getting better?

It might seem like monitoring your progress toward recovery is a no-brainer. After all, you will know if you feel better. Right? Actually, it can be much more difficult than you think. People may have a hard time determining whether they are getting better.

Mood symptom fluctuation

One reason that monitoring treatment response can be difficult is that mood symptoms tend to wax and wane a bit for most people. This typically happens whether the disorder is being treated or not. Some of the variability has to do with external factors. For example, if something good happens, **depression** may improve temporarily. Of course, the opposite also occurs. Stressful events and bad news tend to worsen depression.

Hypomanic episodes can also fluctuate somewhat in response to situations. In addition to mood variations related to situations, symptom severity can go up and down for no apparent reason. This probably has something to do with the **neurobiology** of the disorders that we don't understand yet. In any case, the waxing and waning of symptoms can contribute to difficulties with monitoring progress. The following is an example of how symptom fluctuations can interfere with treatment.

Suppose you have been taking an antidepressant for about four weeks and have a medication follow-up appointment today. Let's say that you have been feeling somewhat better for about two weeks. However, the last three days have been really difficult and you are feeling much more depressed. Most of us are much more likely to focus on the last few days than on the entire two weeks. This is just human nature. What has happened most recently seems more real than what transpired further back in time. Also, we often notice when we feel bad more than when we feel good. So, what is likely to happen at your follow-up appointment? You guessed it. When your prescriber asks how you have been feeling, you tell her, "Really down." Hopefully, through further discussion, the two of you will figure out that it has been a short downturn within a longer period of improvement. But that may not always happen. The risk is that you and she will make a decision based on the belief that you are not getting better when in fact you really are. In that case, perhaps the result will be an unnecessary increase in the dose of your antidepressant. In the worst case scenario, this increase could result in the development of side effects that are so bothersome that you end up stopping the medication and starting over with another agent. Since antidepressants don't work immediately, this whole process might delay your recovery by weeks. The delay could be longer if the second medication isn't effective. The irony is that none of that would have happened if it had been clear that you were actually getting better and there was no reason to change your medication. Unfortunately, scenarios like the one I just described happen all too often. During the acute phase of treatment, it is critical to be absolutely sure of your level of progress. I will tell you how to do that further along in the chapter. First, let's go over some more reasons that it can be hard to be sure about whether you are getting better.

Mood cycles

In the preceding paragraph, we discussed short-term mood variations—in other words, increases and decreases in symptom severity that last for a few hours or a few days. However, longer-term fluctuations also occur, and these changes can last for weeks or months or even years. We typically refer to these as mood cycles. The distinction between a short-term fluctuation and a cycle is somewhat arbitrary. In this book, I use *cycle* to mean a change from one type of **mood episode** to another that lasts for at least one week. By *mood episode*, I mean a period of time during which you meet the criteria for an occurrence of either mood elevation or depression. I also consider a symptom-free period as an episode. We call these periods of full remission and euthymic mood. Please see Chapter 3 for more about mood episodes. Mood cycles must also be taken into consideration when evaluating response to treatment.

Let me give another example. Suppose an individual has been experiencing episodes of depression that typically last two or three weeks and alternate with episodes of full remission that last about the same length of time. As in the preceding example, let's say this person has been taking an antidepressant for about four weeks and has a medication follow-up appointment today. In this case our make-believe patient has been symptom free for about ten days. Is she responding to treatment? The answer is that we don't know. She could be feeling better because of a good response to the medication, or it could be that she has just cycled into euthymia and the antidepressant was not responsible. In this situation, it is going to take a longer period of remission to know whether the treatment is working. The point of this example is that if you know your typical mood cycling pattern, it must be taken into consideration when you evaluate treatment response. That said, some people have very irregular cycling patterns, and even those with generally more regular patterns can have unexpected changes. Still, considering previous cycling patterns can be very helpful when evaluating whether you are getting better.

The nature of treatment response

There is one more reason it can be difficult to assess your progress. This one has to do with the nature of the treatment response. I use the word *treatment* here in a very broad sense to include medications and other biological treatments, psychotherapy, and other complementary approaches such as exercise and meditation. In addition to the individual variations in response discussed above, treatment response typically has a slow onset followed by gradual improvement over time. During that gradual improvement, symptoms often wax and wane somewhat. In other words, changes can be subtle and difficult to notice. We tend to incorrectly think about psychiatric treatment in terms of other experiences we have had with medication. For example, we may take an over-the-counter pain medication for a sore muscle and feel much better within half an hour. Or we might take an antibiotic for an infection and notice improvement within twenty-four hours and a full response within a few days. We have to develop a different mindset in regard to **mood disorders**. Response is almost always much slower and occurs with an up-and-down course. It is essential to have a very specific plan in place to monitor progress. The plan that I recommend is using a mood chart.

Mood charts

There are a couple of ways that you can keep track of your progress. One method is to periodically complete one of the many scales that measure the severity of mood symptoms. A problem with that method is that it takes some time and effort to complete the scales. The approach that I think

---

Table 13.1   Using your mood charts

Daily charts

+ Complete the chart for each day at the end of that day.

+ Count the total number of symptoms of either mood elevation or depression (not both) for the day from the list below. There are eight possible symptoms for mood elevation and ten possible symptoms for depression.

+ If you experience symptoms of both mood elevation and depression in the same day, count only the symptoms from whichever period (elevation or depression) lasted for the longest amount of time.

+ Count a symptom if it was severe enough to be bothersome.

+ Check the box on the daily chart that corresponds to the day and number of symptoms.

+ The bottom line on the daily chart is to help you keep track of medications. Check the box if you have taken all of your medications as prescribed for a given day.

+ Be sure to enter the starting and ending dates and chart number (just start with 1 and number consecutively).

Mood symptoms:

☐ Elevated or irritable mood

☐ Elevated self-esteem or grandiosity

☐ Decreased need for sleep

☐ Talkativeness

☐ Flight of ideas or racing thoughts

---

works best for most people is to use a mood chart. This method doesn't take much time and it provides a very clear picture of how you are doing. Anytime you take a look at the chart, you can see how your recovery is progressing. The chart can also help you decide whether any complementary approaches you have implemented on your own are working. Equally important, such a chart can be invaluable when you have to make treatment decisions with your mental health treatment team.

A key point about mood charts is that they provide trend information. I define *trend* as a general movement in a specific direction beyond

---

Table 13.1 Using your mood charts (*continued*)

☐ Distractibility

☐ Increased goal-directed activity

☐ Excessive involvement in pleasurable activities

☐ No symptoms of mood elevation or depression

☐ Depressed mood

☐ Anhedonia

☐ Increase or decrease in appetite or weight

☐ Insomnia or increased sleeping

☐ Increase or decrease of motor activity

☐ Fatigue or loss of energy

☐ Feelings or thoughts of worthlessness or inappropriate guilt

☐ Difficulty thinking, concentrating, or making decisions

☐ Thoughts of death or suicide

☐ Low self-esteem

Monthly charts

♦ Average the number of daily symptoms separately for elevation and depression for each month (from the two daily charts for that month).

♦ Check the box on the chart that corresponds to the month and the average number of symptoms.

♦ Each month has a column for mood elevations, labeled "E," and depressions, labeled "D."

♦ Be sure to enter the starting and ending dates and the chart number.

---

short-term fluctuations. Because of the short-term fluctuations in both symptoms and treatment response described above, it is critical to know whether your symptoms are trending better or worse over time.

A number of mood charts are available, but the ones I provide are easy to use and contain all of the information you need. Two charts, a daily chart (Form 13.1) and a monthly chart (Form 13.2), are included in this chapter and are also available as PDF files that can be freely downloaded from our website (http://www.bullpub.com/downloads). Detailed instructions are provided in Table 13.1. I suggest including a symptom if it was

Form 13.1
Daily mood chart

Number of symptoms	1	2	3	4	5	6	7	8	9	10	11	12	13	14	15	16
8																
7																
6																
5																
Elevation 4																
3																
2																
1																
None 0																
1																
2																
3																
4																
Depression 5																
6																
7																
8																
9																
10																
Day	1	2	3	4	5	6	7	8	9	10	11	12	13	14	15	16
Medications [check if all doses taken as prescribed]																

Form 13.2
Monthly mood chart

Average number of symptoms from daily chart																									
	E	D	E	D	E	D	E	D	E	D	E	D	E	D	E	D	E	D	E	D	E	D	E	D
8																								
7																								
6																								
5																								
Elevation 4																								
3																								
2																								
1																								
None 0																								
1																								
2																								
3																								
4																								
Depression 5																								
6																								
7																								
8																								
9																								
10																								
Month	1		2		3		4		5		6		7		8		9		10		11		12	

283

severe enough that day to be bothersome. Obviously that will be a judgment call when a symptom is only slightly bothersome. You can decide to count or not in those situations, but please be consistent. The daily chart also provides boxes for you to check if you have taken all of your medications as prescribed on a particular day.

Please start your mood chart today and keep it up to date. This is one of the single most important things you can do for your recovery. Finally, don't forget to take it with you to all appointments with your treatment team members.

Maximizing treatment

As I said at the beginning of this chapter, two key components are involved in achieving a complete recovery and getting well as quickly as possible: monitoring progress, as discussed in the preceding section, and maximizing treatment.

Maximizing treatment boils down to a simple process. The input to the process must be accurate information about progress. The information must be acted upon using logical, evidence-based decision making. The output is a decision that is most likely to result in full recovery.

Inputs to good decision making

This concept of having good inputs applies to anything you are doing to get better, whether it is medication, psychotherapy, or a strategy that you implement on your own, such as exercise. However, it is especially applicable to biological treatments. In many cases, visits with prescribers are relatively infrequent and the duration of the appointment is short. It is critical that you do everything possible to support good decision making during those visits.

We have already discussed the main input during follow-up appointments—that is, information about your progress toward recovery. In other words, are your symptoms trending better or worse or is there no change? However, it is also important for you to provide any other relevant information that may influence treatment decisions. An obvious example is medication side effects. It is critical that you keep track of any problems you may be having so these can be discussed. As with your improvement, it is necessary to track whether the side effect is trending better or worse or if it doesn't seem to be changing. This is important because medication side effects often improve or go away completely after taking a medication for some time. In many cases, if the side effect goes away on its own, nothing further needs to be done and you can keep taking the medication. On the other hand, if the side effect isn't getting better or is getting worse, then a medication adjustment may be indicated. So, it is critical to know the trend when you go in for an appointment. If a side effect was bothersome but is decreasing each day, that may lead to a very different decision than if it were getting worse. As with improvement, I strongly recommend tracking side effects with a chart. I have provided Form 13.3 for your use. It is included in this chapter and is also available as a PDF file that can be freely downloaded from our website (http://www.bullpub.com/downloads). This form is most applicable to medication treatment, but it can also be used with psychotherapy. For example, some people might temporarily have more symptoms if their therapy is exploring painful issues. The form can also be used with approaches that you implement on your own. An example is soreness from starting a new exercise program. The major benefit of the form is that you have good trend information to be able to weigh the pros and cons of continuing the current strategies versus trying something else.

There is one last bit of information that you need to input into the medical decision-making process—any other relevant information. What kind of information? Anything that could affect treatment decisions. Suppose you are a female and want to become pregnant (see Chapter 12 for much more about this). That could certainly influence decisions about medications. Or maybe you are going to move or have an insurance change coming up. Either of these scenarios could cause you to have to change providers. If such a change is upcoming, it might not be a good time to change medications, unless absolutely necessary. Think about anything that should be considered on your next appointment and make a note of it. I

Form 13.3 Adverse effect chart

Severity (higher number = greater severity)	Day	1	2	3	4	5	6	7	8	9	10	11	12	13	14	15
5																
4																
3																
2																
1																
0																

Adverse effect

have included Form 13.4, a summary sheet, for your use. This form is provided in this chapter and is also available as a PDF file that can be freely downloaded from our website (http://www.bullpub.com/downloads). The purpose of this form is to provide a place for you to write down anything that you want to discuss at the appointment. Writing down your questions or any topics you want to discuss, when you think of them, will help you be sure to accomplish everything you want at your follow-up appointments. Just remember to take your mood chart(s), summary form, and (if needed) your side effect chart to the appointment.

Form 13.4   Follow-up appointment summary

1. Appointment date: _____ Time: _____

2. Topics to discuss:

   a. _____

   b. _____

   c. _____

   d. _____

   e. _____

3. Questions to ask:

   a. _____

   b. _____

   c. _____

   d. _____

   e. _____

Evidence-based decision making

This section is about making "the right decision at the right time." I'm sure you remember that I appointed you team captain in Chapter 6. You may also remember that I said that means you are the decider. Of course, you will have help from your providers and perhaps others, but ultimately it is your recovery.

One of my main goals in writing this book is to provide some of the information you will need to make decisions. Also, I want to prepare you for the kinds of decisions you are likely going to have to make BEFORE you go to your appointment. That means that you will have time to think before the appointment. You will also have time to do additional research, talk to friends or family, and do anything else that may be helpful to you. Let's go over some of the decisions that you are likely going to have to make in medication follow-up appointments. In its most basic form, the decision involves two components. The first decision during an acute treatment follow-up visit almost always boils down to this: SHOULD WE KEEP DOING WHAT WE ARE DOING—OR DO SOMETHING DIFFERENT? The answer is based on two pieces of information: (1) Are you able to continue taking the medication? and (2) Is the medication working? We discussed collecting this information earlier in the chapter. Now we will talk about how to use this data.

The answer to the question about being able to continue taking the medication usually involves side effects. However, there are other possible issues. In some cases, the cost of the medication might be prohibitive. In other situations, the new onset of medical problems or the desire to become pregnant could indicate a need to make a change.

It is important to point out that decisions about side effects are not always straightforward because of the limitation we are working with—individual response. Just as we don't have a way to predict whether any given person will actually experience any of the possible side effects associated with a medication, we also don't have a way to predict whether any side effects that do occur will go away. We often have some data about the statistical likelihood of side effects for all individuals who take a given medication, but we can't predict for sure how a medication will turn out for you. Because of this inability to predict, sometimes decisions are "more of an art than a science." Of course, if a side effect is dangerous, then it is an easy decision to stop the medication. But usually that isn't the case. Many of the more common side effects associated with psychiatric medications aren't dangerous and do not cause permanent harm; they are just annoying or uncomfortable. So, as we have said before, it all comes down to weighing the risks and benefits or the pros and cons. Let's go over a few examples.

If a given side effect is really bothersome and isn't getting better, then most of the time the logical decision is to try to fix the side effect by changing the medication or adjusting the dose. But suppose a person has tried several antidepressants for severe depression and none were very effective. Now the medication is working very well but the problem is a daily headache that is very uncomfortable. In this case, the most logical choice might be to try to live with the headache or at least keep taking the medication and see whether the headache eventually goes away. Of course, treating the headache would also be a possibility. On the other hand, a different person who is trying the same medication as the initial treatment for mild depression will most likely not want to tolerate any side effect for long because the depression is mild and there are many other options to try. So, decisions should be based on the individual situation. My goal is to prepare you for some of the kinds of decisions that you may have to make and encourage you to make choices based on the big picture of your recovery by weighing all the pros and cons of the available options.

The other issue is whether a medication is working. But, I need to add one very important point about whether a medication treatment is working: The question is not just, Is it working? The question is whether it is working as expected given the duration of treatment. This is a subtle but very important distinction. As we have discussed, the onset of response to almost all psychiatric medications is gradual. Thus, the expectation will be very different if the treatment has been ongoing for one week or for six weeks. Medical and mental health professionals think in terms of adequate treatment trials. An adequate treatment trial simply means that a treatment was tried at the correct dose for an adequate amount of time. This idea is often applied to full remission of symptoms. In other words, if someone has taken the correct dose for a certain number of weeks, then an adequate trial has been completed. If the person were not in remission, then at that point, a change would likely be in order. The same idea applies to decisions earlier in the course of treatment. If an individual has taken the correct dose for a certain period of time and the response is not at the level that would be expected, then an adjustment should be considered. Specific recommendations are provided on the following pages; here, my aim is to make the concept clear. In summary, acute treatment decisions are based on answering the two questions: (1) Are you able to continue taking the medication; and (2) Is the medication working as would be expected given the dose and duration of treatment? If the answer to both is yes, then the decision should be to continue the same treatment. If the answer to either question is no, then a change is indicated. This brings up the second question: What kind of change should be made?

There are two basic kinds of change to be considered. One is to continue the current medication but change the way it is taken. This might mean increasing or decreasing the milligram dose. Another possibility is to change the timing—for example, changing from morning to evening dosing if the medication is causing sedation. Another strategy might be to split a single dose into two separate doses taken at different times to try to decrease side effects. The second basic change is to start or add a different medication. This might mean stopping one medication entirely and starting another one. Sometimes the choice is to continue the current agent but start a second medication in addition. How are these decisions made? In general, the approach is to follow treatment guidelines, which are summarized in the following sections. However, keep in mind that many situations do not fit neatly within a guideline and a different approach may be optimal for a specific individual. Also, these are just general guidelines; they are not meant to replace advice and treatment by a qualified professional.

Outputs

Once a decision has been made, the process continues to the next assessment point, which is usually the next follow-up appointment. Typically, treatment involves going through several of these decision points until full remission is achieved. Of course, for some people the first medication tried leads to full recovery at the starting dose and there are no side effect problems. In that case, there is probably no decision point until the maintenance phase of treatment (which is discussed in Chapter 14). The next sections will outline the acute treatment options for mood disorders.

Acute treatment for depressive disorders

The first question to address is how long to give the initial treatment before making a change if it is either ineffective or only partially beneficial. The research suggests four to eight weeks for antidepressant treatment.[37] Therefore, I suggest that the first decision point should occur when you have been on your initial treatment AT A THERAPEUTIC DOSE for about a month. Subsequent decision points also occur at four-week intervals. Obviously this is a general recommendation, and changes may need to be made sooner for a variety of reasons, such as significant worsening of symptoms or medication side effects. Further, optimizing treatment (e.g., increasing to the maximum dose) may be warranted sooner than four weeks. Table 13.2 has columns for partial response and no response. The idea of partial response requires some elaboration because the degree of partial response can be variable. For example, an individual with a "partial" improvement might be 10% or 90% better, or anywhere in between. This is an important distinction because having minimal improvement has different implications than if one is significantly (e.g., 60%–90%) better. Therefore, I suggest a definition of partial response as a 50% reduction in symptoms. Table 13.2 lists some recommended strategies if there is either an incomplete or no response to initial treatment using antidepressants for major depression.

Table 13.3 provides another way of looking at the general strategy when antidepressant treatment has no response. Maximizing the dose of the initial medication should almost always be considered before adding a second medication (augmentation) or changing to another agent.[37] This might not be possible in some cases, however, because of side effects or other reasons. Adding psychotherapy or increasing the frequency of sessions should also be considered. If there is a partial response to the maximum

Table 13.2 Strategies for partial or no response to antidepressant treatment[37]

	Full remission or significantly improved (at least 75% reduction in symptoms)	Partial response (at least 50% reduction in symptoms)	No response or less than 50% reduction in symptoms
After approximately four weeks on therapeutic dose of initial treatment with an antidepressant	Continue current treatment. Consider adding psychotherapy if not in full remission or for relapse prevention. Start maintenance treatment if in full remission.	Optimize/maximize dose of initial medication(s). Add psychotherapy.	Optimize/maximize dose of initial medication(s). Add psychotherapy. Increase frequency of psychotherapy. Consider changing to another first-line medication. Consider augmentation with a second medication. Consider ECT for severe depression.
After approximately eight weeks on therapeutic dose of initial treatment with an antidepressant	Optimize/maximize dose of initial medication(s) if not in full remission. Add psychotherapy if not in full remission or for relapse prevention. Start maintenance treatment if in full remission.	Optimize/maximize dose of initial medication(s) if not already accomplished. Add psychotherapy. Augment with a second medication. Consider changing to another first-line medication.	Change to another first-line medication. Add psychotherapy. Increase frequency of psychotherapy. Consider ECT for severe depression.

Table 13.3   General steps to follow for partial or no response to treatment with antidepressants (in chronological order)[37]

First-level steps

- Maximize or optimize dose of antidepressant.
- Add psychotherapy if not already started.
- Increase frequency of psychotherapy if already started.

Second-level steps

- Augment with a second medication, if partial response.
- Change to another first-line agent, if no response.
- Consider ECT for severe depression.

Third-level steps

- Change to a second-line medication.
- Consider ECT.

---

dose that can be tolerated, it is often most logical to try to gain additional improvement by augmenting with a second medication and/or psychotherapy rather than changing the primary medication. This is because there is a risk that trying a different drug could result in less of a response. Of course, if there are significant side effects from the first medication, then changing might be a better option. If the strategies of maximizing the dose, augmenting, and maximizing psychotherapy are not sufficient, the next step is to try another medication. If that strategy is unsuccessful, then switching to a second-line treatment is appropriate.

If the initial medication tried is not effective, the change to a second medication can be to one in the same class (e.g., SSRI to SSRI) or a different class (e.g., SSRI to SNRI).[37] In my opinion, it is generally more logical to change to a different class, unless there is a compelling reason not to do so. An example might be prior trials of agents from other classes in earlier mood episodes.

When there is a partial response to the first or subsequent medication, strategies should be generally aimed at maximizing the response to that drug. Augmentation approaches can be medication, psychotherapy, or both. Medication tactics can include adding lithium, thyroid hormone, an **anticonvulsant**, a psychostimulant, a **second-generation antipsychotic**, or an antidepressant from a different category.[37] Various potential risks and benefits are associated with the different options, and thus a detailed discussion of the options with your prescriber is critical.

The final tier of options include those that have more risk, such as **monoamine oxidase inhibitors (MAOIs)**, MAOIs and **tricyclic antidepressants (TCA)** in combination, electroconvulsive therapy (ECT), or vagus nerve stimulation.[37] Again, a careful risk-benefit analysis must be done. Nonetheless, these approaches may result in remission and should be seriously considered.

Acute treatment for bipolar disorders

Bipolar depression

As with **unipolar** depression, the first question to address with bipolar depression is how long to give the initial treatment before making a change if it is either ineffective or only partially beneficial. The research has not established the optimal time for bipolar depression treatment.[246] One guideline suggests four-week intervals between treatment changes.[411] Based on the limited evidence and my clinical experience, this advice seems reasonable. Therefore, as in the table for unipolar illness, I suggest that the first decision point should occur when you have been on your initial treatment AT A THERAPEUTIC DOSE for about a month. Subsequent decision points also occur at four-week intervals. Obviously, this is a general recommendation and changes might need to be made sooner for a variety of reasons, such as significant worsening of symptoms or medication side effects. Further, optimizing treatment (e.g., increasing to the maximum dose) may be warranted sooner than four weeks. Finally, as in the table for unipolar depression, I suggest a definition of partial response as about a 50% reduction in symptoms. Table 13.4 lists some recommended strategies if there is either an incomplete or no response to initial treatment for bipolar depression. However, the list is not exhaustive and other approaches may be considered depending on your situation.

Table 13.4 Strategies for partial or no response in treatment of bipolar depression[411–14, 423]

	Full remission or significantly improved (at least 75% reduction in symptoms)	Partial response (at least 50% reduction in symptoms)	No response or less than 50% reduction in symptoms
After approximately four weeks on therapeutic dose of initial treatment	Continue current treatment. Consider adding psychotherapy for relapse prevention. Start maintenance treatment if in full remission.	Consider optimizing/maximizing dose of initial medication(s). Consider adding psychotherapy.	Optimize/maximize dose of initial medication(s). Add psychotherapy. Increase frequency of psychotherapy.
After approximately eight weeks on therapeutic dose of initial treatment	Optimize/maximize dose of initial medication(s) if less than full remission. Add frequency of psychotherapy if not in full remission or for relapse prevention. Start maintenance treatment if in full remission.	Optimize/maximize dose of initial medication(s) if not already accomplished. Add psychotherapy. Add quetiapine if on another medication. Add modafinil. Add second mood stabilizer. Increase frequency of psychotherapy.	Change to another first-line medication. Start pramipexole monotherapy. Add ECT for severe depression. Add psychotherapy. Increase frequency of psychotherapy.

Table 13.5   General steps to follow for partial or no response to
treatment for mood elevations (in chronological order)[413]

---

1.   Optimize dose of first medication(s) tried.

2.   Add a second medication or try SGA in combination with lithium or
     valproate.

3.   Consider clozapine.

4.   Consider ECT.

Table 13.4 suggests adding psychotherapy in all cases (if not already started). This advice is based on the literature and my own clinical experience. My strongest recommendation is to start psychotherapy at the beginning of treatment. However, if that was not feasible and if you are not responding to treatment as well as you should, please consider starting psychotherapy along with medication. Even if you are in full remission, adding psychotherapy can help you stay well. See Chapter 9 for more information about psychotherapies.

Mania, hypomania, and mixed episodes

The options to consider when the response to an initial medication is incomplete are not as extensive or well studied for mood elevations as they are for bipolar depression. Recommended strategies are listed in Table 13.5. The first option is to optimize the initial medication. For lithium or valproate, this means adjusting the dose to obtain close to the maximum recommended level in the bloodstream. For an SGA, it means maximizing the dose. Of course, optimization may be limited by side effects. If mood elevation symptoms are still not in full remission, the next recommended strategy is to try a combination of two antimanic agents. An SGA with lithium or valproate is particularly recommended.[413] If this fails, the next option is to try clozapine or ECT.

14

Maintenance Treatment and Relapse Prevention

The goal of the maintenance phase of treatment is to prevent relapse. For medication treatment, maintenance typically means continuing on the same dose of medication that was required to achieve remission in the first place. For psychotherapy, the frequency of sessions might stay the same or decrease depending on your individual situation. This chapter will first review the evidence-based recommendations for maintenance treatment for **unipolar** and bipolar disorders. In the second part of the chapter, I will discuss other aspects of relapse prevention. AS I HAVE STATED BEFORE, I PROVIDE ONLY GENERAL GUIDELINES THAT MAY OR MAY NOT APPLY TO YOUR SPECIFIC SITUATION. THIS CHAPTER DOES NOT REPLACE ADVICE AND TREATMENT FROM A QUALIFED PROFESSIONAL.

Maintenance treatment

Before discussing specific recommendations, let's go over a few general thoughts about maintenance treatment.

The aim of maintenance treatment

The goal of maintenance treatment is to prevent relapse or recurrence of illness. What is the difference between relapse and recurrence? Usually, the word *relapse* is used to mean the return of symptoms either while still receiving treatment or after a short period of remission. *Recurrence* is generally used to indicate a return of symptoms after a relatively long period of remission, with or without treatment. You may find that medical and mental health professionals use the terms interchangeably. The definitions are somewhat arbitrary; the point is that we are talking about the return of symptoms whether it is labeled relapse or recurrence. For the sake of simplicity, I use the term *relapse* to indicate any return of symptoms.

Relapse prevention recommendations range from months of treatment for a single episode of major **depression** to lifelong treatment for recurrent unipolar illness and bipolar spectrum disorders. One general principle guiding maintenance treatment is that, for depressive disorders, the more **mood episodes** that one has experienced, the greater is the likelihood of recurrence. In contrast, for bipolar disorders, **recurrent disorders** almost always occur, so long-term maintenance treatment is almost always recommended. However, like all the recommendations in this book, these guidelines have to be interpreted in light of your individual situation as well as your risk tolerance. Let's discuss these issues next.

Decisions about maintenance treatment

I like to think about relapse prevention using a "risk tolerance" approach. The analogy of investing your hard-earned money might be useful. Financial planners often talk about risk tolerance. For example, individuals with higher risk tolerance may choose investments with a greater chance of high returns but also with a higher probability of loss. In contrast, more conservative investors may want lower risk and therefore accept the possibility of a lower return on investment. What does this have to do with **mood disorders**? Well, the answer is that maintenance treatment decreases the risk of relapse. So, I encourage you to think in terms of your risk tolerance as you make decisions about relapse prevention. In general, the longer you continue maintenance treatment, the longer you minimize the risk of relapse. It's that simple. That said, it is important to keep in mind that maintenance treatment doesn't guarantee that you won't have a relapse; it just decreases the risk.

Another important point is that the more mood episodes one experiences, the greater are the chances of experiencing additional episodes. In other words, having mood episodes seems to make the brain more vulnerable to future illness. Thus, an argument could be made that most people who have experienced even one episode may want to consider lifelong prevention efforts of some type. This is especially true if the episode was severe or if one has a family history of recurrent illness.

How do you decide? One consideration should be your current life situation and your prediction of how your life is going to be during the next year. Times that are very stressful in your life are not times when you want to increase your risk of relapse. For example, suppose you have been in a maintenance phase of treatment for the recommended period of time, but you anticipate that the next few months of your life are going to be highly stressful because of a job change or move. In that case, it might make sense to continue maintenance treatment until you are settled in your new job or home.

Another consideration is whether treatment is causing any adverse effects. Ideally, you and your provider found a biological treatment solution that did not cause side effects for you. Unfortunately, that is not always possible. Obviously, it is easier to make a decision to continue treatment if you are not experiencing side effects. However, in many cases, a perfect solution is not possible and one must choose the proverbial "lesser of evils." Thus, I encourage you to carefully weigh the importance of getting rid of annoying side effects against the risk of possible relapse.

Before moving on to specific recommendations, let's return to the issue of your risk tolerance. If you are in a maintenance phase of treatment and are at a point of deciding whether to continue treatment, then I strongly encourage you to come to a clear decision about your level of risk tolerance over the next year. Then use that information to interpret the information in the remainder of this chapter.

Maintenance treatment for depressive disorders

In general, the recommendation is to continue the same treatment for maintenance as was originally effective in acute treatment, whether this was pharmacotherapy, psychotherapy, or a combination of the two.[37] For medication treatment, continuation of the same dose is recommended. This may be true for psychotherapy (frequency of sessions) as well, at least for the first months of full remission.

Maintenance treatment can be divided into short- and long-term strategies. Some authors use the phrase *continuation treatment* instead of *short-term maintenance*. Who needs long-term maintenance? One recommendation is that those who have experienced three or more depressive episodes should receive long-term (lifelong) maintenance treatment.[37] In contrast, short-term maintenance treatment of four to nine months after achieving full remission is recommended for others who have had fewer episodes.[37]

My opinion is that decisions about the duration of maintenance treatment should be made by carefully considering the evidence. As discussed in Chapter 3, depression is often a recurrent illness. After one episode, the risk of a second is about 50% within the next two years and may be as high as 90% within the following six years.[4] Overall, 75%–95% of individuals who experience one major depressive episode will have at least one more.[4] Finally, after one episode the recurrence rate is at least 50%, after two the risk goes up to 70%, and after a third the risk of relapse is 90%.[1] To me, these statistics suggest that some type of maintenance treatment may be indicated for most, if not all, individuals who have experienced depression.

In addition to the number of episodes, some other factors are thought to increase the risk of recurrent illness.[37] These are listed in Table 14.1. Individuals with one or more of these risk factors may want to consider, at minimum, a longer duration of maintenance treatment after a single depressive episode or long-term maintenance after two episodes. Given the strong evidence for the effectiveness of psychotherapy for preventing relapse, this approach may be a good strategy for those who do

---

Table 14.1   Factors thought to increase the risk of depression recurrence[37]

- Failure to achieve full remission
- More severe episodes
- Early age of first episode
- Psychiatric comorbidity
- Presence of a chronic medical condition
- Family history of mood disorders
- Chronic psychosocial stress

---

not want to take long-term medication. However, both medication and therapy may provide a better chance of staying in remission than either alone. Also since the persistence of any symptoms can increase the risk of having another episode fourfold,[4] one of the best relapse prevention strategies is to do everything possible to achieve full remission. That's why I have suggested that you develop a comprehensive recovery strategy that makes use of more than one approach.

In summary, major depression has a high risk of becoming a **chronic** and recurrent illness, and **dysthymic disorder** is by definition chronic. Thus, my opinion is that the safest strategy is to implement some type of lifelong prevention plan after even one episode of either disorder. I think it is particularly hard to argue against that approach given the fact that some psychotherapy and complementary strategies (see Chapters 9 and 10) are likely to be beneficial for your life in general as well as for relapse prevention. My most important recommendation is to gather as much information as you can and discuss maintenance treatment options with your treatment team in order to find the best approach for your specific situation.

Maintenance treatment for bipolar disorders

For those who have a diagnosis of **bipolar I disorder** (at least one manic or mixed episode), long-term maintenance treatment with medication should be strongly considered.[413] Most experts say it is absolutely necessary because the evidence suggests that bipolar I disorder is almost always a chronic and recurrent illness. Though bipolar maintenance treatment has not been adequately studied, it is thought that prevention of additional mood episodes may lead to a more benign course of illness.[413] Further, having another mood episode can result in significant distress and suffering. I recommend doing whatever you can to avoid that possibility. Maintenance treatment for bipolar I disorder is believed to always require medication, although adjunctive psychotherapy can add significant benefit, as discussed below.

In many cases, maintenance treatment may mean continuing to take some or all of the medications that were effective for the acute treatment of a mood episode. However, in general, long-term treatment should protect against both mood elevations and depression. For those who have had bipolar illness for a number of years, the predominant **mood** can guide maintenance treatment. For example, a person with frequent depressive episodes and rare mood elevations may do better on a regimen targeted primarily at preventing depression. **Lithium** can be a good choice for maintenance treatment in general because it prevents both mood elevations and depressions.[413] Other recommendations include aripiprazole, quetiapine, valproate, and olanzapine for those with predominant mood elevations.[413] For those with predominant depression, quetiapine and lamotrigine are good options.[413] However, these are just general recommendations. Actual decisions need to be made after a detailed discussion with your prescriber of the pros and cons of the various options. All of these treatments have a significant potential to cause serious side effects (see Chapter 8), and no solutions are perfect. Thus, the choice of medications needs to take into account these risks weighed against the potential benefits. It is not uncommon to have to try a number of medications over several years to establish the best long-term prevention strategy for each person.

There is not currently enough evidence to know whether **bipolar II disorder** or other bipolar spectrum disorders should be thought of differently than bipolar I disorder in regard to maintenance treatment. That said, my opinion is that bipolar II disorder should generally be managed like bipolar I for maintenance purposes. I say that because this disorder has the potential to cause significant disability and suffering and is probably a chronic and recurrent illness for most people. We just don't know enough about **cyclothymic disorder** and **bipolar disorder not otherwise specified** (NOS) to be able to make good recommendations. There is probably some risk that either condition may eventually develop into either bipolar I or bipolar II disorder. I think that, at the very least, close monitoring for relapse is indicated. If there is evidence of worsening symptoms, then more aggressive strategies should certainly be considered. If you have either cyclothymia or bipolar disorder NOS, I strongly recommend that you have a detailed discussion of the options with your providers.

As I discussed in Chapters 9 and 11, there is compelling evidence that adjunctive psychotherapies can contribute significantly to relapse prevention in bipolar spectrum disorders. If you have not received psychotherapy, please consider starting now. Complementary approaches to relapse prevention have not been studied for bipolar spectrum illness. However, as I mentioned above in regard to unipolar illness, some may be beneficial for your life in general, and so it seems to me that they can't hurt and might help.

Additional strategies for relapse prevention

Once you are in full remission, the goal is to stay well for life, regardless of the disorder. Maintenance treatment, as described above, may play a role in that process. This section will focus on other aspects of lifelong recovery.

As I have stated a number of times throughout this book, please consider doing everything possible to maximize your chances of achieving a complete and lasting recovery. In some cases this means utilizing both medication and psychotherapy. It also means that you consider implementing some of the complementary approaches discussed in Chapter 10. Now is a good time to take stock of what you are currently doing to support your

---

Table 14.2   Elements of your relapse prevention plan

Relapse triggers
- Identification of triggers
- Strategies to prevent and cope with triggers

Early signs of relapse
- Identification of signs
- Plan of action

---

recovery. Based on that inventory, you can consider whether there are other strategies you can implement. Additionally, I believe it is critical for you to have a written relapse prevention plan.

Developing a relapse prevention plan

If you have the opportunity, I strongly recommend completing a course of psychotherapy that includes relapse prevention planning. For example, family-focused therapy (FFT), discussed in Chapter 9, includes a strong focus on relapse prevention. Also, regardless of the type of therapy you are receiving, I feel certain your therapist will be happy to help you develop a plan. That said, I recognize that there may be a number of reasons that therapy is impractical in your specific situation. Therefore, I have included the following section to walk you through developing a plan. The components of the relapse prevention plan that I recommend are outlined in Table 14.2. This plan is based on the association between stress and mood episodes as well as the fact that psychotherapy approaches that incorporate relapse prevention, such as FFT,[335] are effective. However, the following plan has not been tested for effectiveness; it is common sense–based but not evidence-based. This prevention plan is designed for any mood disorder.

Please complete Form 14.1 to develop your relapse prevention plan. Examples of the components of Form 14.1 are included in this chapter. A form for you to use is included in this chapter and is also available as a PDF file that can be freely downloaded from our website (http://www.bullpub.com/downloads).

Form 14.1 Relapse prevention plan

Last updated on: _____

Section 1: Mood episode triggers

Trigger	Preventable?
_____	Yes No
_____	Yes No
_____	Yes No
_____	Yes No
_____	Yes No

Section 2: Mood episode trigger prevention plan

Preventable trigger	Prevention steps
1. _____	1. _____
2. _____
3. _____
4. _____
2. _____	1. _____
2. _____
3. _____
4. _____
3. _____	1. _____
2. _____
3. _____
4. _____

continues ▶

Form 14.1   Relapse prevention plan (*continued*)

Section 3: Mood episode trigger management plan

Preventable trigger   Management plan

_____   _____

                                            _____

                                            _____

_____   _____

                                            _____

                                            _____

                                            _____

_____   _____

                                            _____

Section 4: Signs of a possible mood episode relapse and your response

Possible signs of relapse

_____

_____

_____

_____

Response to indications of relapse

_____

_____

_____

_____

Your relapse triggers

What are your triggers? You may not know the answer to that question and that's fine. Most of us aren't aware of all the potential triggers that affect our emotional state. The aim of this section is to help you determine yours.

I am going to start this process by asking you to think about any stressful events that may have been associated with the onset of prior mood episodes. You may not be sure whether the stress caused the mood disorder. Don't worry if you can't tell. Frequently it can be difficult to disentangle the relationship between stressful events and our mood. Please just try to remember any stressful events that occurred around the time of the onset of a mood episode. Then, please list those in Section 1 of Form 14.1. After each potential trigger, indicate whether this type of stress is preventable. If you're not sure, that's okay. For now, just make your best guess. Next, please list potential stressors that you think could contribute to a future mood episode. These could be from your "top ten" list of things that stress you the most or stressful events that you foresee arising in the next years or months of your life. Again, decide whether you think each of these is preventable or not.

Form 14.1, Section 1: Mood episode triggers

Trigger   Preventable?

_____   Yes   No

_____   Yes   No

_____   Yes   No

Preventing and managing triggers

Now that you have a list of triggers, the next step is to do something about them. For those that may be preventable, your assignment is to come up with a prevention plan. For those that aren't preventable, my recommendation is that you develop a management plan. Section 2 of Form 14.1 is for your use in developing a prevention plan for each potentially preventable trigger. Since many of the stressors in our lives are complicated, I have provided for more than one step in the prevention process. I have also included a column for a target completion date. Many of us work better with a deadline. Having a deadline has worked for me in writing this book.

Form 14.1, Section 2: Mood episode trigger prevention plan

Preventable trigger	Prevention steps	Target completion date
1. _____	1. _____	_____
	2. _____	_____
	3. _____	_____
2. _____	1. _____	_____
	2. _____	_____
	3. _____	_____

Before we move on, I want to make one important point; it is okay if some of your prevention efforts are unsuccessful. While I strongly encourage you to try to make changes to prevent the occurrence of potential triggers, many of our efforts in life are only partially successful—especially on the first try. Further, the more complicated potential triggers are, the more difficult the resolution process can be. Thus, I hope you will work on preventing relapse triggers AND not become discouraged if the outcome is not always exactly as you had envisioned. The important thing is to learn from each effort and incorporate what you have discovered into the next attempt. If you use this approach, I believe you can little by little decrease potential relapse triggers and enhance your recovery.

Now let's talk about managing triggers that are either not preventable or only partially preventable. Some things in life are just not changeable, at least in the near term. An example is providing care for an elderly parent who has chronic medical problems and is not going to get better. Even when we love someone very much, providing care and assistance can be stressful. Therefore, it can be very helpful to develop a management plan for those stressors that we know we are going to have to live with. Section 3 of Form

14.1 is provided to assist you in identifying potential triggers that are not preventable and outlining specific management steps. There are many possibilities to consider for management steps. Some people might include recreational activities such going to the gym, taking a walk, or listening to music. Other possibilities might include talking to friends or family members or making contact with a member of your treatment team. The main thing is to have management steps that will work for you. It is okay to use the same step for more than one trigger. As I discussed above, it is important to view this as a learning process. Many times our management strategies are not completely successful on the first attempt. Subsequent attempts may not always work perfectly either. I like to use the performance of a professional athlete as an analogy. No matter how talented a player is, she or he will not be 100% successful. Have you ever known of a baseball player who hit a home run every time at bat? We don't expect perfection from others, and we need to be very careful not to expect perfection of ourselves. Thus, it is critical to not become discouraged or make negative judgments about ourselves when our efforts are not completely successful. My view is that the goal is to continue to work on the process of managing relapse triggers with the expectation that our plan will gradually become more and more effective. That, I believe, is a reasonable goal that can make a significant difference in the long run.

Form 14.1, Section 3: Mood episode trigger management plan

Potential trigger   Management plan

_____   _____

                                          _____

                                          _____

                                          _____

I have two more thoughts for your consideration. The first is that some of the steps in managing relapse triggers can occur before the stressor occurs. This is something like prevention, but a bit different. In this situation you may have determined that a particular stress is likely to occur in your life and there isn't much you can do to prevent it. However, you can work on managing your emotional response beforehand. In order to do this, it is helpful to identify exactly what your emotional response is about. To use the analogy of an aging parent with a medical illness again, the stress might involve emotions, such as sadness or guilt. We might feel sad because we recognize that our loved one may not live much longer. Or we might be depressed because of the loss of functioning and independence our parent has suffered because of her illness. Many times, children experience guilt because they feel they have not done enough to help the parent. Whatever the emotion, we can manage it best if we clearly understand what we are feeling and why. Ideally, we do this in advance so that we can develop a response strategy. Often this process might involve working on the response in psychotherapy or perhaps using a **mindfulness** or meditation approach. Being clear about how we respond to particular stresses can guide us in developing a management plan. For example, we might know that whenever we feel sad about mom's health, talking with a particular friend always helps us feel better. Thus, we can add that as a response on Form 14.1 for that specific stressor. The final thought is that some of the stress response strategies may be the same as those you used in Chapter 1 for self-harm prevention. That is fine too. All that matters is that the management steps feel right to you.

Early signs of relapse

In this section, we will talk about early signs of relapse. Mood episodes may have a subtle onset that can remain unrecognized until symptoms are at a moderate or severe level. It is critical to recognize an episode as quickly as possible in order to immediately implement treatment and/or prevention strategies. Section 4 of Form 14.1 will help you identify possible signs of relapse and develop a response plan.

Early signs of relapse are usually mood disorder symptoms. If you have unipolar spectrum illness, then you should list depressive symptoms. In contrast, if you have bipolar spectrum illness, then you should list symptoms of both depression and mood elevation. What symptoms should you list? If you have had prior mood episodes, then you may remember the first symptoms you experienced during the onset of a mood episode. If you don't remember which symptoms occurred first, then I suggest listing the symptoms that were most bothersome for you. I recommend doing the same if this is your first mood episode. The form I have provided is one that you may be able to improve upon over time if you experience more episodes during your life. Perhaps the most important thing is surveillance. By that I mean that it is critical for you to be watching for a possible relapse. Surveillance is more important than making the list of signs. I encourage you to set aside a few minutes every day to complete your mood chart (see Chapter 13) and take an emotional inventory. By comparing your inventory to Form 14.1 and being alert for trends on the mood chart, you should recognize early signs suggesting a possible relapse.

Form 14.1, Section 4: Signs of a possible mood episode relapse and
your response

Possible signs of relapse

_____

_____

_____

Response to indications of relapse

_____

_____

_____

Responding to a potential relapse

Section 4 of Form 14.1 also provides a place for you to list your potential responses to a possible relapse. Some of these responses could be the same as those on your list for managing triggers. However, this list should address two additional areas. The first is deciding whether you are actually experiencing the beginning of a mood episode. One way to do this is to pay very close attention to any symptoms to accurately determine whether you see a trend of more or fewer symptoms as well as their intensity. It may be helpful to ask close friends or family members to keep an eye out too and report to you if they are seeing changes. In many cases, you should consider scheduling an appointment with one or more of your professional team members and soliciting their input. The second area is giving a definitive response. In many cases, this is the best response even if you are not yet sure whether you are having a relapse. In my view, it is always better to take at least some action, such as increasing the frequency of psychotherapy sessions, even if you are not sure. There is little harm in this approach and it may well prevent a full-blown mood episode. If the symptoms resolve quickly, then you can always go back to maintenance treatment. Thus, I suggest that one line of your response plan is to schedule appointments with members of your treatment team. Usually the immediate response means optimizing your current maintenance treatment approaches. This might mean having more frequent therapy sessions as mentioned above, increasing your participation in complementary approaches such as exercise, or optimizing any medications you may be taking.

Final thoughts

The purpose of this book is to empower you to take charge of your recovery and develop a comprehensive plan that will help you to stay safe, get well, and achieve a lifelong full recovery. I hope that you have found the book to be helpful.

Like everything in life, this book is imperfect. I had to make many decisions about what to include and how much detail to provide. So, it is a compromise. Undoubtedly, for some of you, it will be too much information; for others, not enough. Regardless, my hope is that it supports your recovery.

I want to thank everyone who has supported this project. Most of all, I want to thank those of you whom I have personally worked with over the years. All of you have taught me so much. Each of you played a role in my decision to write this book and provided inspiration for me to keep going when I was sick of working on it.

So, dear reader, it is time to say goodbye. I wish the very best for you and your loved ones.

Appendix A

Resources for getting help

Help if you are in crisis

- **National Suicide Prevention Lifeline**
  (http://www.suicidepreventionlifeline.org). This is a free, 24-hour hotline available to anyone in suicidal crisis or emotional distress: 1-800-273-TALK (8255).

Finding treatment

- **American Association for Marriage and Family Therapy** To find a marriage and family therapist, go to the website http://www.aamft.org/ and click on "Therapist Locator."

- **American Association of Pastoral Counselors** To find a pastoral counselor, go to the website http://aapc.org/ and click on "Find a Counselor."

- **Board-certified physicians** To find out whether a physician is board certified, go to the American Board of Medical Specialties website (http://www.abms.org/) and choose "Is Your Doctor Certified?"

- **Call 211** If available in your area, dial 211 for help with food, housing, employment, health care, counseling, and more. You can look up information about your local 211 at http://www.211.org/. Learn more about 211 at http://www.211us.org.

- **Department of Veterans Affairs** You can find health care information for eligible veterans at http://www.va.gov/.

- **Depression and Bipolar Support Alliance** Go to the DBSA "Find a Pro" page at http://findapro.dbsapages.org/ for peer-recommended mental health resources.

- **Mental Health America** The website http://www.nmha.org/ provides helpful information about finding treatment.

- **National Alliance on Mental Illness Information Help Line**
  This resource provides an information and referral service. Call 1-800-950-NAMI (6264), Monday through Friday, 10 AM–6 PM, Eastern time.

- **Psychologists** To find a psychologist, go to the website http://www.apa.org/ and click on "Find a Psychologist."

- *Psychology Today*'s **Therapy Directory** You can conduct an online search for mental health professionals in your area at http://therapists.psychologytoday.com/nmha/.

- **Substance Abuse and Mental Health Services Administration (SAMHSA) Mental Health Treatment Locator** This resource provides information about mental health services at http://store.samhsa.gov/mhlocator.

- **Substance Abuse and Mental Health Services Administration (SAMHSA) Substance Abuse Treatment Facility Locator** You can find information about substance abuse treatment services at http://dasis3.samhsa.gov/.

- **TRICARE** TRICARE provides treatment information for eligible uniformed service members, retirees, and their families at http://tricare.mil/mybenefit/.

Support organizations

- **Mental Health America** (http://www.nmha.org/) is an advocacy organization that aims to inform, advocate, and provide access to quality behavioral health services for all Americans.

- **National Alliance on Mental Illness** (http://www.nami.org/) is an organization dedicated to improving the lives of individuals and families affected by mental illness. NAMI's support and public education efforts are focused on educating America about mental illness as well as offering resources to those in need and advocating that mental illness become a high national priority.

Appendix B

Useful websites

American Academy of Nurse Practitioners
   (http://www.aanp.org/AANPCMS2)

American Academy of Physician Assistants
   (http://www.aapa.org/)

American Association for Marriage and Family Therapy
   (http://www.aamft.org/)

American Association of Pastoral Counselors
   (http://aapc.org/)

American Board of Medical Specialties
   (http://www.abms.org/)

American Psychiatric Association
   (http://www.psych.org/)

American Psychological Association
   (http://www.apa.org/)

American Therapeutic Recreation Association
   (http://www.atra-online.com/)

Depression and Bipolar Support Alliance
   (http://www.dbsalliance.org/)

National Alliance on Mental Illness
   (http://www.nami.org/)

National Association of Social Workers
   (http://www.naswdc.org/)

National Suicide Prevention Lifeline
   (http://www.suicidepreventionlifeline.org)

Appendix C

Recommended reading

Burns, David. (1980). *Feeling Good: The New Mood Therapy*. New York: William Morrow.

Burns, David. (1990). *The Feeling Good Handbook*. New York: Plume.

Germer, Christopher. (2009). *The Mindful Path to Self-Compassion: Freeing Yourself from Destructive Thoughts and Emotions*. New York: Guilford Press.

Hanh, Thich Nhat. (1999). *The Miracle of Mindfulness: A Manual on Meditation*. Boston: Beacon Press.

Jamison, Kay R. (1995). *An Unquiet Mind: A Memoir of Moods and Madness*. New York: Vintage Books.

Kabat-Zinn, Jon. (1990). *Full Catastrophe Living: Using the Wisdom of Your Body and Mind to Face Stress, Pain and Illness*. New York: Delta.

Kabat-Zinn, Jon. (1994). *Wherever You Go, There You Are: Mindfulness Meditation in Everyday Life*. New York: Hyperion.

Kabat-Zinn, Jon. (2005). *Coming to Our Senses: Healing Ourselves and the World through Mindfulness*. New York: Hyperion.

Kornfield, Jack. (1993). *A Path with Heart*. New York: Bantam Books.

Miklowitz, David. (2011). *The Bipolar Disorder Survival Guide: What You and Your Family Need to Know*. New York: Guilford Press.

Rosenberg, Larry (with David Guy). (1998). *Breath by Breath: The Liberating Practice of Insight Meditation*. Boston: Shambhala.

Salzberg, Sharon. (1995). *Loving Kindness: The Revolutionary Art of Happiness*. Boston: Shambhala.

Williams, Mark, et al. (2007). *The Mindful Way through Depression: Freeing Yourself from Chronic Unhappiness*. New York: Guilford Press.

Glossary

Adjustment disorder with depressed mood Depressive symptoms that develop in response to a specific stressor, do not meet the criteria for an episode of major depression, and are not caused by bereavement.

Adjustment disorder with mixed anxiety and depressed mood Symptoms of both anxiety and depression that develop in response to a specific stressor. The symptoms do not meet the criteria for an episode of major depression and are not caused by bereavement.

Affect One's immediate short-term emotional state, such as happy, sad, or annoyed. In contrast, the term *mood* is used to refer to a longer lasting emotional state.

Anhedonia Loss of the ability to experience pleasure from activities usually found enjoyable; a common symptom of depression.

Anorexia nervosa A psychiatric condition that leads to an intense fear of gaining weight and results in consistently maintaining a body weight lower than the minimum required for health.

Anticonvulsants Medications developed to treat epilepsy or seizure disorders. Some are also effective as mood stabilizers for persons with bipolar disorders.

Attention-deficit/hyperactivity disorder (ADHD) A condition that causes problems with attention and concentration (inattentive type) or difficulties related to hyperactivity and impulsiveness (hyperactive-impulsive type) or both

(combined type). To meet the diagnostic criteria, symptoms must start prior to age seven and must cause impairment in social, academic, or occupational functioning. Sometimes the disorder persists into adulthood.

Bipolar I disorder A bipolar spectrum disorder that requires at least one manic or mixed episode, usually with multiple episodes of mood elevations and depressions. Bipolar disorders cause mood changes at both ends of the affective "pole"—that is, both elevations and depressions; also known as manic-depressive disorder. Contrast the term *bipolar* (both mood elevations and depressions) with *unipolar* (either elevations or depressions).

Bipolar II disorder The diagnosis given for one or more major depressive episodes and one or more hypomanic episodes, but no manic or mixed episodes. This disorder is very serious, but the mood elevations are less intense than those in bipolar I disorder.

Bipolar disorder not otherwise specified Also known as bipolar disorder NOS, a bipolar disorder in which the symptom criteria are not met for bipolar I, bipolar II, or cyclothymic disorder.

Bulimia nervosa A disorder characterized by episodes of binge eating and compensatory behaviors to avoid weight gain, such as self-induced vomiting, fasting, or excessive exercise.

Cardinal symptoms The fundamental or essential symptoms of a psychiatric

317

disorder. One or more cardinal symptoms are often required to make a diagnosis of a specific disorder.

Chronic illness A disease or health condition that is long lasting. Depressive disorders are often chronic conditions, and bipolar spectrum disorders are thought to always be chronic illnesses.

Cognitive therapy A psychotherapy that focuses on changing thinking patterns that may be contributing to mood symptoms.

Comorbidity The presence of more than one psychiatric or medical disorder at the same time—for example, major depression and diabetes or bipolar disorder and generalized anxiety disorder.

Compulsions Repetitive behaviors or mental acts that a person feels driven to perform—for example, excessive hand washing, checking, counting, and repeating words.

Cortical midline structures (CMS) The middle surfaces of the cerebral hemispheres, which are thought to be important in mood disorders because of their involvement in thinking about the self and emotional regulation.

Cyclothymic disorder A milder bipolar spectrum disorder consisting of hypomanic episodes as well as depressive episodes that do not meet the criteria for a major depressive episode.

Default mood network A group of areas in the human brain characterized by being more active during rest and less active during task performance. This network has sparked a lot of scientific interest because it may underlie fundamental (or default) processes such as consciousness.

Delusions A general term for beliefs or belief systems that are not consistent with reality or the culture. Common delusions are paranoia (the inaccurate belief that others are against, or out to get, the delusional individual) and grandiosity (the inaccurate inflation of one's self-concept). Delusions are not specific to any disorder. They are a frequent feature of schizophrenia and may also occur with episodes of major depression and mania.

Depression In the context of psychiatric disorders, a period of excessive intensity or duration (usually both) of sadness along with other symptoms.

Depressive disorder not otherwise specified Also known as depressive disorder NOS, a catchall category for depressive symptoms that do not meet the criteria for any specific depressive spectrum disorders.

Discontinuation syndrome A syndrome that can occur if some SSRIs and SNRIs are abruptly discontinued after extended therapy. Symptoms include insomnia, nausea, headache, lightheadedness, chills, body aches, and "electric shock–like" sensations. Usually these symptoms go away without treatment in one or two weeks.

Dopamine An important neurotransmitter in the brain that may play a role in the causes of mood disorders.

Dysthymic disorder A disorder characterized by at least two years of continuous depressive symptoms that do not meet the criteria for an episode of major depression.

Euphoria Intense feelings of elation, happiness, ecstasy, excitement, or joy; often a symptom of mania or hypomania.

GABA Gamma-aminobutyric acid, the primary inhibitory neurotransmitter in the brain. Disordered GABA function may play a role in the causes of mood disorders.

Generalized anxiety disorder (GAD) A psychiatric illness that causes excessive worry and/or anxiety accompanied by physical symptoms.

Glutamate The primary excitatory neurotransmitter in the brain. Disordered glutamate function may play a role in the causes of mood disorders.

Hallucinations A general term for symptoms of experiencing sensations that are not real. The most common hallucinations are the auditory (hearing voices) and visual types. The sensory information is perceived by the individual as being real and is indistinguishable from other "real" sensory inputs. Hallucinations are not specific to any disorder. They are a characteristic of schizophrenia and may also occur with episodes of major depression and mania.

Hypomania A mood elevation episode that can be associated with all bipolar spectrum disorders; less intense than mania.

Lithium A medication used primarily as a mood stabilizer that is effective for the treatment of bipolar disorders.

Major depressive disorder The diagnosis given when someone has experienced one or more episodes of major depression.

Mania Excessive mood elevation associated with bipolar I disorders.

Manic-depressive disorder Older terminology for bipolar spectrum disorders.

Mindfulness Focusing attention in the present moment, as in meditation. Practicing mindfulness facilitates the uncritical awareness and acceptance of the sensations, thoughts, and emotions that one is experiencing in the immediate moment.

Monoamine hypothesis of depression See neurotransmitter hypothesis of depression.

Monoamine oxidase inhibitors (MAOIs) A class of antidepressants that limit the function of monoamine oxidase, which breaks down the mono amine neurotransmitters (dopamine, norepinephrine, and serotonin) in the brain. MAOIs thus make more of these neurotransmitters available for information transfer.

Mood One's emotional state; typically used to refer to a sustained period of being in one particular predominant mood, such as happy or sad. In contrast, the term *affect* is used to refer to one's current emotional state: An analogy is that mood is like climate while affect is like the current weather.

Mood disorder A psychiatric disorder that predominantly involves emotional symptoms. Motor and cognitive symptoms can also occur as a result of mood disorders. The two categories of mood disorders are depressive spectrum and bipolar spectrum conditions. Each of these categories includes several specific disorders.

Mood disorder due to a medical condition A disorder with symptoms similar to those of mood disorder known to be caused by a nonpsychiatric medical illness.

Mood episode A discrete period of a continuous mood state with a definite beginning and end; may last for days, months, or years. For diagnostic purposes, a minimum duration is often required to distinguish an episode of abnormal mood from normal ups and downs.

Neurobiology A general term for the biological processes of the nervous system; can be used to indicate the biological causes of mood disorders—for example, the "neurobiology" of depression.

Neurocircuitry The networks of connected brain regions that function together in support of various processes, such as thinking, interpreting sensory information (hearing, vision, etc.), and controlling motor behavior.

Neuron Another name for a nerve cell; the most fundamental component of the brain. Neurons are electrically excitable cells that transmit information from one point to another in the brain.

Neurotransmitter Chemicals that enable information to be transferred from one neuron to another in the brain by crossing the synapse (gap between neurons). Neurotransmitters can cause a variety of actions, but the most basic function is to cause the electrical signal to be sent along the postsynaptic neuron. The neurotransmitters most relevant to mood disorders are serotonin, norepinephrine, dopamine, glutamate, acetylcholine, and gamma-aminobutyric acid (GABA).

Neurotransmitter hypothesis of depression The idea that depression is caused by a deficiency of certain neurotransmitters; also known as the monoamine hypothesis. This hypothesis, originally proposed in 1965, holds that two monoamine neurotransmitters (serotonin and norepinephrine) and possibly a third (dopamine) are deficient in persons who have unipolar depression. This deficit is often referred to as a "chemical imbalance."

Norepinephrine An important neurotransmitter in the brain that may play a role in the causes of mood disorders.

Obsessions Recurrent and persistent thoughts, impulses, or images that are experienced as intrusive and cause anxiety or distress. Obsessions cause distress because they are inconsistent with an individual's belief system—for example, someone with strong religious convictions experiencing obsessive blasphemous thoughts.

Obsessive-compulsive disorder (OCD) A psychiatric illness that causes either recurrent obsessions or compulsions or both.

Panic attacks Out-of-the-blue attacks of panic that include at least four of the following symptoms: (1) sweating, (2) chest pain, (3) nausea or abdominal distress, (4) a sense that things aren't real, (5) trembling or shaking, (6) shortness of breath or a sense of smothering, (7) rapid heart rate or palpitations, (8) a choking sensation, (9) nausea, (10) dizziness or feeling faint, (11) numbness or a tingling sensation, (12) hot flushes or chills, (13) fear of dying, and (14) fear of going crazy or losing control.

Panic disorder A disorder characterized by recurrent panic attacks and associated symptoms. The additional symptoms associated with panic disorder are (1) persistent worry about having additional attacks; (2) worry that one might die, have a heart attack, or go crazy because of the attacks; and (3) a significant change in one's behavior because of the attacks.

Polygenic A description of inherited disorders that are associated with the effects of multiple genes in combination with lifestyle and environmental factors. Mood disorders fall into this category.

Posttraumatic stress disorder (PTSD) A disorder that occurs as a result of experiencing a traumatic event or events. Symptoms include reexperiencing the trauma, avoidance, and emotional numbing as well as increased emotional arousal.

Psychology The study of the human mind and behavior; the study of animal behavior; the mental characteristics of a particular individual; thoughts, feelings, and unconscious mental processes as well as behaviors that occur as a result of these.

Psychosis A technical term that refers to a specific set of symptoms including hallucinations or delusions. An individual experiencing psychosis (psychotic symptoms) is said to be "psychotic." Psychosis is not specific to any disorder. Psychotic symptoms are a hallmark of schizophrenia and may also occur with episodes of major depression and mania.

Psychotic disorder A disorder that includes conditions such as schizophrenia, schizoaffective disorder, and delusional disorder, which are characterized by distortions of perceptions, including hallucinations and delusions.

Rapid cycling Four or more mood episodes (depressed, manic, or hypomanic) per year in individuals with either bipolar I or II disorder. Some persons may have very rapid cycling, known as "ultradian" or "ultrarapid" cycling. Those with ultrarapid cycling may experience multiple brief occurrences of mania and depression over the course of days or sometimes even hours.

Recurrent illness Disorders or health conditions characterized by multiple episodes over time. Episodes of illness are separated by periods of remission. Depressive disorders are often recurrent, and bipolar spectrum disorders are thought to always be recurrent.

Relapse The return of symptoms, such as a new depressive episode, in a recurrent illness.

Schizoaffective disorder A psychiatric illness manifested by both psychotic and mood symptoms.

Schizophrenia A very severe psychiatric illness characterized by psychotic symptoms (delusions and hallucinations) and significant impairment.

Seasonal affective disorder Also known as SAD, a diagnosis that is given when the following conditions are met: (1) depression onset as well as remission (or switch to mania/hypomania in bipolar spectrum illness) tends to occur at a specific time of year, (2) the mood episodes are not related to season-specific stressors (e.g., the winter holidays), (3) at

least two major depressive episodes have met seasonal criteria during the previous two years and no nonseasonal episodes have occurred, and (4) the total number of seasonal depressive episodes is greater than the number of nonseasonal episodes.

Second-generation antipsychotics (SGAs) A class of antipsychotic medications that are sometimes used as mood stabilizers for persons with bipolar spectrum disorders and as adjunctive agents for the treatment of unipolar illness.

Secondary mood disorder A mood disorder with symptoms caused by another disorder, a medication, or a substance—for example, mood symptoms occurring as a result of hypothyroidism.

Selective serotonin reuptake inhibitors (SSRIs) A class of antidepressants that has been extensively used because of their effectiveness and relatively benign side effect profile. The currently available SSRIs are fluoxetine, sertraline, paroxetine, fluvoxamine, citalopram, and escitalopram. SSRIs, as the name suggests, inhibit the reuptake of serotonin as their primary mechanism of action.

Serotonin An important neurotransmitter in the brain that may play a role in the causes of mood disorders.

Serotonin-norepinephrine reuptake inhibitors (SNRIs) A class of antidepressants that inhibit the reuptake of two neurotransmitters, serotonin and norepinephrine, at the synapse.

Serotonin syndrome A disorder caused by too much serotonergic activity in the body—for example, when a person has taken more than one medication that increases serotonin activity. Symptoms include abdominal pain, diarrhea, flushing, sweating, elevated body temperature, tiredness, confusion, and tremor.

Social phobia A disorder that results in a persistent fear of one or more social or performance situations (e.g., speaking in public, attending parties, dating, eating in public). The anxiety is secondary to a concern that one's actions will result in significant embarrassment or humiliation.

Specific phobia   A disorder characterized by a persistent fear of a specific object or situation (e.g., spiders, blood, heights, flying) that is excessive or unreasonable and causes significant distress or impairment.

Substance-induced mood disorder   A disorder that occurs as a result of substance abuse or dependence.

Synapse   A specialized region in the nervous system where information passes from one neuron to another. Information is usually transmitted through substances known as neurotransmitters.

Tricyclic antidepressants (TCAs)   A class of antidepressants whose primary action is to inhibit reuptake of the neurotransmitters serotonin and norepinephrine. The name *tricyclic* is based on the chemical structure of these medications.

Unipolar   A term used in psychiatric terminology to indicate disorders that cause abnormality along only one pole of the emotional axis; frequently used synonymously with depressive spectrum disorders. In contrast, bipolar disorders are associated with abnormalities along both poles—mood elevations and depressions.

Bibliography

1. Wright, J. H., Beck, A. T., & Thase, M. E. (2003). Cognitive therapy. In R. E. Hales & S. C. Yudofsky (Eds.), *The American Psychiatric Publishing textbook of clinical psychiatry* (pp. 1245–1284). Arlington, VA: American Psychiatric Publishing.
2. Wang, P. S., et al. (2005). Twelve-month use of mental health services in the United States: Results from the National Comorbidity Survey Replication*Archives of General Psychiatry, 62*, 629–640.
3. Substance Abuse and Mental Health Services Administration. (2009). *The NSDUH report: Treatment for substance use and depression among adults, by race/ethnicity.* Rockville, MD: SAMHSA.
4. Dubovsky, S. L., Davies, R., & Dubovsky, A. N. (2003). Mood disorders. In R. E. Hales & S. C. Yudofsky (Eds.), *The American Psychiatric Publishing textbook of clinical psychiatry* (pp. 439–542). Arlington, VA: American Psychiatric Publishing.
5. Rost, K., et al. (1998). Persistently poor outcomes of undetected major depression in primary care. *General Hospital Psychiatry, 20*, 12–20.
6. Hegel, M. T., et al. (2006). Watchful waiting for minor depression in primary care: Remission rates and predictors of improvement. *General Hospital Psychiatry, 28*, 205–212.
7. Posternak, M. A., & Miller, I. (2001). Untreated short-term course of major depression: A meta-analysis of outcomes from studies using wait-list control groups. *Journal of Affective Disorders, 66*, 139–146.
8. Barney, L. J., et al. (2006). Stigma about depression and its impact on help-seeking intentions. *Australian and New Zealand Journal of Psychiatry, 40*, 51–54.
9. Conner, K. O., et al. (2010). Mental health treatment seeking among older adults with depression: The impact of stigma and race. *American Journal of Geriatric Psychiatry, 18*, 531–543.
10. Cook, T. M., & Wang, J. (2010). Descriptive epidemiology of stigma against depression in a general population sample in Alberta. *BMC Psychiatry, 10*, 29.
11. Barney, L. J., et al. (2009). Exploring the nature of stigmatising beliefs about depression and help-seeking: Implications for reducing stigma. *BMC Public Health, 9*, 61.
12. Georg Hsu, L. K., et al. (2008). Stigma of depression is more severe in Chinese Americans than Caucasian Americans. *Psychiatry, 71*, 210–218.
13. Roeloffs, C., et al. (2003). Stigma and depression among primary care patients. *General Hospital Psychiatry, 25*, 311–315.
14. Epstein, R. M., et al. (2010). "I didn't know what was wrong:" How people with undiagnosed depression recognize, name and explain their distress. *Journal of General Internal Medicine, 25*, 954–961.

15. Rochlen, A. B., et al. (2010). Barriers in diagnosing and treating men with depression: A focus group report. *American Journal of Men's Health, 4,* 167–175.

16. Nutt, D. J. (2010). Rationale for, barriers to, and appropriate medication for the long-term treatment of depression. *Journal of Clinical Psychiatry, 71*(suppl. E1), e02.

17. Altshuler, L., et al. (2003). Impact of antidepressant discontinuation after acute bipolar depression remission on rates of depressive relapse at 1-year follow-up. *American Journal of Psychiatry, 160,* 1252–1262.

18. Pacchiarotti, I., et al. (2011). Differential outcome of bipolar patients receiving antidepressant monotherapy versus combination with an antimanic drug. *Journal of Affective Disorders, 129,* 321–326.

19. Lee, M. S., et al. (2010). Variables influencing antidepressant medication adherence for treating outpatients with depressive disorders. *Journal of Affective Disorders, 123,* 216–221.

20. Baldessarini, R. J., Perry, R., & Pike, J. (2008). Factors associated with treatment nonadherence among US bipolar disorder patients. *Human Psychopharmacology, 23,* 95–105.

21. Marchand, W. R., et al. (2011). Aberrant emotional processing in posterior cortical midline structures in bipolar II depression. *Progress in Neuro-Psychopharmacology & Biological Psychiatry, 35,* 1729–1737.

22. Dome, P., et al. (2010). Season of birth is significantly associated with the risk of completed suicide. *Biological Psychiatry, 68,* 148–155.

23. Mann, J. J. (2003). Neurobiology of suicidal behaviour. *Nature Reviews Neuroscience, 4,* 819–828.

24. Carballo, J. J., Akamnonu, C. P., & Oquendo, M. A. (2008). Neurobiology of suicidal behavior. An integration of biological and clinical findings. *Archives of Suicide Research: Official Journal of the International Academy for Suicide Research, 12,* 93–110.

25. Fiori, L. M., & Turecki, G. (2012). Broadening our horizons: Gene expression profiling to help better understand the neurobiology of suicide and depression. *Neurobiology of Disease, 45,* 14–22.

26. McGirr, A., et al. (2009). Familial aggregation of suicide explained by cluster B traits: A three-group family study of suicide controlling for major depressive disorder. *American Journal of Psychiatry, 166,* 1124–1134.

27. von Borczyskowski, A., et al. (2011). Familial factors and suicide: An adoption study in a Swedish National Cohort. *Psychological Medicine, 41,* 749–758.

28. Brent, D. (2009). In search of endophenotypes for suicidal behavior. *American Journal of Psychiatry, 166,* 1087–1089.

29. McGirr, A., et al. (2009). Familial aggregation of suicide explained by cluster B traits: A three-group family study of suicide controlling for major depressive disorder. *American Journal of Psychiatry, 166,* 1124–1134.

30. Mann, J. J., et al. (1999). Toward a clinical model of suicidal behavior in psychiatric patients. *American Journal of Psychiatry, 156,* 181–189.

31. Kasen, S., Cohen, P., & Chen, H. (2011). Developmental course of impulsivity and capability from age 10 to age 25 as related to trajectory of suicide attempt in a community cohort. *Suicide and Life-Threatening Behavior, 41,* 180–192.

32. Neufeld, E., & O'Rourke, N. (2009). Impulsivity and hopelessness as predictors of suicide-related ideation among older adults. *Canadian Journal of Psychiatry, 54*, 684–692.

33. You, J., & Leung, F. (in press). The role of depressive symptoms, family invalidation and behavioral impulsivity in the occurrence and repetition of non-suicidal self-injury in Chinese adolescents: A 2-year follow-up study. *Journal of Adolescence.*

34. Bolton, J. M., et al. (2010). A population-based longitudinal study of risk factors for suicide attempts in major depressive disorder. *Journal of Psychiatric Research, 44*, 817–826.

35. Mukamal, K. J., et al. (2010). Body mass index and risk of suicide among one million US adults. *Epidemiology, 21*, 82–86.

36. Robson, A., et al. (2010). The risk of suicide in cancer patients: A review of the literature. *Psychooncology, 19*, 1250–1258.

37. Work Group on Major Depressive Disorder. (2010). *American Psychiatric Association practice guideline for the treatment of patients with major depressive disorder* (3rd ed.). Arlington, VA: American Psychiatric Publishing.

38. American Psychiatric Association. (2000). *Diagnostic and statistical manual of mental disorders* (4th ed.). Washington, DC: American Psychiatric Association.

39. Melartin, T. K., et al. (2002). Current comorbidity of psychiatric disorders among DSM-IV major depressive disorder patients in psychiatric care in the Vantaa Depression Study. *Journal of Clinical Psychiatry, 63*, 126–134.

40. Simon, N. M., et al. (2004). Anxiety disorder comorbidity in bipolar disorder patients: Data from the first 500 participants in the Systematic Treatment Enhancement Program for Bipolar Disorder (STEP-BD). *American Journal of Psychiatry, 161*, 2222–2229.

41. Baldassano, C. F. (2006). Illness course, comorbidity, gender, and suicidality in patients with bipolar disorder. *Journal of Clinical Psychiatry, 67*(suppl. 11), 8–11.

42. Lee, J. H., & Dunner, D. L. (2008). The effect of anxiety disorder comorbidity on treatment resistant bipolar disorders. *Depression and Anxiety, 25*, 91–97.

43. Singh, J. B., & Zarate, C. A., Jr. (2006). Pharmacological treatment of psychiatric comorbidity in bipolar disorder: A review of controlled trials. *Bipolar Disorders, 8*, 696–709.

44. Kilbane, E. J., et al. (2009). A review of panic and suicide in bipolar disorder: Does comorbidity increase risk? *Journal of Affective Disorders, 115*, 1–10.

45. Currie, S. R., et al. (2005). Comorbidity of major depression with substance use disorders. *Canadian Journal of Psychiatry, 50*, 660–666.

46. Davis, L. L., et al. (2005). Substance use disorder comorbidity in major depressive disorder: An exploratory analysis of the Sequenced Treatment Alternatives to Relieve Depression cohort. *Comprehensive Psychiatry, 46*, 81–89.

47. Rihmer, Z., et al. (2001). Anxiety disorders comorbidity in bipolar I, bipolar II and unipolar major depression: Results from a population-based study in Hungary. *Journal of Affective Disorders, 67*, 175–179.

48. Sonne, S. C., & Brady, K. T. (1999). Substance abuse and bipolar comorbidity. *Psychiatric Clinics of North America, 22*, 609–627.

49. Albert, U., et al. (2008). Impact of anxiety disorder comorbidity on quality of life in euthymic bipolar disorder patients: Differences between bipolar I and II subtypes. *Journal of Affective Disorders, 105*, 297–303.

50. Pini, S., et al. (2006). Social anxiety disorder comorbidity in patients with bipolar disorder: A clinical replication. *Journal of Anxiety Disorders, 20,* 1148–1157.

51. Vieta, E., et al. (2000). Bipolar II disorder and comorbidity. *Comprehensive Psychiatry, 41,* 339–343.

52. Tamam, L., Karakus, G., & Ozpoyraz, N. (2008). Comorbidity of adult attention-deficit hyperactivity disorder and bipolar disorder: Prevalence and clinical correlates. *European Archives of Psychiatry and Clinical Neuroscience, 258,* 385–393.

53. Kessler, R. C., et al. (2005). Prevalence, severity, and comorbidity of 12-month DSM-IV disorders in the National Comorbidity Survey Replication. *Archives of General Psychiatry, 62,* 617–627.

54. Kessler, R. C., et al. (2003). The epidemiology of major depressive disorder: Results from the National Comorbidity Survey Replication (NCS-R). *JAMA, 289,* 3095–3105.

55. Merikangas, K. R., et al. (2007). Lifetime and 12-month prevalence of bipolar spectrum disorder in the National Comorbidity Survey Replication. *Archives of General Psychiatry, 64,* 543–552.

56. Grant, B. F., et al. (2005). Prevalence, correlates, and comorbidity of bipolar I disorder and axis I and II disorders: Results from the National Epidemiologic Survey on Alcohol and Related Conditions. *Journal of Clinical Psychiatry, 66,* 1205–1215.

57. Burton, H., Snyder, A. Z., & Raichle, M. E. (2004). Default brain functionality in blind people. *PNAS, 101,* 15500–15505.

58. Derdikman-Eiron, R., et al. (2011). Gender differences in subjective well-being, self-esteem and psychosocial functioning in adolescents with symptoms of anxiety and depression: Findings from the Nord-Trondelag health study. *Scandinavian Journal of Psychology, 51,* 261–267.

59. Lett, H. S., et al. (2009). Dimensions of social support and depression in patients at increased psychosocial risk recovering from myocardial infarction. *International Journal of Behavioral Medicine, 16,* 248–258.

60. Forsman, A. K., Schierenbeck, I., & Wahlbeck, K. (2011). Psychosocial interventions for the prevention of depression in older adults: Systematic review and meta-analysis. *Journal of Aging and Health, 23,* 387–416.

61. Verheijden, M., et al. (2004). Web-based targeted nutrition counselling and social support for patients at increased cardiovascular risk in general practice: Randomized controlled trial. *Journal of Medical Internet Research, 6,* e44.

62. Brezo, J., et al. (2010). Differences and similarities in the serotonergic diathesis for suicide attempts and mood disorders: A 22-year longitudinal gene-environment study. *Molecular Psychiatry, 15,* 831–843.

63. Gatt, J. M., et al. (2010). Impact of the HTR3A gene with early life trauma on emotional brain networks and depressed mood. *Depression and Anxiety, 27,* 752–759.

64. Mandelli, L., et al. (2007). Interaction between serotonin transporter gene, catechol-O-methyltransferase gene and stressful life events in mood disorders. *International Journal of Neuropsychopharmacology, 10,* 437–447.

65. Zou, Y. F., et al. (in press). Association of DRD2 gene polymorphisms with mood disorders: A meta-analysis. *Journal of Affective Disorders.*

66. Ryu, S. H., et al. (2004). Association between norepinephrine transporter gene polymorphism and major depression. *Neuropsychobiology, 49*, 174–177.

67. Sun, N., et al. (2008). The combined effect of norepinephrine transporter gene and negative life events in major depression of Chinese Han population. *Journal of Neural Transmission, 115*, 1681–1686.

68. Feng, Y., et al. (2010). Association of the GABRD gene and childhood-onset mood disorders. *Genes, Brain and Behavior, 9*, 668–672.

69. Fan, M., et al. (2010). Meta-analysis of the association between the monoamine oxidase-A gene and mood disorders. *Psychiatric Genetics, 20*, 1–7.

70. Feng, Y., et al. (2008). Association of the neurotrophic tyrosine kinase receptor 3 (NTRK3) gene and childhood-onset mood disorders. *American Journal of Psychiatry, 165*, 610–616.

71. Rybakowski, J. K. (2008). BDNF gene: Functional Val66Met polymorphism in mood disorders and schizophrenia. *Pharmacogenomics, 9*, 1589–1593.

72. Milne, B. J., et al. (2009). Predictive value of family history on severity of illness: The case for depression, anxiety, alcohol dependence, and drug dependence. *Archives of General Psychiatry, 66*, 738–747.

73. Marchand, W. R., & Yurgelun-Todd, D. (2010). Striatal structure and function in mood disorders: A comprehensive review. *Bipolar Disorders, 12*, 764–785.

74. Jacobs, D., & Silverstone, T. (1986). Dextroamphetamine-induced arousal in human subjects as a model for mania. *Psychological Medicine, 16*, 323–329.

75. Warrington, L., et al. (2007). Ziprasidone for the treatment of acute manic or mixed episodes associated with bipolar disorder. *CNS Drugs, 21*, 835–849.

76. Fenton, C., & Scott, L. J. (2005). Risperidone: A review of its use in the treatment of bipolar mania. *CNS Drugs, 19*, 429–444.

77. Bhana, N., & Perry, C. M. (2001). Olanzapine: A review of its use in the treatment of bipolar I disorder. *CNS Drugs, 15*, 871–904.

78. Scherk, H., Pajonk, F. G., & Leucht, S. (2007). Second-generation antipsychotic agents in the treatment of acute mania: A systematic review and meta-analysis of randomized controlled trials. *Archives of General Psychiatry, 64*, 442–455.

79. Wang, J., Michelhaugh, S. K., & Bannon, M. J. (2007). Valproate robustly increases Sp transcription factor-mediated expression of the dopamine transporter gene within dopamine cells. *European Journal of Neuroscience, 25*, 1982–1986.

80. Yatham, L. N., et al. (2002). PET study of [(18)F]6-fluoro-L-dopa uptake in neuroleptic- and mood-stabilizer-naive first-episode nonpsychotic mania: Effects of treatment with divalproex sodium. *American Journal of Psychiatry, 159*, 768–774.

81. Ferrie, L., Young, A. H., & McQuade, R. (2006). Effect of lithium and lithium withdrawal on potassium-evoked dopamine release and tyrosine hydroxylase expression in the rat. *International Journal of Neuropsychopharmacology, 9*, 729–735.

82. Ferrie, L., Young, A. H., & McQuade, R. (2005). Effect of chronic lithium and withdrawal from chronic lithium on presynaptic dopamine function in the rat. *Journal of Psychopharmacology, 19*, 229–234.

83. Fichna, J., et al. (2007). The endomorphin system and its evolving neurophysiological role. *Pharmacological Reviews, 59*, 88–123.

84. Heneka, M. T., & O'Banion, M. K. (2007). Inflammatory processes in Alzheimer's disease. *Journal of Neuroimmunology, 184*, 69–91.

85. Hirsch, E. C., & Hunot, S. (2009). Neuroinflammation in Parkinson's disease: A target for neuroprotection? *The Lancet Neurology, 8*, 382–397.

86. Dantzer, R., et al. (2008). Identification and treatment of symptoms associated with inflammation in medically ill patients. *Psychoneuroendocrinology, 33*, 18–29.

87. Dantzer, R., et al. (2008). From inflammation to sickness and depression: When the immune system subjugates the brain. *Nature Reviews Neuroscience, 9*, 46–56.

88. Loftis, J. M., Huckans, M., & Morasco, B. J. (2010). Neuroimmune mechanisms of cytokine-induced depression: Current theories and novel treatment strategies. *Neurobiology of Disease, 37*, 519–533.

89. McNally, L., Bhagwagar, Z., & Hannestad, J. (2008). Inflammation, glutamate, and glia in depression: A literature review. *CNS Spectrums, 13*, 501–510.

90. Miller, A. H. (2009). Norman Cousins Lecture. Mechanisms of cytokine-induced behavioral changes: Psychoneuroimmunology at the translational interface. *Brain, Behavior, and Immunity, 23*, 149–158.

91. Muller, N., & Schwarz, M. J. (2007). The immune-mediated alteration of serotonin and glutamate: Towards an integrated view of depression. *Molecular Psychiatry, 12*, 988–1000.

92. Myint, A. M., & Kim, Y. K. (2003). Cytokine-serotonin interaction through IDO: A neurodegeneration hypothesis of depression. *Medical Hypotheses, 61*, 519–525.

93. Anisman, H., Merali, Z., & Hayley, S. (2008). Neurotransmitter, peptide and cytokine processes in relation to depressive disorder: Comorbidity between depression and neurodegenerative disorders. *Progress in Neurobiology, 85*, 1–74.

94. Raison, C. L., Capuron, L., & Miller, A. H. (2006). Cytokines sing the blues: Inflammation and the pathogenesis of depression. *Trends in Immunology, 27*, 24–31.

95. Zorrilla, E. P., et al. (2001). The relationship of depression and stressors to immunological assays: A meta-analytic review. *Brain, Behavior, and Immunity, 15*, 199–226.

96. Bierhaus, A., et al. (2003). A mechanism converting psychosocial stress into mononuclear cell activation. *PNAS, 100*, 1920–1925.

97. Gavillet, M., Allaman, I., & Magistretti, P. J. (2008). Modulation of astrocytic metabolic phenotype by proinflammatory cytokines. *Glia, 56*, 975–989.

98. Reichenberg, A., et al. (2001). Cytokine-associated emotional and cognitive disturbances in humans. *Archives of General Psychiatry, 58*, 445–452.

99. Kent, S., et al. (1992). Sickness behavior as a new target for drug development. *Trends in Pharmacological Science, 13*, 24–28.

100. Hart, B. L. (1988). Biological basis of the behavior of sick animals. *Neuroscience & Biobehavioral Reviews, 12*, 123–137.

101. Butler, T., et al. (2007). Human fear-related motor neurocircuitry. *Neuroscience, 150*, 1–7.

102. Marchand, W. R. (2010). Cortico-basal ganglia circuitry: A review of key research and implications for functional connectivity studies of mood and anxiety disorders. *Brain Structure & Function, 215*, 73–96.

103. Gorman, J. M., et al. (2000). Neuroanatomical hypothesis of panic disorder, revised. *American Journal of Psychiatry, 157*, 493–505.

104. Northoff, G., & Bermpohl, F. (2004). Cortical midline structures and the self. *Trends in Cognitive Sciences, 8*, 102–107.

105. Amaral, D. G., & Price, J. L. (1984). Amygdalo-cortical projections in the monkey (*Macaca fascicularis*). *Journal of Comparative Neurology, 230*, 465–496.

106. Barbas, H., & De Olmos, J. (1990). Projections from the amygdala to baso-ventral and mediodorsal prefrontal regions in the rhesus monkey. *Journal of Comparative Neurology, 300,* 549–571.

107. Carmichael, S. T., & Price, J. L. (1995). Limbic connections of the orbital and medial prefrontal cortex in macaque monkeys. *Journal of Comparative Neurology, 363,* 615–641.

108. Porrino, L. J., Crane, A. M., & Goldman-Rakic, P. S. (1981). Direct and indirect pathways from the amygdala to the frontal lobe in rhesus monkeys. *Journal of Comparative Neurology, 198,* 121–136.

109. Buckwalter, J. A., Schumann, C. M., & Van Hoesen, G. W. (2008). Evidence for direct projections from the basal nucleus of the amygdala to retrosplenial cortex in the Macaque monkey. *Experimental Brain Research, 186,* 47–57.

110. Haber, S. N., et al. (1995). The orbital and medial prefrontal circuit through the primate basal ganglia. *Journal of Neuroscience, 15,* 4851–4867.

111. Northoff, G., et al. (2006). Self-referential processing in our brain—A meta-analysis of imaging studies on the self. *Neuroimage, 31,* 440–457.

112. St. Jacques, P. L., et al. (2011). Watching my mind unfold versus tours: An fMRI study using a novel camera technology to examine neural differences in self-projection of self versus other perspectives. *Journal of Cognitive Neuroscience, 23,* 1275–1284.

113. Yaoi, K., Osaka, N., & Osaka, M. (2009). Is the self special in the dorsomedial prefrontal cortex? An fMRI study. *Social Neuroscience, 4,* 455–463.

114. Pan, X., et al. (2009). Evaluative-feedback stimuli selectively activate the self-related brain area: An fMRI study. *Neuroscience Letters, 465,* 90–94.

115. Fossati, P., et al. (2003). In search of the emotional self: An fMRI study using positive and negative emotional words. *American Journal of Psychiatry, 160,* 1938–1945.

116. Grimm, S., et al. (2009). Altered negative BOLD responses in the default-mode network during emotion processing in depressed subjects. *Neuropsychopharmacology, 34,* 932–943.

117. Heinzel, A., et al. (2005). How do we modulate our emotions? Parametric fMRI reveals cortical midline structures as regions specifically involved in the processing of emotional valences. *Cognitive Brain Research, 25,* 348–358.

118. Likhtik, E., et al. (2005). Prefrontal control of the amygdala. *Journal of Neuroscience, 25,* 7429–7437.

119. Raichle, M. E., et al. (2001). A default mode of brain function. *PNAS, 98,* 676–682.

120. Gusnard, D. A., & Raichle, M. E. (2001). Searching for a baseline: Functional imaging and the resting human brain. *Nature Reviews Neuroscience, 2,* 685–694.

121. Raichle, M. E., & Snyder, A. Z. (2007). A default mode of brain function: A brief history of an evolving idea. *Neuroimage, 37,* 1083–1090; discussion 1097–1099.

122. George, M. S., et al. (1995). Brain activity during transient sadness and happiness in healthy women. *American Journal of Psychiatry, 152,* 341–351.

123. Mayberg, H. S., et al. (1999). Reciprocal limbic-cortical function and negative mood: Converging PET findings in depression and normal sadness. *American Journal of Psychiatry, 156,* 675–682.

124. Drevets, W. C., Bogers, W., &. Raichle, M. E. (2002). Functional anatomical correlates of antidepressant drug treatment assessed using PET measures of regional glucose metabolism. *European Neuropsychopharmacology, 12,* 527–544.

125. Fu, C. H., et al. (2004). Attenuation of the neural response to sad faces in major depression by antidepressant treatment: A prospective, event-related functional magnetic resonance imaging study. *Archives of General Psychiatry, 61,* 877–889.

126. Neumeister, A., et al. (2006). Effects of a alpha 2C-adrenoreceptor gene polymorphism on neural responses to facial expressions in depression. *Neuropsychopharmacology, 31,* 1750–1756.

127. Sheline, Y. I., et al. (2001). Increased amygdala response to masked emotional faces in depressed subjects resolves with antidepressant treatment: An fMRI study. *Biological Psychiatry, 50,* 651–658.

128. Siegle, G. J., et al. (2002). Can't shake that feeling: Event-related fMRI assessment of sustained amygdala activity in response to emotional information in depressed individuals. *Biological Psychiatry, 51,* 693–707.

129. Peluso, M. A., et al. (2009). Amygdala hyperactivation in untreated depressed individuals. *Psychiatry Research, 173,* 158–161.

130. Holsen, L. M., et al. (2011). Stress response circuitry hypoactivation related to hormonal dysfunction in women with major depression. *Journal of Affective Disorders, 131,* 379–387.

131. Drevets, W. C., et al. (1997). Subgenual prefrontal cortex abnormalities in mood disorders. *Nature, 386,* 824–827.

132. Kegeles, L. S., et al. (2003). Response of cortical metabolic deficits to serotonergic challenge in familial mood disorders. *American Journal of Psychiatry, 160,* 76–82.

133. Liotti, M., et al. (2002). Unmasking disease-specific cerebral blood flow abnormalities: Mood challenge in patients with remitted unipolar depression. *American Journal of Psychiatry, 159,* 1830–1840.

134. Pizzagalli, D. A., et al. (2009). Reduced caudate and nucleus accumbens response to rewards in unmedicated individuals with major depressive disorder. *American Journal of Psychiatry, 166,* 702–710.

135. Dunn, R. T., et al. (2002). Principal components of the Beck Depression Inventory and regional cerebral metabolism in unipolar and bipolar depression. *Biological Psychiatry, 51,* 387–399.

136. Mayberg, H. S., et al. (2000). Regional metabolic effects of fluoxetine in major depression: Serial changes and relationship to clinical response. *Biological Psychiatry, 48,* 830–843.

137. Wu, J., et al. (1999). Prediction of antidepressant effects of sleep deprivation by metabolic rates in the ventral anterior cingulate and medial prefrontal cortex. *American Journal of Psychiatry, 156,* 1149–1158.

138. Pavuluri, M. N., et al. (2009). An fMRI study of the neural correlates of incidental versus directed emotion processing in pediatric bipolar disorder. *Journal of the American Academy of Child and Adolescent Psychiatry, 48,* 308–319.

139. Malhi, G. S., et al. (2004). Cognitive generation of affect in bipolar depression: An fMRI study. *European Journal of Neuroscience, 19,* 741–754.

140. Chen, C. H., et al. (2006). Explicit and implicit facial affect recognition in manic and depressed states of bipolar disorder: A functional magnetic resonance imaging study. *Biological Psychiatry, 59,* 31–39.

141. Monks, P. J., et al. (2004). A functional MRI study of working memory task in euthymic bipolar disorder: Evidence for task-specific dysfunction. *Bipolar Disorders, 6,* 550–564.

142. Adler, C. M., et al. (2004). Changes in neuronal activation in patients with bipolar disorder during performance of a working memory task. *Bipolar Disorders, 6,* 540–549.

143. Lawrence, N. S., et al. (2004). Subcortical and ventral prefrontal cortical neural responses to facial expressions distinguish patients with bipolar disorder and major depression. *Biological Psychiatry, 55,* 578–587.

144. Benedetti, F., et al. (2007). Neural and genetic correlates of antidepressant response to sleep deprivation: A functional magnetic resonance imaging study of moral valence decision in bipolar depression. *Archives of General Psychiatry, 64,* 179–187.

145. Marchand, W. R., et al. (2011). Aberrant emotional processing in posterior cortical midline structures in bipolar II depression. *Progress in Neuropsychopharmacology and Biological Psychiatry, 35,* 1729–1737.

146. Wang, F., et al. (2009). Functional and structural connectivity between the perigenual anterior cingulate and amygdala in bipolar disorder. *Biological Psychiatry, 66,* 516–521.

147. Altshuler, L., et al. (2008). Regional brain changes in bipolar I depression: A functional magnetic resonance imaging study. *Bipolar Disorders, 10,* 708–717.

148. Altshuler, L. L., et al. (2005). Blunted activation in orbitofrontal cortex during mania: A functional magnetic resonance imaging study. *Biological Psychiatry, 58,* 763–769.

149. Elliott, R., et al. (2004). Abnormal ventral frontal response during performance of an affective go/no go task in patients with mania. *Biological Psychiatry, 55,* 1163–1170.

150. Lennox, B. R., et al. (2004). Behavioural and neurocognitive responses to sad facial affect are attenuated in patients with mania. *Psychological Medicine, 34,* 795–802.

151. Ritchey, M., et al. (2011). Neural correlates of emotional processing in depression: Changes with cognitive behavioral therapy and predictors of treatment response. *Journal of Psychiatric Research, 45,* 577–587.

152. Dichter, G. S., Felder, J. N., & Smoski, M. J. (2010). The effects of Brief Behavioral Activation Therapy for Depression on cognitive control in affective contexts: An fMRI investigation. *Journal of Affective Disorders, 126,* 236–244.

153. Siegrist, J. (2008). Chronic psychosocial stress at work and risk of depression: Evidence from prospective studies. *European Archives of Psychiatry and Clinical Neuroscience, 258*(suppl. 5), 115–119.

154. Ehrlich, M., et al. (2010). Loss of resources and hurricane experience as predictors of postpartum depression among women in southern Louisiana. *Journal of Women's Health (Larchmont), 19,* 877–884.

155. Carrera, L., et al. (1998). Depression in women suffering perinatal loss. *International Journal of Gynecology and Obstetrics, 62,* 149–153.

156. Kendler, K. S., et al. (2003). Life event dimensions of loss, humiliation, entrapment, and danger in the prediction of onsets of major depression and generalized anxiety. *Archives of General Psychiatry, 60,* 789–796.

157. Monroe, S. M., et al. (1999). Life events and depression in adolescence: Relationship loss as a prospective risk factor for first onset of major depressive disorder. *Journal of Abnormal Psychology, 108*, 606–614.

158. Turvey, C. L., et al. (1999). Conjugal loss and syndromal depression in a sample of elders aged 70 years or older. *American Journal of Psychiatry, 156*, 1596–1601.

159. Kessing, L. V., Agerbo, E., & Mortensen, P. B. (2004). Major stressful life events and other risk factors for first admission with mania. *Bipolar Disorders, 6*, 122–129.

160. Evans, J., et al. (2005). Negative self-schemas and the onset of depression in women: Longitudinal study. *British Journal of Psychiatry, 186*, 302–307.

161. Miller, L., et al. (1999). Self-esteem and depression: Ten year follow-up of mothers and offspring. *Journal of Affective Disorders, 52*, 41–49.

162. Brewin, C. R., & Firth-Cozens, J. (1997). Dependency and self-criticism as predictors of depression in young doctors. *Journal of Occupational Health Psychology, 2*, 242–246.

163. Fontaine, K. R., & Jones, L. C. (1997). Self-esteem, optimism, and postpartum depression. *Journal of Clinical Psychology, 53*, 59–63.

164. Romney, D. M. (1994). Cross-validating a causal model relating attributional style, self-esteem, and depression: An heuristic study. *Psychology Reports, 74*, 203–207.

165. Kreger, D. W. (1995). Self-esteem, stress, and depression among graduate students. *Psychology Reports, 76*, 345–346.

166. Gara, M. A., et al. (1993). Perception of self and other in major depression. *Journal of Abnormal Psychology, 102*, 93–100.

167. King, C. A., et al. (1993). Global self-worth, specific self-perceptions of competence, and depression in adolescents. *Journal of the American Academy of Child and Adolescent Psychiatry, 32*, 745–752.

168. Sheslow, D., et al. (1993). The relationship between self-esteem and depression in obese children. *Annals of the New York Academy of Sciences, 699*, 289–291.

169. Patton, W. (1991). Relationship between self-image and depression in adolescents. *Psychology Reports, 68*, 867–870.

170. Workman, M., & Beer, J. (1989). Self-esteem, depression, and alcohol dependency among high school students. *Psychology Reports, 65*, 451–455.

171. Brown, G. W., et al. (1990). Self-esteem and depression. II. Social correlates of self-esteem. *Social Psychiatry and Psychiatric Epidemiology, 25*, 225–234.

172. Brown, G. W., Bifulco, A., & Andrews, B. (1990). Self-esteem and depression. III. Aetiological issues. *Social Psychiatry and Psychiatric Epidemiology, 25*, 235–243.

173. Brown, G. W., Bifulco, A., & Andrews, B. (1990). Self-esteem and depression. IV. Effect on course and recovery. *Social Psychiatry and Psychiatric Epidemiology, 25*, 244–249.

174. Brown, G. W., et al. (1990). Self-esteem and depression. I. Measurement issues and prediction of onset. *Social Psychiatry and Psychiatric Epidemiology, 25*, 200–209.

175. Hammen, C. (1988). Self-cognitions, stressful events, and the prediction of depression in children of depressed mothers. *Journal of Abnormal Child Psychology, 16*, 347–360.

176. Battle, J. (1980). Relationship between self-esteem and depression among high school students. *Perceptual & Motor Skills, 51*, 157–158.

177. Schafer, R. B., & Keith, P. M. (1981). Self-esteem discrepancies and depression. *Journal of Psychology, 109*, 43–49.

178. Brown, G. W., et al. (1986). Social support, self-esteem and depression. *Psychological Medicine, 16*, 813–831.

179. Nilsson, K. K., et al. (2010). Self-esteem in remitted bipolar disorder patients: A meta-analysis. *Bipolar Disorders, 12*, 585–592.

180. Knowles, R., et al. (2007). Stability of self-esteem in bipolar disorder: Comparisons among remitted bipolar patients, remitted unipolar patients and healthy controls. *Bipolar Disorders, 9*, 490–495.

181. Pavlova, B., et al. (2011). Reactivity of affect and self-esteem during remission in bipolar affective disorder: An experimental investigation. *Journal of Affective Disorders, 134*, 102–111.

182. Johnson, S. L., et al. (2000). Social support and self-esteem predict changes in bipolar depression but not mania. *Journal of Affective Disorders, 58*, 79–86.

183. Blairy, S., et al. (2004). Social adjustment and self-esteem of bipolar patients: A multicentric study. *Journal of Affectice Disorders, 79*, 97–103.

184. Gonzalez-Isasi, A., et al. (in press). Predictors of good outcome in patients with refractory bipolar disorder after a drug or a drug and cognitive-behavioral treatment. *Comprehensive Psychiatry*.

185. Henning, E. R., et al. (2007). Impairment and quality of life in individuals with generalized anxiety disorder. *Depression and Anxiety, 24*, 342–349.

186. Ehntholt, K. A., Salkovskis, P. M., & Rimes, K. A. (1999). Obsessive-compulsive disorder, anxiety disorders, and self-esteem: An exploratory study. *Behaviour Research and Therapy, 37*, 771–781.

187. Wu, K. D., Clark, L. A., & Watson, D. (2006). Relations between obsessive-compulsive disorder and personality: Beyond Axis I-Axis II comorbidity. *Journal of Anxiety Disorders, 20*, 695–717.

188. Kashdan, T. B., Breen, W. E., & Julian, T. (2010). Everyday strivings in war veterans with posttraumatic stress disorder: Suffering from a hyper-focus on avoidance and emotion regulation. *Behavior Therapy, 41*, 350–363.

189. Boscarino, J. A., & Adams, R. E. (2009). PTSD onset and course following the World Trade Center disaster: Findings and implications for future research. *Social Psychiatry and Psychiatric Epidemiology, 44*, 887–898.

190. Kashdan, T. B., et al. (2006). Fragile self-esteem and affective instability in posttraumatic stress disorder. *Behaviour Research and Therapy, 44*, 1609–1619.

191. Acarturk, C., et al. (2009). Incidence of social phobia and identification of its risk indicators: A model for prevention. *Acta Psychiatrica Scandinavica, 119*, 62–70.

192. Izgic, F., et al. (2004). Social phobia among university students and its relation to self-esteem and body image. *Canadian Journal of Psychiatry, 49*, 630–634.

193. Batelaan, N. M., et al. (2010). The course of panic attacks in individuals with panic disorder and subthreshold panic disorder: A population-based study. *Journal of Affective Disorders, 121*, 30–38.

194. Au, A. C., Lau, S., & Lee, M. T. (2009). Suicide ideation and depression: The moderation effects of family cohesion and social self-concept. *Adolescence, 44*, 851–868.

195. Bhar, S., et al. (2008). Self-esteem and suicide ideation in psychiatric outpatients. *Suicide and Life-Threatening Behavior, 38*, 511–516.

196. Becker, D. F., & Grilo, C. M. (2007). Prediction of suicidality and violence in hospitalized adolescents: Comparisons by sex. *Canadian Journal of Psychiatry, 52*, 572–580.

197. Cox, B. J., Enns, M. W., & Clara, I. P. (2004). Psychological dimensions associated with suicidal ideation and attempts in the National Comorbidity Survey. *Suicide and Life-Threatening Behavior, 34*, 209–219.

198. Kienhorst, C. W., et al. (1990). Characteristics of suicide attempters in a population-based sample of Dutch adolescents. *British Journal of Psychiatry, 156*, 243–248.

199. Evans, E., Hawton, K., & Rodham, K. (2004). Factors associated with suicidal phenomena in adolescents: A systematic review of population-based studies. *Clinical Psychology Review, 24*, 957–979.

200. Kuhlberg, J. A., Pena, J. B., & Zayas, L. H. (2010). Familism, parent-adolescent conflict, self-esteem, internalizing behaviors and suicide attempts among adolescent Latinas. *Child Psychiatry & Human Development, 41*, 425–440.

201. Overholser, J. C., et al. (1995). Self-esteem deficits and suicidal tendencies among adolescents. *Journal of the American Academy of Child and Adolescent Psychiatry, 34*, 919–928.

202. Santos, J. C., Saraiva, C. B., & De Sousa, L. (2009). The role of expressed emotion, self-concept, coping, and depression in parasuicidal behavior: A follow-up study. *Archives of Suicide Research, 13*, 358–367.

203. Thompson, A. H. (2010). The suicidal process and self-esteem. *Crisis, 31*, 311–316.

204. Wild, L. G., Flisher, A. J., & Lombard, C. (2004). Suicidal ideation and attempts in adolescents: Associations with depression and six domains of self-esteem. *Journal of Adolescence, 27*, 611–624.

205. Markowitz, J. C. (2003). Interpersonal therapy. In R. E. Hales & S. C. Yudofsky (Eds.), *The American Psychiatric Publishing textbook of clinical psychiatry* (pp. 1207–1223). Arlington, VA: American Psychiatric Publishing.

206. Johnson, M. K., et al. (2009). Medial cortex activity, self-reflection and depression. *Social Cognitive and Affective Neuroscience, 4*, 313–327.

207. Scheuerecker, J., et al. (2010). Orbitofrontal volume reductions during emotion recognition in patients with major depression. *Journal of Psychiatry & Neuroscience, 35*, 311–320.

208. Smith, G. S., et al. (2009). The functional neuroanatomy of geriatric depression. *International Journal of Geriatric Psychiatry, 24*, 798–808.

209. Grimm, S., et al. (2009). Increased self-focus in major depressive disorder is related to neural abnormalities in subcortical-cortical midline structures. *Human Brain Mapping, 30*, 2617–2627.

210. Brooks, J. O., 3rd, et al. (2009). Decreased prefrontal, anterior cingulate, insula, and ventral striatal metabolism in medication-free depressed outpatients with bipolar disorder. *Journal of Psychiatric Research, 43*, 181–188.

211. Smoski, M. J., et al. (2009). fMRI of alterations in reward selection, anticipation, and feedback in major depressive disorder. *Journal of Affective Disorders, 118*, 69–78.

212. Osuch, E. A., et al. (2009). Brain activation to favorite music in healthy controls and depressed patients. *Neuroreport, 20,* 1204–1208.

213. Lemogne, C., et al. (2010). Negative affectivity, self-referential processing and the cortical midline structures. *Social Cognitive and Affective Neuroscience, 6,* 426–433.

214. Yoshimura, S., et al. (2010). Rostral anterior cingulate cortex activity mediates the relationship between the depressive symptoms and the medial prefrontal cortex activity. *Journal of Affective Disorders, 122,* 76–85.

215. Teasdale, J. D. (1999). Emotional processing, three modes of mind and the prevention of relapse in depression. *Behaviour Research and Therapy, 37*(suppl. 1), S53–77.

216. Watkins, E., & Teasdale, J. D. (2004). Adaptive and maladaptive self-focus in depression. *Journal of Affective Disorders, 82,* 1–8.

217. Rimes, K. A., & Watkins, E. (2005). The effects of self-focused rumination on global negative self-judgements in depression. *Behaviour Research and Therapy, 43,* 1673–1681.

218. Lavender, A., & Watkins, E. (2004). Rumination and future thinking in depression. *British Journal of Clinical Psychology, 43,* 129–142.

219. Williams, A. D., & Moulds, M. L. (2010). The impact of ruminative processing on the experience of self-referent intrusive memories in dysphoria. *Behavior Therapy, 41,* 38–45.

220. Lo, C. S., Ho, S. M., & Hollon, S. D. (2010). The effects of rumination and depressive symptoms on the prediction of negative attributional style among college students. *Cognitive Therapy and Research, 34,* 116–123.

221. Just, N., & Alloy, L. B. (1997). The response styles theory of depression: Tests and an extension of the theory. *Journal of Abnormal Psychology, 106,* 221–229.

222. Kuehner, C., & Weber, I. (1999). Responses to depression in unipolar depressed patients: An investigation of Nolen-Hoeksema's response styles theory. *Psychological Medicine, 29,* 1323–1333.

223. Nolen-Hoeksema, S. (2000). The role of rumination in depressive disorders and mixed anxiety/depressive symptoms. *Journal of Abnormal Psychology, 109,* 504–511.

224. Nolen-Hoeksema, S., Parker, L. E., & Larson, J. (1994). Ruminative coping with depressed mood following loss. *Journal of Personality and Social Psychology, 67,* 92–104.

225. Sakamoto, S. (1999). A longitudinal study of the relationship of self-preoccupation with depression. *Journal of Clinical Psychology, 55,* 109–116.

226. Burwell, R. A., & Shirk, S. R. (2007). Subtypes of rumination in adolescence: Associations between brooding, reflection, depressive symptoms, and coping. *Journal of Clinical Child & Adolescent Psychology, 36,* 56–65.

227. Spasojevic, J., & Alloy, L. B. (2001). Rumination as a common mechanism relating depressive risk factors to depression. *Emotion, 1,* 25–37.

228. Michalak, J., Holz, A., & Teismann, T. (in press). Rumination as a predictor of relapse in mindfulness-based cognitive therapy for depression. *Psychology and Psychotherapy.*

229. Alloy, L. B., et al. (2009). Self-focused cognitive styles and bipolar spectrum disorders: Concurrent and prospective sssociations. *International Journal of Cognitive Therapy, 2,* 354.

230. Johnson, S. L., McKenzie, G., & McMurrich, S. (2008). Ruminative responses to negative and positive affect among students diagnosed with bipolar disorder and major depressive disorder. *Cognitive Therapy and Research, 32,* 702–713.

231. Ingram, R. E. (1990). Self-focused attention in clinical disorders: Review and a conceptual model. *Psychological Bulletin, 107,* 156–176.

232. Northoff, G. (2007). Psychopathology and pathophysiology of the self in depression—Neuropsychiatric hypothesis. *Journal of Affective Disorders, 104,* 1–14.

233. Mor, N., & Winquist, J. (2002). Self-focused attention and negative affect: A meta-analysis. *Psychological Bulletin, 128,* 638–662.

234. Pyszczynski, T., Holt, K., & Greenberg, J. (1987). Depression, self-focused attention, and expectancies for positive and negative future life events for self and others. *Journal of Personality and Social Psychology, 52,* 994–1001.

235. Strack, S., et al. (1985). Pessimistic self-preoccupation, performance deficits, and depression. *Journal of Personality and Social Psychology, 49,* 1076–1085.

236. Shim, R. S., et al. (2011). Prevalence, treatment, and control of depressive symptoms in the United States: Results from the national health and nutrition examination survey (NHANES), 2005–2008. *Journal of the American Board of Family Medicine, 24,* 33–38.

237. Jameson, J. P., & Blank, M. B. (2010). Diagnosis and treatment of depression and anxiety in rural and nonrural primary care: National survey results. *Psychiatric Services, 61,* 624–627.

238. Menchetti, M., et al. (2009). Recognition and treatment of depression in primary care: Effect of patients' presentation and frequency of consultation. *Journal of Psychosomatic Research, 66,* 335–341.

239. Brunoni, A. R., et al. (2009). Placebo response of non-pharmacological and pharmacological trials in major depression: A systematic review and meta-analysis. *PLoS One, 4,* e4824.

240. Walsh, B. T., et al. (2002). Placebo response in studies of major depression: Variable, substantial, and growing. *JAMA, 287,* 1840–1847.

241. Work Group on Schizophrenia. (2004). *American Psychiatric Association practice guideline for the treatment of patients with schizophrenia* (2nd ed.). Arlington, VA: American Psychiatric Publishing.

242. Bech, P., et al. (2002). Citalopram dose-response revisited using an alternative psychometric approach to evaluate clinical effects of four fixed citalopram doses compared to placebo in patients with major depression. *Psychopharmacology (Berlin), 163,* 20–25.

243. Fournier, J. C., et al. (2010). Antidepressant drug effects and depression severity: A patient-level meta-analysis. *JAMA, 303,* 47–53.

244. Khan, A., et al. (2002). Severity of depression and response to antidepressants and placebo: An analysis of the Food and Drug Administration database. *Journal of Clinical Psychopharmacology, 22,* 40–45.

245. Machado, M., et al. (2006). Remission, dropouts, and adverse drug reaction rates in major depressive disorder: A meta-analysis of head-to-head trials. *Current Medical Research & Opinion, 22,* 1825–1837.

246. Nivoli, A. M., et al. (2011). New treatment guidelines for acute bipolar depression: A systematic review. *Journal of Affective Disorders, 129,* 14–26.

247. Vazquez, G., Tondo, L., & Baldessarini, R. J. (2011). Comparison of antidepressant responses in patients with bipolar vs. unipolar depression: A meta-analytic review. *Pharmacopsychiatry, 44*, 21–26.

248. Gijsman, H. J., et al. (2004). Antidepressants for bipolar depression: A systematic review of randomized, controlled trials. *American Journal of Psychiatry, 161*, 1537–1547.

249. Ghaemi, S. N., et al. (2010). Antidepressant discontinuation in bipolar depression: A Systematic Treatment Enhancement Program for Bipolar Disorder (STEP-BD) randomized clinical trial of long-term effectiveness and safety. *Journal of Clinical Psychiatry, 71*, 372–380.

250. Ghaemi, S. N., et al. (2008). Long-term antidepressant treatment in bipolar disorder: Meta-analyses of benefits and risks. *Acta Psychiatrica Scandinavica, 118*, 347–356.

251. Ghaemi, S. N., Lenox, M. S., & Baldessarini, R. J. (2001). Effectiveness and safety of long-term antidepressant treatment in bipolar disorder. *Journal of Clinical Psychiatry, 62*, 565–569.

252. Licht, R. W., et al. (2008). Are antidepressants safe in the treatment of bipolar depression? A critical evaluation of their potential risk to induce switch into mania or cycle acceleration. *Acta Psychiatrica Scandinavica, 118*, 337–346.

253. Balon, R. (2006). SSRI-associated sexual dysfunction. *American Journal of Psychiatry, 163*, 1504–1509; quiz 1664.

254. Olfson, M., Marcus, S. C., & Shaffer, D. (2006). Antidepressant drug therapy and suicide in severely depressed children and adults: A case-control study. *Archives of General Psychiatry, 63*, 865–872.

255. Gibbons, R. D., et al. (2005). The relationship between antidepressant medication use and rate of suicide. *Archives of General Psychiatry, 62*, 165–172.

256. Mulder, R. T., et al. (2008). Antidepressant treatment is associated with a reduction in suicidal ideation and suicide attempts. *Acta Psychiatrica Scandinavica, 118*, 116–122.

257. Kalmar, S., et al. (2008). Antidepressant prescription and suicide rates: Effect of age and gender. *Suicide and Life-Threatening Behavior, 38*, 363–374.

258. Castelpietra, G., et al. (2008). Antidepressant use and suicide prevention: A prescription database study in the region Friuli Venezia Giulia, Italy. *Acta Psychiatrica Scandinavica, 118*, 382–388.

259. Sondergard, L., et al. (2007). Continued antidepressant treatment and suicide in patients with depressive disorder. *Archives of Suicide Research, 11*, 163–175.

260. Nakagawa, A., et al. (2007). Association of suicide and antidepressant prescription rates in Japan, 1999–2003. *Journal of Clinical Psychiatry, 68*, 908–916.

261. Vigo, D. V., & Baldessarini, R. J. (2009). Anticonvulsants in the treatment of major depressive disorder: An overview. *Harvard Review of Psychiatry, 17*, 231–241.

262. Geddes, J. R., Calabrese, J. R., & Goodwin, G. M. (2009). Lamotrigine for treatment of bipolar depression: Independent meta-analysis and meta-regression of individual patient data from five randomised trials. *British Journal of Psychiatry, 194*, 4–9.

263. Bond, D. J., Lam, R. W., & Yatham, L. N. (2010). Divalproex sodium versus placebo in the treatment of acute bipolar depression: A systematic review and meta-analysis. *Journal of Affective Disorders, 124*, 228–234.

264. Wade, J. F., et al. (2010). Emergent complications of the newer anticonvulsants. *Journal of Emergency Medicine, 38*, 231–237.

265. Harden, C. L., et al. (2009). Practice parameter update: Management issues for women with epilepsy—Focus on pregnancy (an evidence-based review): Obstetrical complications and change in seizure frequency: Report of the Quality Standards Subcommittee and Therapeutics and Technology Assessment Subcommittee of the American Academy of Neurology and American Epilepsy Society. *Neurology, 73*, 126–132.

266. Wilby, J., et al. (2005). Clinical effectiveness, tolerability and cost-effectiveness of newer drugs for epilepsy in adults: A systematic review and economic evaluation. *Health Technology Assessment, 9*, 1–157, iii–iv.

267. Bilo, L., & Meo, R. (2008). Polycystic ovary syndrome in women using valproate: A review. *Gynecological Endocrinology, 24*, 562–570.

268. Park, S. P., & Kwon, S. H. (2008). Cognitive effects of antiepileptic drugs. *Journal of Clinical Neurology, 4*, 99–106.

269. Gibbons, R. D., et al. (2009). Relationship between antiepileptic drugs and suicide attempts in patients with bipolar disorder. *Archives of General Psychiatry, 66*, 1354–1360.

270. Miceli, J. J., et al. (2010). Effects of oral ziprasidone and oral haloperidol on QTc interval in patients with schizophrenia or schizoaffective disorder. *Pharmacotherapy, 30*, 127–135.

271. Strom, B. L., et al. (2011). Comparative mortality associated with ziprasidone and olanzapine in real-world use among 18,154 patients with schizophrenia: The Ziprasidone Observational Study of Cardiac Outcomes (ZODIAC). *American Journal of Psychiatry, 168*, 193–201.

272. Schutter, D. J. (2009). Antidepressant efficacy of high-frequency transcranial magnetic stimulation over the left dorsolateral prefrontal cortex in double-blind sham-controlled designs: A meta-analysis. *Psychological Medicine, 39*, 65–75.

273. George, M. S., et al. (2010). Daily left prefrontal transcranial magnetic stimulation therapy for major depressive disorder: A sham-controlled randomized trial. *Archives of General Psychiatry, 67*, 507–516.

274. Driessen, E., et al. (2010). Does pretreatment severity moderate the efficacy of psychological treatment of adult outpatient depression? A meta-analysis. *Journal of Consulting and Clinical Psychology, 78*, 668–680.

275. Miklowitz, D. J. (2008). Adjunctive psychotherapy for bipolar disorder: State of the evidence. *American Journal of Psychiatry, 165*, 1408–1419.

276. Miklowitz, D. J., et al. (2006). Psychotherapy, symptom outcomes, and role functioning over one year among patients with bipolar disorder. *Psychiatric Services, 57*, 959–965.

277. Lauder, S. D., et al. (2010). The role of psychotherapy in bipolar disorder. *Medical Journal of Australia, 193*(suppl.), S31–35.

278. Jones, S. (2004). Psychotherapy of bipolar disorder: A review. *Journal of Affective Disorders, 80*, 101–114.

279. Rizvi, S., & Zaretsky, A. E. (2007). Psychotherapy through the phases of bipolar disorder: Evidence for general efficacy and differential effects. *Journal of Clinical Psychology, 63*, 491–506.

280. Scott, J., Colom, F., & Vieta, E. (2007). A meta-analysis of relapse rates with adjunctive psychological therapies compared to usual psychiatric treatment for bipolar disorders. *International Journal of Neuropsychopharmacology, 10*, 123–129.

281. Gibbons, C. J., et al. (2010). The clinical effectiveness of cognitive therapy for depression in an outpatient clinic. *Journal of Affective Disorders, 125*, 169–176.

282. Kabat-Zinn, J. (2005). *Full catastrophe living: Using the wisdom of your body and mind to face stress, pain, and illness* (15th anniv. ed.). New York: Bantam Dell.

283. Goldin, P. R., & Gross, J. J. (2010). Effects of mindfulness-based stress reduction (MBSR) on emotion regulation in social anxiety disorder. *Emotion, 10*, 83–91.

284. Evans, S., et al. (2008). Mindfulness-based cognitive therapy for generalized anxiety disorder. *Journal of Anxiety Disorders, 22*, 716–721.

285. Gross, C. R., et al. (2011). Mindfulness-based stress reduction versus pharmacotherapy for chronic primary insomnia: A randomized controlled clinical trial. *EXPLORE: The Journal of Science and Healing, 7*, 76–87.

286. Birnie, K., Garland, S. N., & Carlson, L. E. (2010). Psychological benefits for cancer patients and their partners participating in mindfulness-based stress reduction (MBSR). *Psychooncology, 19*, 1004–1009.

287. Esmer, G., et al. (2010). Mindfulness-based stress reduction for failed back surgery syndrome: A randomized controlled trial. *JAOA: Journal of the American Osteopathic Association, 110*, 646–652.

288. Gross, C. R., et al. (2010). Mindfulness-based stress reduction for solid organ transplant recipients: A randomized controlled trial. *Alternative Therapies in Health and Medicine, 16*, 30–38.

289. Joo, H. M., et al. (2010). Effects of mindfulness based stress reduction program on depression, anxiety and stress in patients with aneurysmal subarachnoid hemorrhage. *Journal of Korean Neurosurgical Society, 47*, 345–351.

290. Lengacher, C. A., et al. (2009). Randomized controlled trial of mindfulness-based stress reduction (MBSR) for survivors of breast cancer. *Psychooncology, 18*, 1261–1272.

291. Grossman, P., et al. (2007). Mindfulness training as an intervention for fibromyalgia: Evidence of postintervention and 3-year follow-up benefits in well-being. *Psychotherapy and Psychosomatics, 76*, 226–233.

292. Sephton, S. E., et al. (2007). Mindfulness meditation alleviates depressive symptoms in women with fibromyalgia: Results of a randomized clinical trial. *Arthritis & Rheumatism, 57*, 77–85.

293. Campbell, T. S., et al. (in press). Impact of mindfulness-based stress reduction (MBSR) on attention, rumination and resting blood pressure in women with cancer: A waitlist-controlled study. *Journal of Behavioral Medicine.*

294. Carlson, L. E., et al. (2007). One year pre-post intervention follow-up of psychological, immune, endocrine and blood pressure outcomes of mindfulness-based stress reduction (MBSR) in breast and prostate cancer outpatients. *Brain, Behavior, and Immunity, 21*, 1038–1049.

295. Carlson, L. E., & Garland, S. N. (2005). Impact of mindfulness-based stress reduction (MBSR) on sleep, mood, stress and fatigue symptoms in cancer outpatients. *International Journal of Behavioral Medicine, 12*, 278–285.

296. Ledesma, D., & Kumano, H. (2009). Mindfulness-based stress reduction and cancer: A meta-analysis. *Psychooncology, 18*, 571–579.

297. Gayner, B., et al. (in press). A randomized controlled trial of mindfulness-based stress reduction to manage affective symptoms and improve quality of life in gay men living with HIV. *Journal of Behavioral Medicine.*

298. Flugel Colle, K. F., et al. (2010). Measurement of quality of life and participant experience with the mindfulness-based stress reduction program. *Complementary Therapies in Clinical Practice, 16*, 36–40.

299. Rosenzweig, S., et al. (2010). Mindfulness-based stress reduction for chronic pain conditions: Variation in treatment outcomes and role of home meditation practice. *Journal of Psychosomatic Research, 68*, 29–36.

300. Perlman, D. M., et al. (2010). Differential effects on pain intensity and unpleasantness of two meditation practices. *Emotion, 10*, 65–71.

301. Ernst, S., et al. (2008). Effects of mindfulness-based stress reduction on quality of life in nursing home residents: A feasibility study. *Forschende Komplementärmedizin, 15*, 74–81.

302. Chiesa, A., & Serretti, A.(2009). Mindfulness-based stress reduction for stress management in healthy people: A review and meta-analysis. *Journal of Alternative and Complementary Medicine, 15*, 593–600.

303. Winbush, N. Y., Gross, C. R., & Kreitzer, M. J. (2007). The effects of mindfulness-based stress reduction on sleep disturbance: A systematic review. *EXPLORE: The Journal of Science and Healing, 3*, 585–591.

304. Grossman, P., et al. (2004). Mindfulness-based stress reduction and health benefits. A meta-analysis. *Journal of Psychosomatic Research, 57*, 35–43.

305. Evans, S., et al. (2011). Mindfulness-based stress reduction (MBSR) and distress in a community-based sample. *Clinical Psychology & Psychotherapy, 18*, 553–558.

306. Fang, C. Y., et al. (2010). Enhanced psychosocial well-being following participation in a mindfulness-based stress reduction program is associated with increased natural killer cell activity. *Journal of Alternative and Complementary Medicine, 16*, 531–538.

307. Jam, S., et al. (2010). The effects of mindfulness-based stress reduction (MBSR) program in Iranian HIV/AIDS patients: A pilot study. *Acta Medica Iranica, 48*, 101–106.

308. Kieviet-Stijnen, A., et al. (2008). Mindfulness-based stress reduction training for oncology patients: Patients' appraisal and changes in well-being. *Patient Education and Counseling, 72*, 436–442.

309. Martin-Asuero, A., & Garcia-Banda, G. (2010). The mindfulness-based stress reduction program (MBSR) reduces stress-related psychological distress in healthcare professionals. *Spanish Journal of Psychology, 13*, 897–905.

310. Pradhan, E. K., et al. (2007). Effect of mindfulness-based stress reduction in rheumatoid arthritis patients. *Arthritis & Rheumatism, 57*, 1134–1142.

311. Bohlmeijer, E., et al. (2010). The effects of mindfulness-based stress reduction therapy on mental health of adults with a chronic medical disease: A meta-analysis. *Journal of Psychosomatic Research, 68*, 539–544.

312. Segal, Z. V., Williams, J. M. G., & Teasdale, J. D. (2002). *Mindfulness-based cognitive therapy for depression: A new approach to preventing relapse.* New York: Guilford Press.

313. Teasdale, J. D. (1988). Cognitive vulnerability to persistent depression. *Cognition & Emotion, 2*, 247–274.

314. Bondolfi, G., et al. (2010). Depression relapse prophylaxis with mindfulness-based cognitive therapy: Replication and extension in the Swiss health care system. *Journal of Affective Disorders, 122,* 224–231.

315. Godfrin, K. A., & van Heeringen, C. (2010). The effects of mindfulness-based cognitive therapy on recurrence of depressive episodes, mental health and quality of life: A randomized controlled study. *Behaviour Research and Therapy, 48,* 738–746.

316. Kuyken, W., et al. (2008). Mindfulness-based cognitive therapy to prevent relapse in recurrent depression. *Journal of Consulting and Clinical Psychology, 76,* 966–978.

317. Manicavasgar, V., Parker, G., & Perich, T. (2011). Mindfulness-based cognitive therapy vs cognitive behaviour therapy as a treatment for non-melancholic depression. *Journal of Affective Disorders, 130,* 138–144.

318. Mathew, K. L., et al. (2010). The long-term effects of mindfulness-based cognitive therapy as a relapse prevention treatment for major depressive disorder. *Behavioural and Cognitive Psychotherapy, 38,* 561–576.

319. Segal, Z. V., et al. (2010). Antidepressant monotherapy vs sequential pharmacotherapy and mindfulness-based cognitive therapy, or placebo, for relapse prophylaxis in recurrent depression. *Archives of General Psychiatry, 67,* 1256–1264.

320. Kim, B., et al. (2010). Effectiveness of a mindfulness-based cognitive therapy program as an adjunct to pharmacotherapy in patients with panic disorder. *Journal of Anxiety Disorders, 24,* 590–595.

321. Lovas, D. A., & Barsky, A. J. (2010). Mindfulness-based cognitive therapy for hypochondriasis, or severe health anxiety: A pilot study. *Journal of Anxiety Disorders, 24,* 931–935.

322. Piet, J., et al. (2010). A randomized pilot study of mindfulness-based cognitive therapy and group cognitive-behavioral therapy for young adults with social phobia. *Scandinavian Journal of Psychology, 51,* 403–410.

323. Chiesa, A., & Serretti, A. (2011). Mindfulness based cognitive therapy for psychiatric disorders: A systematic review and meta-analysis. *Psychiatry Research, 187,* 441–453.

324. Barnhofer, T., et al. (2009). Mindfulness-based cognitive therapy as a treatment for chronic depression: A preliminary study. *Behaviour Research and Therapy, 47,* 366–373.

325. Britton, W. B., et al. (2010). Polysomnographic and subjective profiles of sleep continuity before and after mindfulness-based cognitive therapy in partially remitted depression. *Psychosomatic Medicine, 72,* 539–548.

326. Hofmann, S. G., et al. (2010). The effect of mindfulness-based therapy on anxiety and depression: A meta-analytic review. *Journal of Consulting and Clinical Psychology, 78,* 169–183.

327. Williams, J. M., et al. (2008). Mindfulness-based cognitive therapy (MBCT) in bipolar disorder: Preliminary evaluation of immediate effects on between-episode functioning. *Journal of Affective Disorders, 107,* 275–279.

328. Weber, B., et al. (2010). Mindfulness-based cognitive therapy for bipolar disorder: A feasibility trial. *European Psychiatry, 25,* 334–337.

329. Chadwick, P., et al. (2011). Experience of mindfulness in people with bipolar disorder: A qualitative study. *Psychotherapy Research, 21,* 277–285.

330. Williams, J. M., et al. (2006). Mindfulness-based cognitive therapy for prevention of recurrence of suicidal behavior. *Journal of Clinical Psychology, 62*, 201–210.

331. Barnhofer, T., et al. (2007). Effects of meditation on frontal alpha-asymmetry in previously suicidal individuals. *Neuroreport, 18*, 709–712.

332. Hepburn, S. R., et al. (2009). Mindfulness-based cognitive therapy may reduce thought suppression in previously suicidal participants: Findings from a preliminary study. *British Journal of Clinical Psychology, 48*, 209–215.

333. Hargus, E., et al. (2010). Effects of mindfulness on meta-awareness and specificity of describing prodromal symptoms in suicidal depression. *Emotion, 10*, 34–42.

334. Williams, J. M., et al. (2010). Staying well after depression: Trial design and protocol. *BMC Psychiatry, 10*, 23.

335. Morris, C. D., Miklowitz, D. J., & Waxmonsky, J. A. (2007). Family-focused treatment for bipolar disorder in adults and youth. *Journal of Clinical Psychology, 63*, 433–445.

336. Miklowitz, D. J., et al. (2003). A randomized study of family-focused psychoeducation and pharmacotherapy in the outpatient management of bipolar disorder. *Archives of General Psychiatry, 60*, 904–912.

337. Miklowitz, D. J., et al. (2000). Family-focused treatment of bipolar disorder: 1-year effects of a psychoeducational program in conjunction with pharmacotherapy. *Biological Psychiatry, 48*, 582–592.

338. Rea, M. M., et al. (2003). Family-focused treatment versus individual treatment for bipolar disorder: Results of a randomized clinical trial. *Journal of Consulting and Clinical Psychology, 71*, 482–492.

339. Frank, E., Swartz, H. A., & Kupfer, D. J. (2000). Interpersonal and social rhythm therapy: Managing the chaos of bipolar disorder. *Biological Psychiatry, 48*, 593–604.

340. Frank, E. (2007). Interpersonal and social rhythm therapy: A means of improving depression and preventing relapse in bipolar disorder. *Journal of Clinical Psychology, 63*, 463–473.

341. Frank, E., et al. (2005). Two-year outcomes for interpersonal and social rhythm therapy in individuals with bipolar I disorder. *Archives of General Psychiatry, 62*, 996–1004.

342. Frank, E., et al. (2008). The role of interpersonal and social rhythm therapy in improving occupational functioning in patients with bipolar I disorder. *American Journal of Psychiatry, 165*, 1559–1565.

343. Colom, F., et al. (2003). A randomized trial on the efficacy of group psychoeducation in the prophylaxis of recurrences in bipolar patients whose disease is in remission. *Archives of General Psychiatry, 60*, 402–407.

344. Chiesa, A., & Serretti, A. (2010). A systematic review of neurobiological and clinical features of mindfulness meditations. *Psychological Medicine, 40*, 1239–1252.

345. Ives-Deliperi, V. L., Solms, M., & Meintjes, E. M. (2011). The neural substrates of mindfulness: An fMRI investigation. *Social Neuroscience, 6*, 231–242.

346. Farb, N. A., et al. (2010). Minding one's emotions: Mindfulness training alters the neural expression of sadness. *Emotion, 10*, 25–33.

347. Holzel, B. K., et al. (2011). Mindfulness practice leads to increases in regional brain gray matter density. *Psychiatry Research, 191*, 36–43.

348. Chiesa, A., Calati, R., & Serretti, A. (2011). Does mindfulness training improve cognitive abilities? A systematic review of neuropsychological findings. *Clinical Psychology Review, 31*, 449–464.

349. Luo, W. Z., Zhang, Q. Z., & Lai, X. S. (2010). [Effect of acupuncture treatment of relieving depression and regulating mind on insomnia accompanied with depressive disorders]. *Zhongguo Zhen Jiu, 30*, 899–903.

350. Manber, R., et al. (2010). Acupuncture for depression during pregnancy: A randomized controlled trial. *Obstetrics & Gynecology, 115*, 511–520.

351. Zhang, W. J., Yang, X. B., & Zhong, B. L. (2009). Combination of acupuncture and fluoxetine for depression: A randomized, double-blind, sham-controlled trial. *Journal of Alternative and Complementary Medicine, 15*, 837–844.

352. Manber, R., et al. (2004). Acupuncture: A promising treatment for depression during pregnancy. *Journal of Affective Disorders, 83*, 89–95.

353. Allen, J. J., et al. (2006). Acupuncture for depression: A randomized controlled trial. *Journal of Clinical Psychiatry, 67*, 1665–1673.

354. Schroer, S., & Adamson, J. (2011). Acupuncture for depression: A critique of the evidence base. *CNS Neuroscience & Therapeutics, 17*, 398–410.

355. Pilkington, K. (2010). Anxiety, depression and acupuncture: A review of the clinical research. *Autonomic Neuroscience, 157*, 91–95.

356. Ernst, E., Lee, M. S., & Choi, T. Y. (2011). Acupuncture for depression? A systematic review of systematic reviews. *Evaluation & the Health Professions, 34*, 403–412.

357. Smith, C. A., & Hay, P. P. (2005). Acupuncture for depression. *Cochrane Database of Systematic Reviews*, p. CD004046.

358. Smith, C. A., Hay, P. P., & Macpherson, H. (2010). Acupuncture for depression. *Cochrane Database of Systematic Reviews*, p. CD004046.

359. Strohle, A. (2009). Physical activity, exercise, depression and anxiety disorders. *Journal of Neural Transmission, 116*, 777–784.

360. Dinas, P. C., Koutedakis, Y., & Flouris, A. D. (2011). Effects of exercise and physical activity on depression. *Irish Journal of Medical Science, 180*, 319–325.

361. Gill, A., Womack, R., & Safranek, S. (2010). Clinical inquiries: Does exercise alleviate symptoms of depression? *Journal of Family Practice, 59*, 530–531.

362. Mead, G. E., et al. (2009). Exercise for depression. *Cochrane Database of Systematic Reviews*, p. CD004366.

363. Daley, A. (2008). Exercise and depression: A review of reviews. *Journal of Clinical Psychology in Medical Settings, 15*, 140–147.

364. Hoffman, B. M., et al. (2011). Exercise and pharmacotherapy in patients with major depression: One-year follow-up of the SMILE study. *Psychosomatic Medicine, 73*, 127–133.

365. Sylvia, L. G., Ametrano, R. M., & Nierenberg, A. A. (2010). Exercise treatment for bipolar disorder: Potential mechanisms of action mediated through increased neurogenesis and decreased allostatic load. *Psychotherapy and Psychosomatics, 79*, 87–96.

366. Alsuwaidan, M. T., et al. (2009). Exercise and bipolar disorder: A review of neurobiological mediators. *Neuromolecular Medicine, 11*, 328–336.

367. Perraton, L. G., Kumar, S., & Machotka, Z. (2010). Exercise parameters in the treatment of clinical depression: A systematic review of randomized controlled trials. *Journal of Evaluation in Clinical Practice, 16*, 597–604.

368. Fava, M. (2010). Using complementary and alternative medicines for depression. *Journal of Clinical Psychiatry, 71,* e24.

369. Fava, M., & Mischoulon, D. (2009). Folate in depression: Efficacy, safety, differences in formulations, and clinical issues. *Journal of Clinical Psychiatry, 70*(suppl. 5), 12–7.

370. Freeman, M. P. (2009). Omega-3 fatty acids in major depressive disorder. *Journal of Clinical Psychiatry, 70*(suppl. 5), 7–11.

371. Kris-Etherton, P. M., Harris, W. S., & Appel, L. J. (2003). Fish consumption, fish oil, omega-3 fatty acids, and cardiovascular disease. *Arteriosclerosis, Thrombosis, and Vascular Biology, 23,* e20–30.

372. Rocha Araujo, D. M., Vilarim, M. M., & Nardi, A. E. (2010). What is the effectiveness of the use of polyunsaturated fatty acid omega-3 in the treatment of depression? *Expert Review of Neurotherapeutics, 10,* 1117–1129.

373. Carney, R. M., et al. (2009). Omega-3 augmentation of sertraline in treatment of depression in patients with coronary heart disease: A randomized controlled trial. *JAMA, 302,* 1651–1657.

374. Borja-Hart, N. L., & Marino, J. (2010). Role of omega-3 fatty acids for prevention or treatment of perinatal depression. *Pharmacotherapy, 30,* 210–216.

375. Yashodhara, B. M., et al. (2009). Omega-3 fatty acids: A comprehensive review of their role in health and disease. *Postgraduate Medical Journal, 85,* 84–90.

376. Calder, P. C., & Yaqoob, P. (2009). Omega-3 polyunsaturated fatty acids and human health outcomes. *Biofactors, 35,* 266–272.

377. Papakostas, G. I. (2009). Evidence for S-adenosyl-L-methionine (SAM-e) for the treatment of major depressive disorder. *Journal of Clinical Psychiatry, 70*(suppl. 5), 18–22.

378. Shelton, R. C. (2009). St. John's wort (*Hypericum perforatum*) in major depression. *Journal of Clinical Psychiatry, 70*(suppl. 5), 23–27.

379. Zhou, S. F., & Lai, X. (2008). An update on clinical drug interactions with the herbal antidepressant St. John's wort. *Current Drug Metabolism, 9,* 394–409.

380. Lantz, M. S., Buchalter, E., & Giambanco, V. (1999). St. John's wort and antidepressant drug interactions in the elderly. *Journal of Geriatric Psychiatry and Neurology, 12,* 7–10.

381. van Olphen, J., et al. (2003). Religious involvement, social support, and health among African-American women on the east side of Detroit. *Journal of General Internal Medicine, 18,* 549–557.

382. Koenig, H. G. (2007). Religion and depression in older medical inpatients. *American Journal of Geriatric Psychiatry, 15,* 282–291.

383. Koenig, H. G. (2007). Religion and remission of depression in medical inpatients with heart failure/pulmonary disease. *Journal of Nervous and Mental Disease, 195,* 389–395.

384. Braam, A. W., et al. (2001). Religion as a cross-cultural determinant of depression in elderly Europeans: Results from the EURODEP collaboration. *Psychological Medicine, 31,* 803–814.

385. Cruz, M., et al. (2009). The association of public and private religious involvement with severity of depression and hopelessness in older adults treated for major depression. *American Journal of Geriatric Psychiatry, 17,* 503–507.

386. Kaplan, G. A., et al. (1987). Psychosocial predictors of depression. Prospective evidence from the human population laboratory studies. *American Journal of Epidemiology, 125*, 206–220.

387. Hays, J. C., et al. (1997). Psychosocial and physical correlates of chronic depression. *Psychiatry Research, 72*, 149–159.

388. Boyce, P., et al. (1998). Psychosocial factors associated with depression: A study of socially disadvantaged women with young children. *Journal of Nervous and Mental Disease, 186*, 3–11.

389. Ezquiaga, E., et al. (1999). Psychosocial predictors of outcome in major depression: A prospective 12-month study. *Journal of Affective Disorders, 52*, 209–216.

390. O'Sullivan, C. (2004). The psychosocial determinants of depression: A lifespan perspective. *Journal of Nervous and Mental Disease, 192*, 585–594.

391. Boyce, P., & Hickey, A. (2005). Psychosocial risk factors to major depression after childbirth. *Social Psychiatry and Psychiatric Epidemiology, 40*, 605–612.

392. Sherbourne, C. D., Hays, R. D., & Wells, K. B. (1995). Personal and psychosocial risk factors for physical and mental health outcomes and course of depression among depressed patients. *Journal of Consulting and Clinical Psychology, 63*, 345–355.

393. Cohen, A. N., et al. (2004). Effects of stress and social support on recurrence in bipolar disorder. *Journal of Affective Disorders, 82*, 143–147.

394. Johnson, L., et al. (2003). Social support in bipolar disorder: Its relevance to remission and relapse. *Bipolar Disorders, 5*, 129–137.

395. Johnson, S. L., et al. (1999). Social support and the course of bipolar disorder. *Journal of Abnormal Psychology, 108*, 558–566.

396. Munoz Lasa, S., et al. (2011). Animal-assisted interventions in internal and rehabilitation medicine: A review of the recent literature. *Panminerva Medica, 53*, 129–136.

397. Moretti, F., et al. (2011). Pet therapy in elderly patients with mental illness. *Psychogeriatrics: The Official Journal of the Japanese Psychogeriatric Society, 11*, 125–129.

398. Orlandi, M., et al. (2007). Pet therapy effects on oncological day hospital patients undergoing chemotherapy treatment. *Anticancer Research, 27*, 4301–4303.

399. Stasi, M. F., et al. (2004). Pet-therapy: A trial for institutionalized frail elderly patients. *Archives of Gerontology and Geriatrics. Supplement*, 407–412.

400. Scogin, F., Jamison, C., & Davis, N. (1990). Two-year follow-up of bibliotherapy for depression in older adults. *Journal of Consulting and Clinical Psychology, 58*, 665–667.

401. Smith, N. M., et al. (1997). Three-year follow-up of bibliotherapy for depression. *Journal of Consulting and Clinical Psychology, 65*, 324–327.

402. Jorm, A. F., et al. (2002). Effectiveness of complementary and self-help treatments for depression. *Medical Journal of Australia, 176*(suppl.), S84–96.

403. Floyd, M., et al. (2004). Cognitive therapy for depression: A comparison of individual psychotherapy and bibliotherapy for depressed older adults. *Behavior Modification, 28*, 297–318.

404. Markowitz, J. C. (1996). Psychotherapy for dysthymic disorder. *Psychiatric Clinics of North America, 19*, 133–149.

405. Dunner, D. L., et al. (1996). Cognitive therapy versus fluoxetine in the treatment of dysthymic disorder. *Depression, 4*, 34–41.

406. Browne, G., et al. (2002). Sertraline and/or interpersonal psychotherapy for patients with dysthymic disorder in primary care: 6-month comparison with longitudinal 2-year follow-up of effectiveness and costs. *Journal of Affective Disorders, 68*, 317–330.

407. Gradus, J. L., et al. (2010). The association between adjustment disorder diagnosed at psychiatric treatment facilities and completed suicide. *Clinical Epidemiology, 2*, 23–28.

408. Casey, P. (2009). Adjustment disorder: Epidemiology, diagnosis and treatment. *CNS Drugs, 23*, 927–938.

409. Hameed, U., et al. (2005). Antidepressant treatment in the primary care office: Outcomes for adjustment disorder versus major depression. *Annals of Clinical Psychiatry, 17*, 77–81.

410. Carta, M. G., et al. (2009). Adjustment disorder: Epidemiology, diagnosis and treatment. *Clinical Practice and Epidemiology in Mental Health, 5*, 15.

411. Grunze, H., et al. (2010). The World Federation of Societies of Biological Psychiatry (WFSBP) Guidelines for the Biological Treatment of Bipolar Disorders: Update 2010 on the treatment of acute bipolar depression. *World Journal of Biological Psychiatry, 11*, 81–109.

412. NICE Clinical Guidelines. *The management of bipolar disorder in adults, children and adolescents in primary and secondary care*, update 2009. London: National Institute for Health and Clinical Excellence.

413. Goodwin, G. M. (2009). Evidence-based guidelines for treating bipolar disorder: Revised second edition—Recommendations from the British Association for Psychopharmacology. *Journal of Psychopharmacology, 23*, 346–388.

414. Yatham, L. N., et al. (2009). Canadian Network for Mood and Anxiety Treatments (CANMAT) and International Society for Bipolar Disorders (ISBD) collaborative update of CANMAT guidelines for the management of patients with bipolar disorder: Update 2009. *Bipolar Disorders, 11*, 225–255.

415. Bisol, L. W., & Lara, D. R. (2010). Low-dose quetiapine for patients with dysregulation of hyperthymic and cyclothymic temperaments. *Journal of Psychopharmacology, 24*, 421–424.

416. Hellerstein, D. J., et al. (2004). Citalopram in the treatment of dysthymic disorder. *International Clinical Psychopharmacology, 19*, 143–148.

417. Bakish, D., et al. (1994). Psychopharmacological treatment response of patients with a DSM-III diagnosis of dysthymic disorder. *Psychopharmacology Bulletin, 30*, 53–59.

418. Dunner, D. L., et al. (2002). Dysthymic disorder: Treatment with citalopram. *Depression and Anxiety, 15*, 18–22.

419. Devanand, D. P., et al. (2004). An open treatment trial of venlafaxine for elderly patients with dysthymic disorder. *Journal of Geriatric Psychiatry and Neurology, 17*, 219–224.

420. Dunner, D. L., et al. (1997). Venlafaxine in dysthymic disorder. *Journal of Clinical Psychiatry, 58*, 528–531.

421. Dunner, D. L., et al. (1999). Dysthymic disorder: Treatment with mirtazapine. *Depression and Anxiety, 10*, 68–72.

422. Hellerstein, D. J., et al. (2001). Bupropion sustained-release for the treatment of dysthymic disorder: An open-label study. *Journal of Clinical Psychopharmacology, 21*, 325–329.

423. Kasper, S., et al. (2008). International Consensus Group on the evidence-based pharmacologic treatment of bipolar I and II depression. *Journal of Clinical Psychiatry, 69,* 1632–1646.

424. Miranda, J., et al. (1998). Unmet mental health needs of women in public-sector gynecologic clinics. *American Journal of Obstetrics & Gynecology, 178,* 212–217.

425. Miranda, J., et al. (1998). Unmet mental health needs of women in public-sector gynecologic clinics. *American Journal of Obstetrics & Gynecology, 178,* 212–217.

426. O'Hara, M. W., Neunaber, D. J., & Zekoski, E. M. (1984). Prospective study of postpartum depression: Prevalence, course, and predictive factors. *Journal of Abnormal Psychology, 93,* 158–171.

427. Faisal-Cury, A., & Rossi Menezes, P. (2007). Prevalence of anxiety and depression during pregnancy in a private setting sample. *Archives of Women's Mental Health, 10,* 25–32.

428. American Psychiatric Association. (2000). *Diagnostic and statistical manual of mental disorders* (4th ed.). Washington, DC: American Psychiatric Association.

429. Segre, L. S., et al. (2007). The prevalence of postpartum depression: The relative significance of three social status indices. *Social Psychiatry and Psychiatric Epidemiology, 42,* 316–321.

430. Gavin, N. I., et al. (2005). Perinatal depression: A systematic review of prevalence and incidence. *Obstetrics & Gynecology, 106,* 1071–1083.

431. Banti, S., et al. (2011). From the third month of pregnancy to 1 year postpartum. Prevalence, incidence, recurrence, and new onset of depression. Results from the perinatal depression-research & screening unit study. *Comprehensive Psychiatry, 52,* 343–351.

432. Peindl, K. S., Wisner, K. L., & Hanusa, B. H. (2004). Identifying depression in the first postpartum year: Guidelines for office-based screening and referral. *Journal of Affective Disorders, 80,* 37–44.

433. Kendell, R. E., et al. (1981). Mood changes in the first three weeks after childbirth. *Journal of Affective Disorders, 3,* 317–326.

434. Wisner, K. L., et al. (2009). Major depression and antidepressant treatment: Impact on pregnancy and neonatal outcomes. *American Journal of Psychiatry, 166,* 557–566.

435. Chung, T. K., et al. (2001). Antepartum depressive symptomatology is associated with adverse obstetric and neonatal outcomes. *Psychosomatic Medicine, 63,* 830–834.

436. Jablensky, A. V., et al. (2005). Pregnancy, delivery, and neonatal complications in a population cohort of women with schizophrenia and major affective disorders. *American Journal of Psychiatry, 162,* 79–91.

437. Hedegaard, M., et al. (1996). The relationship between psychological distress during pregnancy and birth weight for gestational age. *Acta Obstetricia et Gynecologica Scandinavica, 75,* 32–39.

438. Orr, S. T., & Miller, C. A. (1995). Maternal depressive symptoms and the risk of poor pregnancy outcome. Review of the literature and preliminary findings. *Epidemiologic Reviews, 17,* 165–171.

439. Steer, R. A., et al. (1992). Self-reported depression and negative pregnancy outcomes. *Journal of Clinical Epidemiology, 45,* 1093–1099.

440. Sohr-Preston, S. L., & Scaramella, L. V. (2006). Implications of timing of maternal depressive symptoms for early cognitive and language development. *Clinical Child and Family Psychology Review, 9*, 65–83.

441. Pilowsky, D. J., et al. (2006). Children of currently depressed mothers: A STAR*D ancillary study. *Journal of Clinical Psychiatry, 67*, 126–136.

442. Kim-Cohen, J., et al. (2005). Maternal depression and children's antisocial behavior: Nature and nurture effects. *Archives of General Psychiatry, 62*, 173–181.

443. Weissman, M. M., et al. (2004). Depressed mothers coming to primary care: Maternal reports of problems with their children. *Journal of Affective Disorders, 78*, 93–100.

444. Hammen, C., et al. (1990). Longitudinal study of diagnoses in children of women with unipolar and bipolar affective disorder. *Archives of General Psychiatry, 47*, 1112–1117.

445. Grupp-Phelan, J., Whitaker, R. C., & Naish, A. B. (2003). Depression in mothers of children presenting for emergency and primary care: Impact on mothers' perceptions of caring for their children. *Ambulatory Pediatrics, 3*, 142–146.

446. Andrade, S. E., et al. (2008). Use of antidepressant medications during pregnancy: A multisite study. *American Journal of Obstetrics & Gynecology, 198*, 194.e1–5.

447. Newport, D. J., & Stowe, Z. N. (2006). Psychopharmacology during pregnancy and lactation. In A. F. Schatzberg & C. B. Nemeroff (Eds.), *Essentials of clinical psychopharmacology* (pp. 745–777). Arlington, VA: American Psychiatric Publishing.

448. Kalra, S., et al. (2005). The safety of antidepressant use in pregnancy. *Expert Opinion on Drug Safety, 4*, 273–284.

449. Koren, G., Pastuszak, A., & Ito, S. (1998). Drugs in pregnancy. *New England Journal of Medicine, 338*, 1128–1137.

450. Payne, J. L., & Meltzer-Brody, S. (2009). Antidepressant use during pregnancy: Current controversies and treatment strategies. *Clinical Obstetrics and Gynecology, 52*, 469–482.

451. Grzeskowiak, L. E., Gilbert, A. L., & Morrison, J. L. (2011). Investigating outcomes following the use of selective serotonin reuptake inhibitors for treating depression in pregnancy: A focus on methodological issues. *Drug Safety: An International Journal of Medical Toxicology and Drug Experience, 34*, 1027–1048.

452. O'Brien, L., et al. (2007). Longitudinal study of depression, anxiety, irritability, and stress in pregnancy following evidence-based counseling on the use of antidepressants. *Journal of Psychiatric Practice, 13*, 33–39.

453. Marcus, S. M., et al. (2005). A screening study of antidepressant treatment rates and mood symptoms in pregnancy. *Archives of Women's Mental Health, 8*, 25–27.

454. Cohen, L. S., et al. (2004). Relapse of depression during pregnancy following antidepressant discontinuation: A preliminary prospective study. *Archives of Women's Mental Health, 7*, 217–221.

455. Cohen, L. S., et al. (2004). Reintroduction of antidepressant therapy across pregnancy in women who previously discontinued treatment. A preliminary retrospective study. *Psychotherapy and Psychosomatics, 73*, 255–258.

456. Cohen, L. S., et al. (2006). Relapse of major depression during pregnancy in women who maintain or discontinue antidepressant treatment. *JAMA, 295*, 499–507.

457. Yonkers, K. A., et al. (2011). Does antidepressant use attenuate the risk of a major depressive episode in pregnancy? *Epidemiology, 22,* 848–854.

458. Lorenzo, L., Byers, B., & Einarson, A. (2011). Antidepressant use in pregnancy. *Expert Opinion on Drug Safety, 10,* 883–889.

459. Simoncelli, M., Martin, B. Z., & Berard, A. (2010). Antidepressant use during pregnancy: A critical systematic review of the literature. *Current Drug Safety, 5,* 153–170.

460. Einarson, A., et al. (2009). Incidence of major malformations in infants following antidepressant exposure in pregnancy: Results of a large prospective cohort study. *Canadian Journal of Psychiatry, 54,* 242–246.

461. Reis, M., & Kallen, B. (2010). Delivery outcome after maternal use of antidepressant drugs in pregnancy: An update using Swedish data. *Psychological Medicine, 40,* 1723–1733.

462. Gentile, S. (2010). On categorizing gestational, birth, and neonatal complications following late pregnancy exposure to antidepressants: The prenatal antidepressant exposure syndrome. *CNS Spectrums, 15,* 167–185.

463. Einarson, A., et al. (2010). Adverse effects of antidepressant use in pregnancy: An evaluation of fetal growth and preterm birth. *Depression and Anxiety, 27,* 35–38.

464. Hemels, M. E., et al. (2005). Antidepressant use during pregnancy and the rates of spontaneous abortions: A meta-analysis. *Annals of Pharmacotherapy, 39,* 803–809.

465. Croen, L. A., et al. (2011). Antidepressant use during pregnancy and childhood autism spectrum disorders. *Archives of General Psychiatry, 68,* 1104–1112.

466. Louik, C., et al. (2007). First-trimester use of selective serotonin-reuptake inhibitors and the risk of birth defects. *New England Journal of Medicine, 356,* 2675–2683.

467. Alwan, S., et al. (2007). Use of selective serotonin-reuptake inhibitors in pregnancy and the risk of birth defects. *New England Journal of Medicine, 356,* 2684–2692.

468. Kallen, B., & Olausson, P. O. (2008). Maternal use of selective serotonin re-uptake inhibitors and persistent pulmonary hypertension of the newborn. *Pharmacoepidemiology and Drug Safety, 17,* 801–806.

469. Chambers, C. D., et al. (2006). Selective serotonin-reuptake inhibitors and risk of persistent pulmonary hypertension of the newborn. *New England Journal of Medicine, 354,* 579–587.

470. Andrade, S. E., et al. (2009). Antidepressant medication use and risk of persistent pulmonary hypertension of the newborn. *Pharmacoepidemiology and Drug Safety, 18,* 246–252.

471. McElhatton, P. R., et al. (1996). The outcome of pregnancy in 689 women exposed to therapeutic doses of antidepressants. A collaborative study of the European Network of Teratology Information Services (ENTIS). *Reproductive Toxicology, 10,* 285–294.

472. Pastuszak, A., et al. (1993). Pregnancy outcome following first-trimester exposure to fluoxetine (Prozac). *JAMA, 269,* 2246–2248.

473. Chambers, C. D., et al. (1996). Birth outcomes in pregnant women taking fluoxetine. *New England Journal of Medicine, 335,* 1010–1015.

474. Goldstein, D. J. (1995). Effects of third trimester fluoxetine exposure on the newborn. *Journal of Clinical Psychopharmacology, 15,* 417–420.

475. Goldstein, D. J., Corbin, L. A., & Sundell, K. L. (1997). Effects of first-trimester fluoxetine exposure on the newborn. *Obstetrics & Gynecology, 89,* 713–718.

476. Hendrick, V., et al. (2003). Birth outcomes after prenatal exposure to antidepressant medication. *American Journal of Obstetrics & Gynecology, 188,* 812–815.

477. Suri, R., et al. (2004). The impact of depression and fluoxetine treatment on obstetrical outcome. *Archives of Women's Mental Health, 7,* 193–200.

478. Ericson, A., Kallen, B., & Wiholm, B. (1999). Delivery outcome after the use of antidepressants in early pregnancy. *European Journal of Clinical Pharmacology, 55,* 503–508.

479. Simon, G. E., Cunningham, M. L., & Davis, R. L. (2002). Outcomes of prenatal antidepressant exposure. *American Journal of Psychiatry, 159,* 2055–2061.

480. Cohen, L. S., et al. (2000). Birth outcomes following prenatal exposure to fluoxetine. *Biological Psychiatry, 48,* 996–1000.

481. Addis, A., & Koren, G. (2000). Safety of fluoxetine during the first trimester of pregnancy: A meta-analytical review of epidemiological studies. *Psychological Medicine, 30,* 89–94.

482. Nulman, I., et al. (1997). Neurodevelopment of children exposed in utero to antidepressant drugs. *New England Journal of Medicine, 336,* 258–262.

483. Nulman, I., et al. (2002). Child development following exposure to tricyclic antidepressants or fluoxetine throughout fetal life: A prospective, controlled study. *American Journal of Psychiatry, 159,* 1889–1895.

484. Costei, A. M., et al. (2002). Perinatal outcome following third trimester exposure to paroxetine. *Archives of Pediatrics & Adolescent Medicine, 156,* 1129–1132.

485. Kulin, N. A., et al. (1998). Pregnancy outcome following maternal use of the new selective serotonin reuptake inhibitors: A prospective controlled multicenter study. *JAMA, 279,* 609–610.

486. Lanza di Scalea, T., & Wisner, K. L. (2009). Antidepressant medication use during breastfeeding. *Clinical Obstetrics and Gynecology, 52,* 483–497.

487. Wisner, K. L., et al. (2004). Prevention of postpartum depression: A pilot randomized clinical trial. *American Journal of Psychiatry, 161,* 1290–1292.

488. Wisner, K. L., et al. (2006). Postpartum depression: A randomized trial of sertraline versus nortriptyline. *Journal of Clinical Psychopharmacology, 26,* 353–360.

489. Appleby, L., et al. (1997). A controlled study of fluoxetine and cognitive-behavioural counselling in the treatment of postnatal depression. *BMJ, 314,* 932–936.

490. Misri, S., et al. (2004). The use of paroxetine and cognitive-behavioral therapy in postpartum depression and anxiety: A randomized controlled trial. *Journal of Clinical Psychiatry, 65,* 1236–1241.

491. Stowe, Z. N., et al. (2003). The pharmacokinetics of sertraline excretion into human breast milk: Determinants of infant serum concentrations. *Journal of Clinical Psychiatry, 64,* 73–80.

492. Kristensen, J. H., et al. (1998). Distribution and excretion of sertraline and N-desmethylsertraline in human milk. *British Journal of Clinical Pharmacology, 45,* 453–457.

493. Stowe, Z. N., et al. (1997). Sertraline and desmethylsertraline in human breast milk and nursing infants. *American Journal of Psychiatry, 154,* 1255–1260.

494. Hendrick, V., et al. (2001). Fluoxetine and norfluoxetine concentrations in nursing infants and breast milk. *Biological Psychiatry, 50*, 775–782.

495. Kristensen, J. H., et al. (1999). Distribution and excretion of fluoxetine and norfluoxetine in human milk. *British Journal of Clinical Pharmacology, 48*, 521–527.

496. Taddio, A., Ito, S., & Koren, G. (1996). Excretion of fluoxetine and its metabolite, norfluoxetine, in human breast milk. *Journal of Clinical Pharmacology, 36*, 42–47.

497. Rampono, J., et al. (2000). Citalopram and demethylcitalopram in human milk; distribution, excretion and effects in breast fed infants. *British Journal of Clinical Pharmacology, 50*, 263–268.

498. St-Andre, M. (1993). Psychotherapy during pregnancy: Opportunities and challenges. *American Journal of Psychotherapy, 47*, 572–590.

499. Mackie-Ramos, R. L., & Rice, J. M. (1988). Group psychotherapy with methadone-maintained pregnant women. *Journal of Substance Abuse Treatment, 5*, 151–161.

500. Henker, F. O., 3rd. (1976). Psychotherapy as adjunct in treatment of vomiting during pregnancy. *Southern Medical Journal, 69*, 1585–1587.

501. Destounis, N. (1966). Psychotherapy in pregnancy. *Delaware Medical Journal, 38*, 78–82.

502. Spinelli, M. G., & Endicott, J. (2003). Controlled clinical trial of interpersonal psychotherapy versus parenting education program for depressed pregnant women. *American Journal of Psychiatry, 160*, 555–562.

503. Cooper, P. J., et al. (2003). Controlled trial of the short- and long-term effect of psychological treatment of post-partum depression. I. Impact on maternal mood. *British Journal of Psychiatry, 182*, 412–419.

504. O'Hara, M. W., et al. (2000). Efficacy of interpersonal psychotherapy for post-partum depression. *Archives of General Psychiatry, 57*, 1039–1045.

505. Cohen, L. S. (2007). Treatment of bipolar disorder during pregnancy. *Journal of Clinical Psychiatry, 68*(suppl. 9), 4–9.

506. Viguera, A. C., et al. (2007). Risk of recurrence in women with bipolar disorder during pregnancy: Prospective study of mood stabilizer discontinuation. *American Journal of Psychiatry, 164*, 1817–1824; quiz 1923.

507. Freeman, M. P., et al. (2002). The impact of reproductive events on the course of bipolar disorder in women. *Journal of Clinical Psychiatry, 63*, 284–287.

508. Jones, I., & Craddock, N. (2001). Familiality of the puerperal trigger in bipolar disorder: Results of a family study. *American Journal of Psychiatry, 158*, 913–917.

509. Yonkers, K. A., et al. (2004). Management of bipolar disorder during pregnancy and the postpartum period. *American Journal of Psychiatry, 161*, 608–620.

510. Cohen, L. S., et al. (1994). A reevaluation of risk of in utero exposure to lithium. *JAMA, 271*, 146–150.

511. Gentile, S. (2006). Prophylactic treatment of bipolar disorder in pregnancy and breastfeeding: Focus on emerging mood stabilizers. *Bipolar Disorders, 8*, 207–220.

512. Vigod, S. N., Ross, L. E., & Steiner, M. (2009). Understanding and treating premenstrual dysphoric disorder: An update for the women's health practitioner. *Obstetrics and Gynecology Clinics of North America, 36*, 907–924, xii.

513. Lustyk, M. K., et al. (2009). Cognitive-behavioral therapy for premenstrual syndrome and premenstrual dysphoric disorder: A systematic review. *Archives of Women's Mental Health, 12*, 85–96.

514. Brown, J., et al. (2009). Selective serotonin reuptake inhibitors for premenstrual syndrome. *Cochrane Database of Systematic Reviews*, p. CD001396.
515. Shah, N. R., et al. (2008). Selective serotonin reuptake inhibitors for premenstrual syndrome and premenstrual dysphoric disorder: A meta-analysis. *Obstetrics & Gynecology, 111*, 1175–1182.

Index